IRELAND

N T I C

E A N

Londonderry
Donegal
Belfast
Sligo
Newry
Westport
Drogheda
I R E L A N D
Galway
Dublin
Kilrush
Limerick
New Ross
Tralee
Waterford
Wexford
Cork
Youghal

THE FAMINE SHIPS

THE FAMINE SHIPS

THE IRISH EXODUS
TO AMERICA
1846–51

EDWARD LAXTON

BLOOMSBURY

To all the brave Irish men and women and their children
who survived the Atlantic crossing between 1846 and 1851.

First published in Great Britain 1996
Bloomsbury Publishing Plc, 38 Soho Square, London W1V 5DF

Copyright © 1996 Edward Laxton

The moral right of the author has been asserted

A CIP catalogue record for this book is available from the British Library

ISBN 0 7475 2535 8

10 9 8 7 6 5 4 3 2 1

Typeset by Hewer Text Composition Services, Edinburgh
Printed by in Great Britain by Clays Ltd, St Ives plc

Contents

CONTENTS

Foreword

The only encouragement we hold out to strangers are a good climate, fertile soil, wholesome air and water, plenty of provisions, good pay for labor, kind neighbors, good laws, a free government and a hearty welcome.

These words were spoken by Benjamin Franklin, who did so much to promote the American cause of independence, a hundred years before the Famine Emigration. But they held true for a million and more citizens of Ireland, the men, women and children who sailed to America between 1846 and 1851, so that they might escape the Famine and survive. For as little as US $10, a passenger could sail 3,000 miles across the Atlantic Ocean, a voyage of fear, hunger, sickness, misery . . . and hope. But a million more would die at home, from starvation and fever, after the failure of the potato crop in successive seasons.

Were those voyagers alive today, what stories they could tell, of the agonizing decision to leave their beloved Isle of Erin, of the lamentions on their last night at home and the

1

American Wake, as it came to be known, of the arduous journey to the port and the search for a ship, of the misery they endured on the voyage! But what joy when they arrived, what relief they must have savoured as they stepped ashore! They were released from tyranny, no longer tormented tenants. Free at last, they could start to live again.

A *famous drawing from the* Illustrated London News, *July 6th 1850, 'The Departure'.*

In fact emigration from Ireland to America had begun in the early 1700s. A trickle swelled to an average of 5,000 a year by 1830 and grew steadily until the Famine arrived and the exodus began, 150 years ago. The emigrants sailed to New York and Boston, to Philadelphia, Baltimore and New Orleans, and they spread across America's heartland. They sailed to Canada, a British colony to which the passage was cheaper, from where an estimated 200,000 immediately went south across the border.

Before the Famine the population of America had risen to around 23 million. The Statue of Liberty, with its famous welcome for immigrants, was not yet built – Ellis Island was many years away. But the Irish looked upon America as their natural choice and by 1850 the residents of New York were 26 per cent Irish.

Seven million are believed to have left Ireland for America over the last three centuries. For a million, over a period of six years, there was no option. Now more than 40 million American citizens can claim Irish blood.

While books on the Famine period have dealt with the journey, no publication has dealt specifically with the Irish-owned ships, the Irish crews who sailed them, the Irish ports they sailed from and the Irish passengers they carried in those years.

The ships featured in this book made these crossings on the dates shown, at the times stated; passenger lists are from US Immigration files, crew's papers for the specific voyages from marine archives, and a wealth of first-hand reports have contributed to the stories. Details have been taken from eye-witness accounts; original Certificates of Registration, paintings and contemporary lithograph drawings have been reproduced.

SOURCES: National Library, Dublin; Linen Hall Library, Belfast; American-Ulster Folk Park; Famine Museum, Strokestown, County Roscommon; Royal Maritime Museum, Greenwich; Liverpool Maritime Museum; Public Record Office and Guildhall Library, London; the libraries of Cork, Cobh, Galway, Limerick; the Bodleian and Rhodes House Libraries, Oxford; Irish Historical Society, New York; Balch Institute and Maritime Museum, Philadelphia.

Introduction: These Desperate People

For 700 years prior to the Great Famine, the Irish had gradually become a nation of tenants in their own homeland. Ireland's estates and farms were continually seized and redistributed by their oppressors, the invading armies and the avaricious kings and noblemen of England. The land was let and sub-let, divided and sub-divided, often to be rented and worked by the original owners. In 1841 a census revealed that the population of Ireland had peaked at just above 8 million. Fully two-thirds of those depended on agriculture for their survival, but they rarely received a working wage in return for the patch of land they needed to grow enough food for their own families.

The rich maintained their wealth through ownership of the land and wielded the political power in Ireland, yet a number of the absentee landlords living in England had never set foot in Ireland. They extracted profitable rents from their impoverished tenants or paid them minimal wages to raise crops and livestock for export. This was the system which forced Ireland and so many of her people to rely on a single crop, and only the potato could be grown in sufficient quantity on these tiny scraps of soil.

The rights to a piece of land meant the difference between life and death in Ireland in the early 1800s. The population was exploding, and with hundreds of thousands without work, entire families managed to exist on a section no bigger than half an acre, growing nothing more than row after row of potatoes. If they were lucky, they might have enough land to raise a pig each year, to slaughter, salt and eat through the worst of the winter months. They might go hungry for a few weeks at the end of the summer, when the previous season's potatoes were no longer edible, but what was the alternative?

There were famine years before the blight struck and the English rulers were well aware of the problems arising out of the economic structure they had forced on the Irish. During the first 45 years of the last century at least 150 committees and commissions of inquiry, appointed by the British Parliament, had made their reports on the State of Ireland. But nothing happened.

Emigration to America began in earnest more than a hundred years earlier, but the Famine years, from 1846 to 1851, were marked by an urgency to get away as never seen before. Ships had always sailed in the spring and summer months. Now, the clamour for a passage saw vessels of every kind and size, with bunks hastily raised in the holds, departing in the autumn and winter too. They braved the worst of the weather – the bitter cold, ice, gales, fog, storms and heavy seas, short days and long nights, could not deter these desperate people. Desperation was the distinctive feature of the Famine sailings.

As the potato crop was wiped out in successive years, Ireland started to starve and the exodus to America began. On tiny two- and three-masted ships they sailed from Dublin and Donegal, from Sligo, Galway and Limerick, from Waterford and Wexford, New Ross, Belfast, Londonderry and

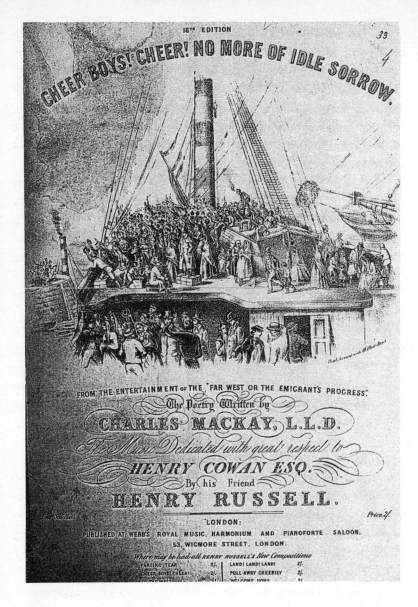

A selection of Charles Mackay's poetry, dedicated to the Irish Emigration.

Cork, from Tralee, Drogheda, Newry, Kilrush, Westport and Youghal, directly to America.

More often, however, they were ferried across the Irish Sea to Liverpool on the hated British mainland, to seek bigger ships for the Atlantic crossing. Liverpool was the ill-famed slavers' port, where human cargo always had a value, and the Irish would travel in no greater comfort than the slaves before them.

For ship owners, captains, crews and agents, this sudden increase in the passenger trade all the year round, was very welcome. Whereas in previous years they had operated a lucrative three-sided business – timber, iron, tools, salt and varied cargo down to West Africa; slaves out to America; cotton, tobacco, wheat and provisions back to Europe – outward-bound passages had been losing money. The Napoleonic Wars had ended around the turn of the century, completely upsetting the balance of trade in Europe. In particular, the price of timber had soared five-fold: the forests of Canada had more than enough wood to satisfy demand in Europe, and it was cheaper to buy there and ship it home. It was cheaper still if cargo could be found for the westward crossings and once again the human cargo, emigrants instead of slaves, provided the answer. Within a year or two it would provide more revenue than Canadian timber sailing eastwards.

Five thousand ships sailed across the Atlantic with Irish emigrants in the six years of the Famine Emigration. They were diverse in size, safety and comfort, or the lack of it, and they varied in many other respects – in age and in the experience and quality of their crews, their speed on the voyage, provisions on board, and the fares they charged.

American packet ships of more than 1,000 tons, with triple-decks were built in the late 1840s specifically for the emigrant trade. They would carry more than 400 passengers, some in private cabins. But by no means all the ships were custom-built. When the *British Queen* first put to sea in 1785 she needed several major repairs before she could carry passengers on regular voyages from Liverpool to New York. And when the *Elizabeth and Sarah* achieved infamy in the fever year of 1847, she had been at sea for 83 years.

Undoubtedly, many of the Famine ships would have carried African slaves in the early years of the 19th century. The European slave traders finally ended their activities barely a dozen years before the onset of the Famine and the Arab slavers continued to ply well into the 1860s.

There were tiny vessels like *The Hannah* with a crew of six and measuring only 59 feet – about the same length as four family cars parked bumper-to-bumper. She was converted from a coaster by the addition of a third mast to enable her to go into deeper waters, and sailed to New York five times, from Dublin, Cork and Limerick, with a complement of only 50 or 60 passengers crammed below in a single hold.

These Irish men and women were not always welcome on arrival in their new homeland, for this desperate migration represented cheap labour, a threat to the established American workforce. But they dug canals, built roads and laid railways, they became seamstresses and servants.

The alternative was to stay at home and starve. A meal, a job, a place to rest, a chance to survive was all the Famine emigrants asked. They left Ireland by sailing ship every day, summer and winter, for six years while the Famine lasted, to make the 3,000 mile journey across the Atlantic Ocean. This is their story.

1

From Dublin's Fair City

For an island nation during the last century, the sea was the only link with the outside world. The black waters of the River Liffey, where they enter Dublin Bay, provided perfect anchorage for as many as 4,000 ships, registered to the port of Dublin, in the mid-1800s. Small cutters and sloops carried the mail, cattle and agricultural produce for the English markets and the expanding passenger trade to Liverpool. Colliers and schooners kept local industry thriving while the big three-masted barques and brigs traded on the high seas. Dublin was the home port for 300 square-rigged ships sailing to every corner of the world, though few were fitted out to carry human cargo until the Famine arrived. Every day the cobblestones on Custom House Quay would ring with the sound of horses' hooves and creaking cart wheels and the shouts of men in a hurry. Dockside gangs unloaded cargoes from recent arrivals on to barges plying busily along the canals leading into the old city.

The year 1846, which marked the beginning of the Famine Emigration, saw the start of a dramatic change in the scene on Dublin's quays. The *Irish Quarterly Review* would subsequently record this scene as follows:

> A procession fraught with most striking and most melancholy interest, wending its painful and mournful way along the whole line of the river, to where the beautiful pile of the Custom House is distinguishable in the far distance, towering amongst the masts of the shipping.
>
> Melancholy, most melancholy, is the sight to the eye not only of the Dublin citizen or resident, but to the eye of every Irishman who is worthy of being so called and indeed, the spectacle is one of sadness and foreboding. A long continuous procession . . . a mixed stream of men, women and children, with their humble baggage, who are hurrying to quit for ever their native land!
>
> It is not a departing crowd of paupers but unhappily an exodus of those who may be regarded as having constituted, as it were, the bone and sinew of the land; the farmers and comfortable tenantry, the young and strong, the hale and hearty, the pride and the prime of our Nation!

In later years the *Irish Quarterly Review* stated that the procession, or queue, would stretch a mile-and-a-half from the railway station to the Custom House, which today is still the most beautiful building in Dublin's fair city.

The London architect James Gandon had refused a commission in Tsarist Russia to build a palace for Catherine the Great in St Petersburg, in favour of taking his ideas to Dublin where he also built the magnificent Four Courts and King's Inns. His splendid grey-stone structure standing on the quayside was begun in 1781 and took ten years to finish. It carries statues representing Navigation, Industry, Commerce and Wealth. Prophetically, the architect also included in his design stone figures symbolizing Neptune chasing away Famine and Despair.

Dublin at this time was a thriving city with grand Georgian mansions and elegant houses lining the newly laid-out streets and squares, a gracious city to rival any of Europe's capitals. The name is taken from the Gaelic *Dubh-linn*, meaning Black Pool, suggested by the waters of the Liffey which flows only a few miles from the Wicklow Mountains and through the city and into Dublin Bay before it reaches the sea.

As Ireland's capital city, Dublin was by far the biggest and busiest of all the ports around the Irish coast, and the passengers for one of the first voyages of the Famine period, directly to New York, boarded here on St Patrick's Day in 1846. The sweet smell from the hatches of the *Perseverance* still hung in the air, for Demerara, the old Dutch colony in the West Indies, was her last port of call and sugar, rum and molasses had recently been unloaded.

The passengers were full of wonder and apprehension, with little or no idea of what lay ahead, but they were fortunate in their choice of ship. She was commanded by a man who knew his craft so well that some years earlier the owners had entrusted him with overseeing the building of new vessels for their fleet. Martin and Sons were long-established Dublin merchants, and when the Atlantic trade replaced the nearer but less profitable markets of Europe, the place to build and buy ships was on the eastern seaboard of British North America, as Canada was then known.

The abundant Canadian forests had more than enough wood to equip the expanding fleets on either side of the ocean and timber was only a fraction of the price compared with Europe. So Martin and Sons despatched their senior captain, William Scott, to Saint John in New Brunswick, to build, buy and commission new ships to sail under their flag, to be registered in the port of Dublin.

A native of the Shetland Isles in the north of Scotland, Captain William Scott was a veteran of the Atlantic crossing.

At around the time when most men would be thinking of retiring, he gave up his desk job and his home in Saint John and returned to his adopted city. When he took the *Perseverance* out of Dublin that day, he was an astonishing 74 years old.

For the first time Captain Scott's barque of 597 tons was carrying passengers, the vanguard of a million Famine emigrants. He would cut short the farewells, scorning the quayside tears, anxious to get this strange cargo down below while he prepared his ship to catch the late afternoon tide the following day, on Wednesday, March 18th. The crew had cleared the holds, and ship's carpenter James Gray had fitted out bunks four tiers high and 6 feet square. The fare in steerage was £3 (around US $15). In the cramped conditions for 210 passengers, pots and pans to cook their meagre rations were a priority, as were a tradesman's tools to earn a living in America. The mate Shadrack Stone checked the passengers and their belongings as they stepped on board. Perhaps there was also room for a couple of fiddles, maybe a squeezebox or a set of Irish pipes.

Catherine Halligan was a seamstress – was she forced to abandon her spinning wheel? Michael McSollough, a young blacksmith, would surely have no room for even a small anvil, and nor would Patrick Byrne or Tom Hanbury who shared his craft. John Butler was lucky, he was a watchmaker and his tools would fit easily into a pocket. George and Patrick Dermody were not so fortunate, as they were cabinet makers.

In reasonable weather groups of 20 or 30 passengers at a time would be allowed on deck to breathe fresh air for a change, wash their clothing and clean themselves, and to cook whatever rations were still intact and fit to eat. In bad weather they would be forced to remain below, in complete darkness if the seas were really rough, the heaving waves bringing all kinds of discomfort as well as the inevitable sea-sickness for poor travellers. Most of the time they stayed on their bunks: despite the lack of space, it was usually more comfortable there than on deck.

The caulking of the boards on the floor of the hold was often slack and the gaps between the planks, as they closed up with the movement of the ship, would catch the passengers' clothing, particularly the women's skirts. Sometimes they would be pinned in one position for hours on end, until the ship shifted in the wind on to a new course. Clothing would be released as the ship went over, although the smaller and weaker passengers might go with her, tossed to the other side of the hold, and become trapped again.

As we have seen, Irish emigration to America and Canada had been growing since 1835, but the potato failure ten years later had broken all records. There was bound to be an increase in emigration in 1846, and when the crop failed again, more than 100,000 had crossed the Atlantic by year's end. Anxiety to get away was replaced by an indiscriminate rush, and round-the-year sailings became necessary so that the number of ships available to make the voyage could cope with the numbers.

Later in 1846 Dublin politicians would appeal to the British Government in London, 'We would recommend that free emigrants should be treated at least as well as convicts in transport ships . . .' The plight of the Irish Famine emigrants was compared to that of the English prisoners sentenced to be transported to the Colonies, which usually meant to the other side of the world in Australia.

That humane plea would be ignored, and soon enough every port in Ireland would bear witness to the sad departures of the Famine ships. Scavengers would converge on to the quays, picking over abandoned bundles: it was the same for every voyage. For those on board the *Perseverance* in early 1846, the chiselled statues on the domed Custom House looked down on all this activity, the noise echoing from its porticoed entrance. The voyage would not be an easy one. It lasted for two months, although the *Perseverance* was reckoned to be a fast ship with, as we now know, a determined and experienced master in Captain William Scott although he was very likely a hard task-master and unpopular with his crew. More than four years would pass before his ship made another such journey, carrying emigrant passengers to America.

The *Perseverance* arrived on May 18th 1846, and 216 went ashore – all the passengers plus the mate Shadrack Stone and the bosun Michael Kelly, both from Dublin, two seamen, Thomas Branagan from Rush and Patrick Maguire from Drogheda, and two young apprentices. According to the original ship's papers for this voyage the entire crew deserted in New York.

NAMES OF PASSENGERS		AGE	SEX	OCCUPATIONS	DATE PORT SHIP
NNON, Biddy		16	F	None	18Ma02Gn
TCHINSON, Hannah		16	F	None	18Ma02Gn
UL, Wm.		24	M	Laborer	18Ma02Gn
U	(W)	25	F	None	18Ma02Gn
James	(S)	.00	M	Infant	18Ma02Gn
ERCE, Henry		20	M	Laborer	18Ma02Gn
STRANGE, Bridget		35	F	None	18Ma02Gn
Michl.	(S)	.00	M	Infant	18Ma02Gn
IGNE, Philip		40	M	Laborer	18Ma02Gn
Margaret	(W)	40	F	None	18Ma02Gn
Mary	(D)	20	F	None	18Ma02Gn
Cath.	(D)	18	F	None	18Ma02Gn
Ann	(D)	17	F	None	18Ma02Gn
Wm.	(S)	15	M	Laborer	18Ma02Gn
Jane	(D)	09	F	Child	18Ma02Gn
Elizabeth	(D)	07	F	Child	18Ma02Gn
Philip	(S)	05	M	Child	18Ma02Gn
RRAY, Cath.		13	F	None	18Ma02Gn
RKE, John		25	M	Laborer	18Ma02Gn
Bridget		20	F	None	18Ma02Gn
NNELL, Mary		22	F	None	18Ma02Gn
RT, Sarah		30	F	None	18Ma02Gn
HRY, Bridget		24	F	None	18Ma02Gn
AY, Cath.		20	F	None	18Ma02Gn
NLAN, Ellen		10	F	Child	18Ma02Gn
CHDALE, John		20	M	Laborer	18Ma02Gn
LAND, Mich.		20	M	Laborer	18Ma02Gn
VITT, Mary		21	F	None	18Ma02Gn
ELY, John		25	M	Laborer	18Ma02Gn
HILL		22	M	None	18Ma02Gn
RNER, Jane		20	F	None	18Ma02Gn
Nancy		18	F	None	18Ma02Gn
NNER, John		20	M	Laborer	18Ma02Gn
EILE, Susan		22	F	None	18Ma02Gn
Elizabeth		24	F	None	18Ma02Gn
NNER, Wm.		45	M	Laborer	18Ma02Gn
Bridget	(D)	22	F	None	18Ma02Gn
Cath.	(D)	18	F	None	18Ma02Gn
John	(S)	16	M	None	18Ma02Gn
Martin	(S)	13	M	None	18Ma02Gn
May	(D)	11	F	Child	18Ma02Gn
ADBY, Francis		19	M	Laborer	18Ma02Gn
TCHELL, Margt.		20	F	None	18Ma02Gn
LLEN, Ann		22	F	None	18Ma02Gn
LLY, Mickl.		20	M	Laborer	18Ma02Gn
RLEY, Peter		25	M	Laborer	18Ma02Gn
IVER, Joseph		45	M	Laborer	18Ma02Gn
Mary	(W)	45	F	None	18Ma02Gn
Mary	(D)	13	F	None	18Ma02Gn
Joseph	(S)	08	M	Child	18Ma02Gn
CCALLUM, Ellen		30	F	None	18Ma02Gn
CRACKEN, John		20	M	Laborer	18Ma02Gn
ADY, Hugh		22	M	Laborer	18Ma02Gn
LLAGHER, Phillip		20	M	Laborer	18Ma02Gn
ILLY, Judy		20	F	None	18Ma02Gn
NCH, Marla		13	F	None	18Ma02Gn
ODEN, James		20	M	Laborer	18Ma02Gn
IX, Patt		22	M	Laborer	18Ma02Gn
ODEN, Thomas		24	M	Laborer	18Ma02Gn
RTIN, Bridget		18	F	None	18Ma02Gn
Eliz.		13	F	None	18Ma02Gn
OOK, Edward		24	M	Laborer	18Ma02Gn
LSH, James		22	M	Laborer	18Ma02Gn
ON, Anthony		21	M	Laborer	18Ma02Gn
RPHY, Francis		21	M	Laborer	18Ma02Gn
ARKE, Thomas		20	M	Laborer	18Ma02Gn
LLOY, John		20	M	Laborer	18Ma02Gn
NLEY, John		20	M	Laborer	18Ma02Gn
EST, Andrew		20	M	Laborer	18Ma02Gn
Patt		20	M	Laborer	18Ma02Gn
LMES, John		20	M	Laborer	18Ma02Gn
ON, Bridget		20	F	None	18Ma02Gn
ADY, Peggy		20	F	None	18Ma02Gn
LMES, Cath.		20	F	None	18Ma02Gn
EYNOLDS, Mary		19	F	None	18Ma02Gn

NAMES OF PASSENGERS		AGE	SEX	OCCUPATIONS	DATE PORT SHIP
BOYLE, Mary		22	F	None	18Ma02Gn
GILMARTIN, Mary		21	F	None	18Ma02Gn
KERRON, Bridget		20	F	None	18Ma02Gn
Phlobe		18	F	None	18Ma02Gn
HOPE, John		25	M	Laborer	18Ma02Gn
RODGERS, Pat		24	M	Laborer	18Ma02Gn
RAFFERTY, Wm.		21	M	Laborer	18Ma02Gn
MCMULLIN, James		18	M	Laborer	18Ma02Gn
WARD, Wm.		18	M	Laborer	18Ma02Gn
RAFFERTY, Teresa		22	F	Laborer	18Ma02Gn
MCCANDLE, Ann		21	F	Laborer	18Ma02Gn
KEARNY, Ann		20	F	Laborer	J8Ma02Gn
LYNCH, Mathew		24	M	Laborer	18Ma02Gn
Mary		22	F	None	18Ma02Gn
GLYNN, Biddy		20	F	None	18Ma02Gn
MCANEENY, Cath.		22	F	None	18Ma02Gn
CURRAN, Bridget		20	F	None	18Ma02Gn
Mary		28	F	None	18Ma02Gn
HANLEY, Anthony		24	M	Laborer	18Ma02Gn
THOMAS, Peter		35	M	Laborer	18Ma02Gn
U	(W)	35	F	None	18Ma02Gn
Wm.	(S)	10	M	Child	18Ma02Gn
John	(S)	07	M	Child	18Ma02Gn
Hannah	(D)	03	F	Child	18Ma02Gn
Peter	(S)	.00	M	Infant	18Ma02Gn
DAVIDSON, John		20	M	Laborer	18Ma02Gn
CONDON, Wm.		20	M	Laborer	18Ma02Gn
HARRIGAN, Peter		22	M	Laborer	18Ma02Gn
BOWYER, Mary		21	F	Unknown	18Ma02Gn

PERSEVERANCE 18 MAY 1846

From Dublin

NAMES OF PASSENGERS		AGE	SEX	OCCUPATIONS	DATE PORT SHIP
ARCHBOLD, Christe		20	M	Laborer	18Ma20Go
CASHEN, Pat		22	M	Laborer	18Ma20Go
MARRINAN, Ann		24	F	Servant	18Ma20Go
GRAHAM, U-Mrs.		21	F	Servant	18Ma20Go
ARCHBOLD, John		22	M	Laborer	18Ma20Go
MORGAN, James		19	M	Laborer	18Ma20Go
MCNULTY, Charles		24	M	Laborer	18Ma20Go
MITCHELTON, Sarah		40	F	Wife	18Ma20Go
DOWLING, Maria		20	F	Servant	18Ma20Go
MCPARLIN, John		20	M	Laborer	18Ma20Go
Rose		16	F	Servant	18Ma20Go
FITZPATRICK, Ann		22	F	Servant	18Ma20Go
HAY, U		22	F	Lady'S Maid	18Ma20Go
Jane		20	F	Lady'S Maid	18Ma20Go
SPENCER, U		25	M	Clerk	18Ma20Go
MONKS, Laurence		22	M	Butcher	18Ma20Go
GALOGHLIN, Jos.		22	M	Tailor	18Ma20Go
BAKER, Christopher		18	M	Tailor	18Ma20Go
CUMMING, Richd.		20	M	Clerk	18Ma20Go
LYNN, Ann		20	F	Wife	18Ma20Go
FLOOD, Eliza		22	F	Dressmaker	18Ma20Go
MORRISON, James		25	M	Weaver	18Ma20Go
CARROLIN, Rose		30	F	Weaver	18Ma20Go
LEONARD, Julia		20	F	Laborer	18Ma20Go
LAWLESS, John		30	M	Laborer	18Ma20Go
U	(W)	25	F	Wife	18Ma20Go
Peter	(S)	02	M	Child	18Ma20Go
Catharine	(D)	01	F	Child	18Ma20Go
RIDDLE, Wm.		25	M	Carpenter	18Ma20Go
FLYNN, Mary		20	F	Servant	18Ma20Go
DOYLE, Ann		22	F	Servant	18Ma20Go
COSTELLO, Michael		25	M	Servant	18Ma20Go
CULLIN, Bridge		20	F	Servant	18Ma20Go
MAGUIRE, Patrick		30	M	Laborer	18Ma20Go
BYRNE, Peter		25	M	Laborer	18Ma20Go

The Perseverance's *passenger list, handed to US Immigration officials in New York in May 1846.*

15

NAMES OF PASSENGERS		AGE	SEX	OCCUPATIONS	DATE PORT SHIP
CAUFIELD, Cathne.		17	F	Seamstress	18Ma20Go
MAXWELL, John		26	M	Carpenter	18Ma20Go
U	(W)	20	F	Wife	18Ma20Go
FLANNIGAN, Joseph		20	M	Laborer	18Ma20Go
FENERAL, James		26	M	Laborer	18Ma20Go
SHANNON, Edward		24	M	Laborer	18Ma20Go
CAROLIN, Bridget		18	F	Servant	18Ma20Go
NOON, Mark		23	M	Carpenter	18Ma20Go
CLOONE, John		21	M	Carpenter	18Ma20Go
FINNIGAN, Cathne.		22	F	Servant	18Ma20Go
CARROLL, Bessy		17	F	Servant	18Ma20Go
Sally		15	F	Servant	18Ma20Go
SHARP, William		20	M	Baker	18Ma20Go
LYONS, Michael		25	M	Laborer	18Ma20Go
KENNY, Peter		24	M	Laborer	18Ma20Go
FARRELLY, A.		25	F	Wife	18Ma20Go
Mary-Ann	(D)	02	F	Child	18Ma20Go
HALLIGAN, Cathrn.		20	F	Seamstress	18Ma20Go
KILLIEN, Michl.		50	M	Laborer	18Ma20Go
Bridget	(M)	80	F	None	18Ma20Go
REGAN, Jas.		24	M	Servant	18Ma20Go
Bridget	(W)	22	F	Servant	18Ma20Go
Thomas	(S)	02	M	Child	18Ma20Go
KENNY, Pat		21	M	Laborer	18Ma20Go
MALONE, Mary		20	F	Servant	18Ma20Go
HANBURY, Thos.		30	M	Blacksmith	18Ma20Go
RYAN, Thos.		26	M	Laborer	18Ma20Go
Ellen	(W)	20	F	Wife	18Ma20Go
NYSELL, Peter		27	M	Butler	18Ma20Go
SWEETMAN, Mary		20	F	Servant	18Ma20Go
CREATION, Pat		24	M	Laborer	18Ma20Go
GOUGH, Pat		18	M	Laborer	18Ma20Go
STOKES, James		21	M	Laborer	18Ma20Go
HUGHES, Richard		18	M	Laborer	18Ma20Go
RAIL, John		21	M	Laborer	18Ma20Go
Mary	(W)	18	F	Wife	18Ma20Go
TRAINER, John		20	M	Carpenter	18Ma20Go
GILL, Bessy		19	F	Wife	18Ma20Go
RYAN, Patrick		19	M	Butcher	18Ma20Go
CUNNINGHAM, Margt.		20	F	Servant	18Ma20Go
BURK, Francis		25	M	Laborer	18Ma20Go
FEGAN, Ann		20	F	Servant	18Ma20Go
MAGUIRE, Julia		20	F	Servant	18Ma20Go
Manilia		21	F	Servant	18Ma20Go
DOOLEY, Pat		27	M	Tailor	18Ma20Go
MAGRETT, Margt.		18	F	Servant	18Ma20Go
FEHALLY, Margt.		20	F	Servant	18Ma20Go
GERAGHTY, Margt.		21	F	Servant	18Ma20Go
LONG, Patrick		20	M	Baker	18Ma20Go
CLABBY, Mary		20	F	Dressmaker	18Ma20Go
MOORE, John		25	M	Cooper	18Ma20Go
GAGHAGAN, Margt.		20	F	Servant	18Ma20Go
KELLY, Ann		20	F	Servant	18Ma20Go
FARRELL, Mary		20	F	Servant	18Ma20Go
AYRES, Eliza		20	F	Servant	18Ma20Go
MCCORMACK, Michl.		24	M	Barber	18Ma20Go
Tessy	(W)	18	F	Wife	18Ma20Go
COLLINS, Mary-Ann		24	F	Servant	18Ma20Go
SANFORD, U-Mrs.		20	F	Servant	18Ma20Go
NEWMAN, Patk.		24	M	Walter	18Ma20Go
KELLY, Mary		21	F	Seamstress	18Ma20Go
DUNCAN, Patt		18	M	Laborer	18Ma20Go
BRAHAM, Mary		20	F	Servant	18Ma20Go
DOYLE, William		18	M	Laborer	18Ma20Go
MCCABE, Patt		20	M	Laborer	18Ma20Go
MONAGHAN, Bridget		20	F	Spinster	18Ma20Go
SHERIDAN, Henry		20	M	Spinner	18Ma20Go
MCSOLLOUGH, Michl.		25	M	Blacksmith	18Ma20Go
BURKE, Julia		20	F	Spinster	18Ma20Go
KENNY, Bridget		22	F	Spinster	18Ma20Go
MALEY, John		24	M	Servant	18Ma20Go
MCCABE, Bridget		22	F	Servant	18Ma20Go
MCCUE, Ann		20	F	Servant	18Ma20Go
WHITE, Henry		50	M	Laborer	18Ma20Go
Ellen		20	F	Servant	18Ma20Go
CARTY, Margt.		19	F	Servant	18Ma20Go
COSGILL, Patt		25	M	Laborer	18Ma20Go
GRADY, Michael		23	M	Laborer	18Ma20Go
DEMPSEY, Mary		20	F	Servant	18Ma20Go
GLENNIN, Margt.		21	F	Servant	18Ma20Go
PENDER, Mary		21	F	Servant	18Ma20Go
BUTLER, John		25	M	Watchmaker	18Ma20Go
Patt		22	M	Laborer	18Ma20Go
EGAN, Winiford		20	M	Laborer	18Ma20Go
TREACY, Mary		20	F	House Maid	18Ma20Go
DEEGAN, Mary		20	F	House Maid	18Ma20Go
KENNY, Cathne.		20	F	House Maid	18Ma20Go
WALSH, Michael		27	M	Laborer	18Ma20Go
LYONS, John		22	M	Laborer	18Ma20Go
GATSBY, John		09	M	Child	18Ma20Go
CUNNINGHAM, Patt		24	M	Laborer	18Ma20Go
BURK, Thomas		22	M	Laborer	18Ma20Go
MCAVOCK, Richie		20	M	Laborer	18Ma20Go
KENNY, John		27	M	Laborer	18Ma20Go
CONLON, William		20	M	Laborer	18Ma20Go
MCNULTY, Sally		24	F	Servant	18Ma20Go
TYGUE, Mary		26	F	Servant	18Ma20Go
MULLALLY, Watt		20	M	Laborer	18Ma20Go
NEWMAN, Peter		20	M	Laborer	18Ma20Go
WINEN, Thos.		53	M	Laborer	18Ma20Go
Eliza	(W)	50	F	Servant	18Ma20Go
Francis	(S)	24	M	Cooper	18Ma20Go
Bridget	(D)	20	F	Servant	18Ma20Go
Onney	(D)	18	F	Servant	18Ma20Go
Barney	(S)	26	M	Baker	18Ma20Go
Ellen	(D)	16	F	Servant	18Ma20Go
Ann	(D)	09	F	Child	18Ma20Go
REILLY, Cathn.		20	F	Servant	18Ma20Go
Michael		15	M	Laborer	18Ma20Go
LOWE, Ann		18	F	Wife	18Ma20Go
LEIBY, Mary		20	F	Servant	18Ma20Go
DUFFY, Bridget		20	F	Servant	18Ma20Go
MURRAY, Cathn.		18	F	Servant	18Ma20Go
BRADY, Catherine		20	F	Servant	18Ma20Go
DERMODY, Geo.		24	M	Cbtmkr	18Ma20Go
Patt		22	M	Cbtmkr	18Ma20Go
U	(W)	25	F	Wife	18Ma20Go
Thomas		20	M	Servant	18Ma20Go
BURKE, James		20	M	Laborer	18Ma20Go
CONNOLLY, John		30	M	Laborer	18Ma20Go
RENNOLDS, Owen		24	M	Laborer	18Ma20Go
KING, Ann		28	F	House Maid	18Ma20Go
REILLY, Bridget		18	F	House Maid	18Ma20Go
HEGAN, Cathn.		20	F	House Maid	18Ma20Go
REYNOLDS, Mary		20	F	House Maid	18Ma20Go
HAY, John		20	M	Watchmaker	18Ma20Go
Cathne.		25	F	Wife	18Ma20Go
JORDAN, Mary		20	F	Servant	18Ma20Go
GARDNER, Richd.		40	M	Laborer	18Ma20Go
U	(W)	46	F	Wife	18Ma20Go
Robert	(S)	03	M	Child	18Ma20Go
WEBB, U-Mrs.		60	F	Wife	18Ma20Go
HOPKINS, Jas.		24	M	Shoemaker	18Ma20Go
PENDER, Thomas		24	M	Shoemaker	18Ma20Go
MCNALLY, Terence		20	M	Laborer	18Ma20Go
Patt		22	M	Laborer	18Ma20Go
WHITNEY, Michael		20	M	Laborer	18Ma20Go
DWYER, Richd.		20	M	Laborer	18Ma20Go
SWEETMAN, Michael		20	M	Laborer	18Ma20Go
KELLY, Rose		20	F	Servant	18Ma20Go
FLYNN, Sally		22	F	Servant	18Ma20Go
BYRNE, Edward		20	M	Laborer	18Ma20Go
DUNN, Patt		20	M	Laborer	18Ma20Go
FLEMMON, John		34	M	Laborer	18Ma20Go
ONEILL, Cathne.		20	F	Servant	18Ma20Go
BRUANYHAND, Geo.		20	M	Laborer	18Ma20Go
COLLIGAN, Barny		20	M	Laborer	18Ma20Go
REILLY, Edward		22	M	Laborer	18Ma20Go
MCKENNAN, Biddy		20	F	House Maid	18Ma20Go
GAFNEY, James		20	M	Baker	18Ma20Go

94

16

NAMES OF PASSENGERS	AGE	SEX	OCCUPATIONS	DATE PORT SHIP	NAMES OF PASSENGERS	AGE	SEX	OCCUPATIONS	DATE PORT SHIP
BOYD, U	20	F	Servant	18Ma20Go	MANGHAN, Patrick	40	M	Laborer	19Ma11Gp
CASEY, Ann	20	F	Servant	18Ma20Go	KELLY, Catherine	18	F	Spinster	19Ma11Gp
MURRAY, Margt.	24	F	Servant	18Ma20Go	BEAMAN, Biddy	38	F	Wi	19Ma11Gp
MILLER, Margt.	20	F	Servant	18Ma20Go	FEENEY, John	19	M	Servant	19Ma11Gp
MCDONALD, Pat	20	M	Baker	18Ma20Go	Catherine (W)	19	F	Wife	19Ma11Gp
WIELON, Ann	20	F	Wife	18Ma20Go	MAHONY, Bridget	27	F	Spinster	19Ma11Gp
MILLER, Ann	20	F	Servant	18Ma20Go	Ellen	25	F	Spinster	19Ma11Gp
DALY, Bessy	24	F	Servant	18Ma20Go	LEONARD, Catharine	18	F	Spinster	19Ma11Gp
FLATTERY, Cathne.	20	F	Servant	18Ma20Go	FORD, Malachi	38	M	Laborer	19Ma11Gp
KELLY, John	20	M	Farmer	18Ma20Go	MCMAHON, John	39	M	Laborer	19Ma11Gp
FOX, Ann	20	F	Servant	18Ma20Go	HARE, Jane	27	F	Spinster	19Ma11Gp
FITZPATRICK, John	25	M	Laborer	18Ma20Go	OBRIEN, James	36	M	Laborer	19Ma11Gp
LOWE, Michael	20	M	Laborer	18Ma20Go	MCDONNELL, Mary	27	F	Wife	19Ma11Gp
CARTLEY, Ann	20	F	Servant	18Ma20Go	DARCY, Darby	40	M	Laborer	19Ma11Gp
FEGAN, Mary	20	F	Servant	18Ma20Go	FLAHERTY, Michael	43	M	Laborer	19Ma11Gp
BYRNE, Pat	25	M	Blacksmith	18Ma20Go	NEVIN, John	21	M	Laborer	19Ma11Gp
MCCORMICK, Cathne.	20	F	Servant	18Ma20Go	CAHILAN, John	36	M	Laborer	19Ma11Gp
BURK, John	26	M	Farmer	18Ma20Go	WARD, Mary	27	F	Spinster	19Ma11Gp
Sally (W)	22	F	Wife	18Ma20Go	CALLAGHY, Patrick	46	M	Laborer	19Ma11Gp
James	20	M	Laborer	18Ma20Go	CARTY, Thomas	41	M	Laborer	19Ma11Gp
SULLIVAN, Michl.	24	M	Laborer	18Ma20Go	FLEMMING, Thomas	38	M	Laborer	19Ma11Gp
John	20	M	Laborer	18Ma20Go	Catherine	37	F	Spinster	19Ma11Gp
BUTLER, Saml.	22	M	Laborer	18Ma20Go	LAWLESS, Biddy	42	F	Spinster	19Ma11Gp
WALL, Mary	16	F	House Maid	18Ma20Go	BRODERICK, Kittty	61	F	Wife	19Ma11Gp
FOLEY, Sally	27	F	Cook	18Ma20Go	BURKE, Bridget	18	F	Spinster	19Ma11Gp
					Margaret	19	F	Spinster	19Ma11Gp
					FLEMMING, Michael	47	M	Laborer	19Ma11Gp
					Mary (W)	40	F	Wife	19Ma11Gp
CLARENCE 19 MAY 1846					Mary (D)	07	F	Child	19Ma11Gp
					Patt (S)	09	M	Child	19Ma11Gp
From Galway					CANNON, John	40	M	Laborer	19Ma11Gp
					LALLEY, Mary	21	F	Spinster	19Ma11Gp
					FINEGAN, John	27	M	Laborer	19Ma11Gp
FLANIGAN, Mary	27	F	Wife	19Ma11Gp	Michael	30	M	Laborer	19Ma11Gp
John	00	M	None	19Ma11Gp	OBRIEN, Mary	16	F	Spinster	19Ma11Gp
Kate	06	F	Child	19Ma11Gp	COPPINGER, John	30	M	Carpenter	19Ma11Gp
MAGUIRE, Peter	47	M	None	19Ma11Gp	KEHILL, John	41	M	Laborer	19Ma11Gp
Mary	40	F	Spinster	19Ma11Gp	HARDIMAN, Mary	60	F	None	19Ma11Gp
DOMADY, Thomas	36	M	Laborer	19Ma11Gp	CARRICK, Bridget	27	F	Spinster	19Ma11Gp
GALVIN, Ellen	42	F	Spinster	19Ma11Gp	FINEGAN, Mary	26	F	Spinster	19Ma11Gp
DILLON, William	36	M	Laborer	19Ma11Gp	PLEESE, Catherine	21	F	Spinster	19Ma11Gp
HUGHES, James	54	M	Laborer	19Ma11Gp	Margaret	20	F	Spinster	19Ma11Gp
CARRICK, Patrick	41	M	Laborer	19Ma11Gp	FLAHERTY, John	40	M	Laborer	19Ma11Gp
Catherine (W)	40	F	Wife	19Ma11Gp	KENNY, Ann	25	F	Spinster	19Ma11Gp
TIERNEY, Martin	22	M	Laborer	19Ma11Gp	SILVER, Ann	27	F	Spinster	19Ma11Gp
WALTERS, Matthew	30	M	Laborer	19Ma11Gp	CONNELLY, Pat	36	M	Laborer	19Ma11Gp
DOOLARTY, Patrick	26	M	Laborer	19Ma11Gp	RAFTERY, Nancy	24	F	Spinster	19Ma11Gp
CREW, John	39	M	Laborer	19Ma11Gp	MANNION, Michael	32	M	Tailor	19Ma11Gp
WARD, James	21	M	Laborer	19Ma11Gp	Mary (W)	28	F	Wife	19Ma11Gp
Mary	20	F	Servant	19Ma11Gp	MURRAY, John	46	M	Laborer	19Ma11Gp
HEAGANY, Owen	39	M	Laborer	19Ma11Gp	BURNS, Mary	25	F	Spinster	19Ma11Gp
NEILAN, James	27	M	Laborer	19Ma11Gp	DARCY, Mary	39	F	Wife	19Ma11Gp
PRENDERGAST, Patrick	42	M	Laborer	19Ma11Gp	KEALY, Mary	23	F	Spinster	19Ma11Gp
Ellen (W)	17	F	Wife	19Ma11Gp	BOYLE, Biddy	27	F	Spinster	19Ma11Gp
FARRELL, Martin	42	M	Laborer	19Ma11Gp	BUTLER, Michael	40	M	Laborer	19Ma11Gp
CONNER, Thomas	36	M	Laborer	19Ma11Gp	FLEMMING, Michael	50	M	Laborer	19Ma11Gp
DUANE, John	37	M	Laborer	19Ma11Gp	HYNES, Thomas	27	M	Laborer	19Ma11Gp
Mary (W)	32	F	Wife	19Ma11Gp	MCDERMOT, William	37	M	Laborer	19Ma11Gp
Bridget (D)	08	F	Child	19Ma11Gp	HANE, Pat	21	M	Laborer	19Ma11Gp
Mary (D)	06	F	Child	19Ma11Gp	GLYNN, John	19	M	Laborer	19Ma11Gp
Judy (D)	04	F	Child	19Ma11Gp	QUIN, John	32	M	Laborer	19Ma11Gp
John (S)	02	F	Child	19Ma11Gp					
HEAGANY, John	49	M	Mason	19Ma11Gp					
Margaret (W)	47	F	Wife	19Ma11Gp					
Mary (D)	23	F	None	19Ma11Gp	**SARDINIA 20 MAY 1846**				
John (S)	20	M	None	19Ma11Gp					
James (S)	18	M	None	19Ma11Gp	**From Liverpool**				
Judy (D)	16	F	None	19Ma11Gp					
COST, Patrick	47	M	Laborer	19Ma11Gp					
Betty (W)	46	F	Wife	19Ma11Gp	BREADY, Rose	21	F	Servant	20Ma02Gt
Kate (D)	10	F	Child	19Ma11Gp	BAGHT, James	30	M	Carpenter	20Ma02Gt
LYNCH, Patrick	48	M	Carpenter	19Ma11Gp	CAUGHLIN, Carney	16	M	Laborer	20Ma02Gt

95

17

2

Catholic Persecution

For many an Irish citizen, today's journey to New York, door-to-door, would take perhaps 12 hours. A hundred and fifty years later it is impossible to imagine the horrendous passage endured aboard the Famine ships, lasting four weeks if they were lucky, though twice as long was by no means exceptional. Even the captains and their crews were unwilling to repeat the experience too often, as the following simple statistic will reveal. The port of New York received more than half of Ireland's Famine emigrants: passenger lists recovered from US Immigration files show that 651,931 arrived on 2,743 voyages during the Famine period. Yet only 325 ships made more than one voyage.

Of those 325, only one, the 520-ton barque *Brothers*, made the voyage in each of those six years. She made a total of ten Atlantic crossings in the Famine period, all from Newry in County Down, Northern Ireland. Newry is not many miles from the site of the infamous Battle of the Boyne, and here we can see a little more of Ireland's bitter history. Though the battle was fought more than 300 years ago, it is still commemorated every year on July 12th, which remains a public holiday, by the Orange Marches celebrating a victory for the Protestant cause throughout the province of Ulster.

Perhaps the most disgraceful aspect of the Famine was that in each of its six years there was probably sufficient food exported out of Ireland to sustain the nation, certainly enough to have saved the million who died. The bulk of the agricultural produce, most of the cattle, butter, wheat, barley, vegetables, went to the markets in England. Politicians in London, and some in Dublin as well, determined that market forces should dictate the outcome. They were not disposed towards introducing food tariffs, and the starving Irish could not afford the market prices.

Notwithstanding, how did a nation of 8 million people come to rely to such a degree on a solitary crop, the humble potato? Admittedly, much of Ireland's soil is infertile, consisting of peat-bog, marsh and mountain, but the true reason lies in the division and ownership of the land – Catholic land.

Ireland has suffered from religious discord for centuries. The Civil War in England in the mid-1600s saw the removal and execution of the Catholic King Charles I. Support for the deposed Catholic monarchy remained strong in Ireland, and the people, land-owners and peasants alike, paid dearly for that. The ruler who succeeded King Charles to become Lord Protector of England, Scotland and Ireland, was a commoner, a soldier turned statesman, the Protestant Oliver Cromwell. In a series of brutal battles, Cromwell put down the Irish insurrections, slaughtering thousands and imposing savage punishments on his devout enemies. He also transported a term, 'deportation', used then to describe the sentence of deportation from their own country for petty criminals, trouble-makers and anyone deemed an enemy of the State. During Cromwell's rule, 100,000 Irish were transported to America, one of Britain's colonies. Unwittingly, the hated Lord Protector may have started a movement which has lasted for 350 years, although the flow of emigrants from Ireland to America is not deemed to have started in earnest until 1730.

The savagery of Oliver Cromwell's government was continued by his successors – still worse was to follow some 40 years later. After Cromwell died the monarchy was restored in England; then King James II, a converted Roman Catholic, was forced to abdicate in 1688. He fled to Ireland to live in exile and to raise an army as he fought to recover his throne. Once again Catholic supporters in Ireland rallied to the royal cause but James's final demise came at the Battle of the Boyne. Here, in July 1690, he led a 21,000-strong Catholic army, consisting mostly of French and Irish troops, who were outfought and outmanouevred by a Protestant force of 35,000 containing detachments of Dutch Guards, French Huguenots and English cavalry, plus Danish, Prussian, Finnish and Swiss mercenaries.

With King James in exile, the English had invited the intensely anti-Catholic Dutch ruler, William of Orange to assume the throne in London and be crowned King William III, as joint sovereign with his wife Queen Mary. William, who was also a soldier, never happier than on the battlefield, led the Protestant army himself on that fateful day, encircling his opponents on the banks of the River Boyne. Although 2,000 men perished he allowed the vast majority of his opponents to escape, and the war continued in Ireland, with battles and skirmishes, major and minor, for another year.

The loyal Irish already had good reason to loathe this cruel monarch, but in 1695, when he introduced the Penal Laws, he left his mark on them forever. All public practices of the Roman Catholic religion were banned, and various decrees stripped the huge Catholic majority of their wealth and position, homes and estates, and gradually turned them into paupers.

In time, barely 5 per cent of the land remained in Catholic ownership. Catholics were barred from purchasing land, and any acreage owned at death had to be distributed equally between all the sons in a family, unless the eldest turned Protestant, in which case he could keep the entire estate. Historians long ago identified an estate in County Clare farmed by one owner in 1793 and by 96 tenants in 1847. No Catholic could vote, hold office, practise law, join the army, carry a sword, keep a gun or own a horse worth more than £5, the equivalent of US $25 then, but today, not much more than US $7.

Education was virtually impossible: Catholic schools were closed and priests ran secret hedge schools. Morale was shattered as churches were shut, religious devotions were forbidden and priests were hunted down. The penal ways – paths followed by the faithful as they went from their villages to worship together and take Mass at isolated meeting places – can be clearly seen to this day etched into the Irish countryside. And the Penal Laws were not entirely repealed until 1829, 16 years before the Famine.

It was tiny strips of tenanted land, planted year after year with potatoes, that kept the Irish alive. Individual consumption varied from 6-9lbs a day, sometimes more, and a family were doing well if they raised a pig each year, feeding the animal on raw potatoes too small to cook. Few could afford to buy extra food, though the plate of potatoes might be fortified with buttermilk and salt. An average family of five needed to grow 6 tons of potatoes a year, and recovery from a bad year was difficult, with too few good tubers to plant for the following season.

Strangely enough, the 1845 potato rot is believed to have emanated from America a year earlier, transported in tubers destined for Europe. It was in Holland and the southern counties of England that the first signs of the blight were seen, many weeks before making an appearance in Ireland.

Those with the foresight and sufficient funds made their departure early on in those trying years, immediately after the Famine struck. Many people, especially from the Protestant communities in the north, who had suffered no religious persecution in the previous two centuries and had managed to hold on to their farms and wealth, decided to sell up and emigrate not because they were hungry or destitute but because they could see that Ireland would take so long to recover from the dreadful Famine.

Newry in Ulster at the time of the Famine.

Newry was a thriving town with a population of around 15,000 in 1845, and with daily departures of small ships for Liverpool 120 miles away, carrying agricultural produce, timber, leather, linen and Mourne granite, the inland port had long been important. It stands on the River Clanrye, 15 miles from the sea, and many a symbol of the religious hatred which has dogged Ireland for so long can be found in its magnificent surrounding countryside. Rivers and streams wind through the valleys to fill Carlingford Lough, where purple hues of the granite slopes above contrast with the green and honey-coloured farmlands below and just as the song proclaims, the Mountains of Mourne sweep down to the sea.

To be forced to leave their homes, however small and cramped, in such beautiful surroundings must have broken the hearts of many an emigrant as they boarded the big square-riggers moored on the lough at Warrenpoint, Newry's deep-water port. The Irish name for Newry is derived from the yew trees planted at the head of the strand in the fifth century to last for a thousand years, and of course, legend has it that the original yew, symbol of immortality, was planted by St Patrick himself who is alleged to have landed in Ireland at this very spot, in 432. Also in terms of religious symbolism, it may be no coincidence that it was here in Newry that the first Protestant church in Ireland was built.

The *Brothers* made the first of her ten Famine voyages early in 1846. The local newspaper, the *Newry Telegraph,* advertised all through February:

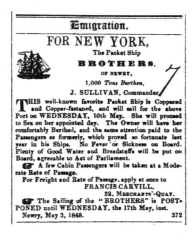

An advertisement for a later sailing of the Brothers, 'a well-known favourite packet ship'. In truth, she was a converted cargo ship.

No fare was mentioned but tickets for similar sailings in following years cost £3 10s (roughly US $17.50). On April 23rd the *Brothers* arrived in America with her full complement of passengers.

Back home, records in the once thriving community of Newry reveal that by 1848 the town's workhouse was vastly overcrowded. It held 1,283 and half of those were children, including 29 infants under the age of two.

In 1838 the Poor Law had been introduced on mainland Britain as well, but it was in Ireland that, as we shall see later, it would have its most dire effect. The new Act decreed that a portion of the rates paid by landowners should be used to build and support the workhouses where the destitute could at least survive. Throughout Ireland 130 workhouses were built: in Newry the workhouse was designed to accommodate a maximum of 800.

The workhouse at Newry, built in 1841 to accommodate a maximum of 800 people. In 1848 it housed 1,283 – half of them children.

3

Land of the Free

Famine is a word still very much part of today's vocabulary. In war-torn, poor, Third World countries such as Ethiopia, Sudan, and Cambodia, the people go hungry, their bodies wither and they die from starvation and disease. But here we are looking at Europe, at a country which was at that time the most densely populated European country, part of the British Empire, the mightiest the world has seen.

The Famine in Ireland, the starving of an entire nation 150 years ago, may seem an age away today. Yet there are still people living in America who can remember their grandparents telling personal tales of the crossing following the Potato Famine. Of course, they were really repeating their own parents' stories, but they were there aboard the ships which sailed 3,000 miles across the Atlantic. So just a few people in their 80s and 90s now, have listened to their grandmothers or grandfathers who would have been small children themselves when they became emigrants. Looked at in this way, Ireland's awful six-year-long Famine does not seem so very long ago.

The Irish arriving on America's eastern seaboard usually

settled in lodgings close to the port, especially in New York where a staggering average of 300 were disembarking daily, every day for six years: on some days more than 1,000 would

Another drawing from the Illustrated London News, *showing a raid of Galway potato store.*

arrive on a single tide. As we know, this was the favoured destination of the Irish exodus, which immediately raised its status to that of the busiest port in the world. Whether their original intention had been to move on to other cities or out on to the plains and lush farmlands, to head for the frontier or to join the Gold Rush, the majority of the Irish emigrants stayed right there, in New York.

The exodus to Canada was different: the vast majority moved on. Though many thousands sailed to the colony known as British North America, their true destination was the United States. Canada was cold, sparsely inhabited, and many of its people spoke only French. Job prospects were poor, and worse still, to remain there meant a continued existence under the hated British flag. Boston had only a tenth of New York's direct traffic but its Irish population was swollen by the masses coming from Canada.

Many had sworn an oath to settle north of the border, in return for a cheaper Atlantic passage to Halifax or Saint John, and, if they were sailing into Quebec, a free place on a barge to carry them up the St Lawrence River to Montreal. English politicians and civil servants were anxious to populate the country and subsidized fares as low as £2 (US $11), were made available. Many thousands of families were not given a say in the matter. Canada was the destination for destitute tenants on the huge estates in Ireland, cleared by their landlords, who paid the fares and chartered the ships, and the passage to Canada was far more economical than to the United States.

Once they landed, however, a great many emigrants went south. If they had a little money they took the lake steamers, small coasters and schooners, or whatever means of transport was available. If not, they walked across the border. For six months of the year the larger Canadian ports and the St Lawrence seaway were ice-bound and closed but even in the warmer half of the year, the great majority of Ireland's Famine emigrants an − estimated 200,000 − merely used those ports as staging posts.

New York and Boston were by no means alone along the east coast in receiving the emigrant ships. Baltimore and Philadelphia had regular sailings of trading ships going east across the Atlantic and captains would pick up whatever cargo was available for the return journey. During the Famine, they were well aware of the constant availability of the human cargo. It took only two or three days, a few planks of wood and some nails, for the ship's carpenter to erect bunks in the hold.

Savannah and Charleston joined in the emigrant trade too. Further south, and to a greater extent, so did New Orleans which had great appeal for those who wanted to continue their journey westwards into Texas or up the Mississippi River to the frontier lands. But the longer the journey, the higher the fare, and that choice was not open to many.

The records of two shipping firms in Londonderry have survived over the years. William McCorkell & Company and Messrs J & J Cooke, regularly advertised fares for Quebec and Saint John between £2 5s and £3 (US $12 to $15). The fare to New York started at £3 10s (US $17.50) and to Philadelphia at £4 (US $20). The cheapest steerage fare to New Orleans from Liverpool, was £5 (US $25). And a healthier and wealthier body was required to withstand that 5,000-mile voyage.

AMERICAN PASSENGER OFFICE, LONDONDERRY

PASSENGERS CONTRACT TICKET
LONDONDERRY, 18TH MAY, 1844

Ship "Provincialist" of 880 tons Register burden will sail from Londonderry for Philadelphia on the 18th day of May 1844.

We engage that the parties herein named, will be provided with a steerage passage to Philadelphia in the Ship "Provincialist" with not less than 10 cubic feet for luggage for each adult, for the sum of £4 : 0 : 0 including head money, if any, at the place of landing, and every other charge, and we hereby acknowledge to have received the sum of £2 : 0 : 0 in part payment.

Names.
Ann McElkinney   11 years.

Balance to be paid at the office of Wm. McCorkell & Co., on the 16th May, 1844.

Water and provisions according to the annexed scale will be supplied by the ship as required by law, and also fires and suitable hearths for cooking. Bedding and utensils for eating and drinking must be provided by the passenger.

A ticket *for the* Provincialist, *from Londonderry to Philadelphia.*

The variation in some fares depended on the season and the comfort of the different ships, rather than the accommodation on board. There were steerage fares, down in the holds. Cabin passengers would pay much more – £12 to £15

(US $60 to $75) – but cabins, and they were few and far between, even on the biggest vessels, were usually available only on packet ships, in regular service back and forth across the Atlantic.

A typical ticket for the voyage, from Londonderry to Philadelphia, purchased from either ship owner's office, would state:

> We engage that the parties herein named . . . will be provided with a steerage passage with not less than 10 cubic feet for luggage for each adult, for the sum of £4, including head money, if any, at the place of landing, and every other charge.
>
> Water and provision according to the annexed scale will be supplied by the ship as required by law, and also fires and suitable hearths for cooking. Bedding and utensils for eating and drinking must be provided by the passenger.

The hearths were nothing more than rudimentary boxes lined with bricks, a crude form of barbecue. When the weather was rough, no fires would be allowed, but there would often be a period of calm at the end of the day, as dusk was settling on the ocean, when a few passengers would be allowed on deck to cook for their families and friends below. Then it would be the turn of the youngest apprentice seaman on board, Jack in the Shrouds as he was known, to clamber up the rigging carrying a jug of water to douse the flames. Many a protest was raised, but no argument was heeded.

The water ration was supposed to be 6 pints per person per day, to drink, wash and cook. If the journey lasted beyond the estimated period, passengers and crew alike went thirsty and dirty, and those on board could soon gauge if they were going to be on the sea for longer than expected when the daily water allocation was reduced. Head money covered the dues which might be payable by the captain at the port before any passengers were allowed to disembark.

During the six years of the Famine Emigration the Passengers' Acts, which covered the provision of food, were changed, and different versions of these Acts were imposed by American and British governments. A glaring example of the contrast between the legislation of the two countries was in the number of passengers allowed on board. America decreed only two people be allowed for every 5 tons of the vessel's registered tonnage, while in Britain, the allowance was three for every 5 tons. Thus, British ships could carry half as many passengers, again 300 instead of 200, as American ships of similar size. Not surprisingly, American ships were considered to be faster, safer, more comfortable, more modern, and sailed by more competent crews.

Rigid enforcement of the Acts was impossible. There were regularly too many passengers aboard too many ships and too few Customs and Immigration officers. These were hard times, desperate times: with so many ships carrying emigrants for only one voyage, the politicians in Washington and London could easily be ignored, and many a captain was guilty of failing to care properly for the people in his ship. Changes in the Passengers' Acts were aimed at making ocean travel safer, for the protection of the passengers, but their effect was to drive up the fares, bringing despair to the impoverished people in Ireland.

In the first year of the Famine sailings the ships were supposed to provide each passenger, each week, with a total of 7lbs of bread, biscuit, flour, rice, oatmeal or potatoes. One pound of food a day was nothing more than an insurance against starvation: the passengers themselves were supposed to be responsible for anything else they required. Three years later, in 1849, the Acts were amended, decreeing that twice a week tea, sugar and molasses were to be given out. Ship owners were also directed to provide more space on board for each passenger. The new Act laid down a minimum of 12 square feet, so now the bunks were 6 feet long and 2 feet wide where previously they had been only 20 inches wide.

Let us imagine the scene during the last few hours on board for those emigrants bound for New York. They would have been sailing for a week or a day with the coastline in sight, depending on the winds and the weather, and on how soon the captain had sought some protection from the land. Danger from the ocean was not yet past, but eventually they would arrive at Sandy Hook and the lighthouse signalling the last run into the port, where freelance pilots would patrol in their dinghies waiting to go on board the brigs and barques to take them on the last few miles of their journey.

Staten Island then consisted of farmland and wooded hills, nor would the banks of the East River yield many clues to the spectacle in store when the emigrants reached the quayside in South Street Seaport, where the bustling wharves and piers greeted more than half a million of these new Irish-Americans. Ships' captains were responsible for listing their passengers for the Immigration authorities but there were times when these few officials would be swamped, when ten or a dozen emigrant ships from Ireland and Liverpool might tie up on one day.

At that time the city's buildings were rarely more than three or four storeys high – only the church steeples reached for the sky. At last the waters were calm, the decks level, the ship was still, groggy sea-legs would soon recover, the voyage would soon be a distant memory. So this was America . . . a land of plenty, where people had a purpose in life, and were not merely struggling to stay alive. No search for food, no distant landlords . . . At long last, the Land of the Free, a land of opportunity!

In truth, life in America proved very hard, a bitter struggle for the new arrivals. Work was not so easy to find, and job advertisements were soon accompanied by the phrase, 'No Irish Need Apply', shortened to NINA. Native Americans were worried about their own jobs and the desperate Irish immigrants represented a cheap labour force which they feared would depress wages. The natural clannishness of the Irish also threatened the political balance and many a fight or riot broke out between the nativists and the Irish and other immigrant communities, or between Catholics and Protestants. The British were held responsible for all this, blamed for deliberately dumping the poor, the vicious and the degraded on the United States of America.

Emigrant populations around the world have created ghettoes, and the Irish were no exception. People in a strange land feel comfortable living among their own, helping their neighbours, identifying with each other's problems in foreign surroundings. The Irish moved if they had to in their search for work and America's early network of roads, railways and canals right across the country owes much to the Irishman with his strong back and ability to wield a shovel or pickaxe from dawn till dusk.

But the majority of those fleeing the Famine, largely from the agricultural and poorer provincial regions of Ireland, were attracted to the city in their new country. Perhaps they felt that rural life had dealt with them cruelly and that working in industry would be preferable to labouring on the land again. They had just undergone a tumultuous experience on the high seas, and many had never seen the ocean, let alone a sailing ship, before reaching the port. Now they had arrived in not just any city, but New York, the third largest in the Western world.

Quite apart from the splendid shops with their window displays, the clothing stores and horsedrawn buses, imagine

32

going into a studio and having your photograph taken! Mind, that was a luxury, it cost a dollar. Food was sold on barrows and carts and there were more than a hundred restaurants, some specializing in French or Italian cuisine. There were bars and hotels, books and newspapers on sale, candy stalls, grand brownstone houses, jewellers, dispensaries, banks, and the more familiar sight of churches, of many denominations. Of course, there were shops and restaurants and hotels in Dublin, but not on such a scale, and how many of these people had ever been to Dublin? New York was vast – half-way through the Famine the population was approaching 500,000 and for anyone who had just left a home, which was nothing more than a stick-and-mud-built hovel without a window or a chimney, and possibly with the family's pig for a bedfellow, these new surroundings were mind-boggling.

But there were pigs in New York too, hundreds of them roamed the city along with hordes of dogs, and the rubbish lay ankle-deep in side-streets and alleyways. There were also drab and dirty lodging houses and all kinds of villains ready to batten off the gullible emigrants the moment they set foot ashore: runners to guide them to rogue landlords, friendly porters to help them with baggage which soon disappeared, ticket sellers peddling onward journeys which might not exist. Soon enough there were protection societies, almshouse commissioners and churchmen to advise the new arrivals.

The year 1846 saw the beginning of a regular, direct trade of passenger ships from the Irish ports to America. Throughout the Famine period three-quarters of Ireland's million-strong exodus would make the Atlantic crossing through Liverpool. For them it was little more than a day's sailing over the Irish Sea, perhaps three days if they were travelling from the west coast.

But Irish ships were generally much smaller, few had been built with passenger-traffic in mind and owners were not all that quick to see the opportunities. The New York port authorities list only three ships from Dublin for instance, the *Wave* and *Charlotte* as well as the *Perseverance*. Waterford had one sailing, the *Louisa*. Cork, which would later become a major influence on emigrant traffic and remain so for nearly a hundred years, sent four ships, the *Adirondack, Alhambra, Liberty* and *Alert*. From Limerick came the *Dorcas*, and from Galway the *Clarence* and the *Kate*. Only the *Mary Harrington* sailed from Londonderry, but as this port had established a strong commercial trade with Philadelphia, her early emigrants went there. And Newry sent the *Brothers* just once that first year.

The pattern of autumn and winter sailings had not yet been established from the Irish ports but it was affecting the larger vessels going out of Liverpool, particularly when, towards the end of that year, the potato crop had still shown no real signs of recovery. And there was worse, much worse, to follow.

4

Hunger and Exile

A Celtic cross stands high above the waters at the western end of Canada's Grosse Isle. Hewn out of sombre grey granite, the memorial is nearly 50 feet tall and rises like a pulpit above the mass graves on this island in the St Lawrence River. The cross bears inscriptions in Gaelic, French and English, carved on ebony panels. Built and unveiled in 1909 by the Ancient Order of Hibernians in America, it is dedicated to the victims of ship fever, or typhus, in the dreadful second and third years of the Famine emigration.

Children of the Gael died in their thousands on this island
having fled from the laws of the foreign tyrants and an
artificial famine in the years 1847–48.
God's loyal blessing upon them.
Let this monument be a token to their name and honour
from the Gaels of America.
God Save Ireland.

That is the translation from the Gaelic inscription. The bitterness of the accusatory Gaelic inscription is absent from the English dedication, which reads:

Sacred to the memory of thousands of Irish immigrants, who, to preserve the faith, suffered hunger and exile in 1847–48, and stricken with fever ended here their sorrowful pilgrimage.

The French dedication is similarly lacking in bitterness:

. . . à la pieuse mémoire de milliers d'Irlandaise qui pour garder la foi, souffrirent le faim et l'exil et, victimes du typhus, finirent ici leur douloureux pélérinage, consolés et fortifiés par le prêtre Canadian. Ceux qui sement dans les larmes moissonneront dans la joie.

Translated, it says:

. . . to the sacred memory of thousands of Irish who, in order to preserve their faith, suffered famine and exile, and, victims of typhus, ended their sorrowful pilgrimage here, comforted and strengthened by the Canadian priests. Those who sow in tears will reap in joy.

The potato crop had failed again, so it was not surprising that the direct shipping trade picked up dramatically, and 1847 lives in the memory as the worst year of the Famine, the year of the coffin ships. Thousands of passengers who suffered in these few months were not willing emigrants, they had not voluntarily given up their homes to seek a better life. They were the evicted tenants of wealthy landlords, sent out of Ireland aboard ageing ships on cheaper fares, the victims of landlord clearance.

This was really a phenomenon particular to the Canadian sailings and various estimates of the number of deaths have been voiced over the years. They can only be estimates, as so many died unreported on board ship and by no means all the

The
Grosse=Isle Tragedy

and the

Monument to the Irish Fever Victims

1847

REPRINTED, WITH ADDITIONAL INFORMATION AND ILLUSTRATIONS, FROM
THE DAILY TELEGRAPH'S COMMEMORATIVE SOUVENIR, ISSUED ON
THE OCCASION OF THE UNVEILING OF THE NATIONAL
MEMORIAL ON THE 15TH AUGUST, 1909, INCLUDING
A FULL ACCOUNT OF THE DEDICATORY
CEREMONIES, SERMON,
SPEECHES, ETC.

By J. A. Jordan

ERIN GO BRAGH

Quebec
Published and Printed by
The Telegraph Printing Company
A. D. Nineteen Hundred and Nine

A simple memorial to the coffin ship victims, unveiled 62 years later.

burials on land could be recorded. In 1847 the emigration to Canada swelled enormously for several reasons. Considerably more than 100,000 set out for the Canadian ports, as compared with 43,000 in 1846, and began arriving as early in the spring as the melting ice would allow. The death toll was similarly out of all proportion: the most conservative estimates show that around 30,000 were struck down with typhus. One third of passengers managed to survive but there were at least 20,000 deaths, over 5,000 at sea, and 8,000 in Quebec and 7,000 in Montreal.

Typhus is a fever, one of the most contagious diseases in existence, and the conditions endured in almost every facet of the emigrants' lives, in the weeks and days leading up to departure, on the ocean, detained on board awaiting inspection and then in the quarantine centres, were ideal for its survival and propagation. Workhouses, lodging houses, ship's holds without any form of sanitation, hospital wards and tents were perfect, and the typhus spread like wildfire.

In 1847 it was called ship fever but before then it was known as hospital fever, gaol fever or camp fever. The microorganism is carried in the faeces of body lice and fleas which dries into a fine dust. The dust can be absorbed through the eyes or by being inhaled, and even people who were fit, healthy and clean, and not living in overcrowded conditions, went down with typhus.

Avoiding typhus was difficult indeed, and some emigrants contracted the disease at home before they travelled. In the first half of the year 300,000 Irish were crammed on to tiny vessels to reach Liverpool, where they slept as many as 20 to a room in boarding houses while awaiting passage, and there is no doubt that the fever started to spread in that environment. Residents of Liverpool suffered too, and in May alone, 1,500 cases were reported; the local landlords were as much to blame as the recently arrived Irish who then had to spend weeks at sea, jammed together in a ship's hold, on their way to Canada.

The body lice which spread the fever are easily dealt with today by fumigation but the disease was a killer 150 years ago, with the surrounding problems. Doctors, nurses and priests in Canada, working in the quarantine hospitals and immigration sheds, died trying to save the lives of their new patients.

At this distance in time it seems that the Immigration authorities in Canada were ill-prepared for what happened when the emigrant ships of 1847 began to disembark. Yet an outstanding case had occurred the previous year when the barque *Elizabeth and Sarah* arrived at Quebec. Again, figures vary according to source, but this was a ship built in 1763 which should have carried no more than 155 statute adults. Taking into account that two children under 14 counted as one adult, she was still dangerously overloaded, with 276 names on the manifest, when she sailed from the tiny port of Killala in County Mayo. Compared with what was to come 12 months later, the death toll was relatively minor – fever killed the captain and some 20 passengers during the voyage but the remainder were in a sorry state on arrival. Many of the hastily erected berths in the 83-year-old ship had fallen down as soon as she sailed and there were only 32 to be shared by all those in the hold; the rest spent the voyage on the floor. The water was putrid and no food had been supplied by the crew.

This was a rare but not entirely isolated case in the later part of 1846, and America was swift to impose stringent health regulations at her ports to be ready for the following emigrant season. These appear to have worked very well, for Boston escaped the epidemic in 1847, and although New York had 1,400 reported deaths from fever, this figure was considered not too high in proportion to the numbers of

APPENDIX TO THE SIXTH VOLUME

OF THE

JOURNALS

OF THE

LEGISLATIVE ASSEMBLY

OF THE

PROVINCE OF CANADA.

ROM THE 2ND DAY OF JUNE TO THE 28TH DAY OF JULY, 1847,

BOTH DAYS INCLUSIVE,

AND IN THE TENTH AND ELEVENTH YEARS OF THE REIGN OF OUR SOVEREIGN LADY

QUEEN VICTORIA.

BEING THE THIRD SESSION OF THE SECOND PROVINCIAL PARLIAMENT OF CANADA.

SESSION, 1847.

Throughout 1847 endless debates in the Canadian Parliament failed to find a solution to the flow of sick emigrants from Ireland.

passengers arriving there and certainly compared extremely favourably with figures in Canada.

The new Passengers' Acts introduced by Congress (see page 30–31) had dramatically cut the numbers allowed on each ship, so fares to America were suddenly increased and cost twice as much as the tickets to British North America where these Acts did not apply. Although the US regulations were virtually impossible to enforce, many ship owners and their captains were unwilling to risk heavy fines. In May 1847, the English ship *Amelia Mary*, a small barque of 150 tons, left Donegal, in north-west Ireland, to sail direct for New York. The coast of Donegal is wild and even today is largely deserted with huge beaches and high cliffs over which the Atlantic Ocean, on more savage days, will shoot its spray 100 feet high. The quay in Donegal is very small, and passengers might well have embarked out in the bay from small rowing boats or the captain might have been duped by unscrupulous agents who pocketed the fares. In any event when the captain got out onto the ocean and checked his manifest, he discovered he was carrying 17 passengers too many. If this discrepancy showed up on arrival he faced a year in prison or a total fine of $850, $50 for each passenger over the allotted number. The *Amelia Mary* hove to and 17 of her passengers were deposited on the beach before she set sail again. The one official reference to the incident reveals that both the agents and the captain escaped punishment. Emigration from Ireland was handled in London by the Colonial Office whose Minister Earl Gray reported on June 9th, 1847:

The *Amelia Mary* cleared out of Donegal having on board 111 souls, equal to 103 adults [16 children counted as eight adults]. The ship was bound for New York and as the United States Passengers' Act would not admit to her taking so many the Master, as it is presumed with a view to avoiding the penalties imposed by that statute, suddenly re-landed 17 passengers on the beach and then sailed.

The letter then referred to the section of the British Passengers' Act forbidding the dumping of passengers after the ship has sailed, adding:

The master is liable to a fine not exceeding £50 on conviction. But there is a difficulty in taking proceedings . . . from want of evidence of the passengers left behind.

The same letter revealed that the *Lady Milton* sailed from Liverpool on April 21st but put back after being damaged in a storm on the 30th. We are not told why but when she sailed again on May 5th she left more than half her passengers, a total of 143, in port.

By this proceeding families are stated to be separated and the passengers left behind, besides the loss of their passage, have been deprived of their clothes, bedding and provisions . . . Owners or charterers and masters of vessels are required to enter into a joint and several bond to Her Majesty in the sum of £1,000 to ensure that rules and regulations for the carriage of passengers shall be well and truly performed before and during the intended voyage.

In closing, Earl Grey promised to consult the Attorney General to see whether all or part of the £1,000 bond should be forfeited. Nothing more was recorded in either case. The owners, charterers and masters escaped any punishment.

So the emigrant traffic turned towards Canada, and with Parliament in London anxious to transfer the Irish issue 3,000 miles away to the other side of the ocean, populating British

North America solved two problems. Free government passage was provided to some emigrants, and as the coffin ships went up the St Lawrence River, there were many sad accounts of the fever sheds and the burial grounds, and of the exchanges between politicians in Quebec and Montreal, and those in Dublin and London. It was a shameful period for which Britain has never officially admitted any guilt.

There was further motivation for the huge increase in Canadian emigration. The Poor Laws of 1838 meant that every landlord's rates were assessed on the value of his estate, and he was also responsible for paying rates for every one of his tenants with land worth less than £4 (just US $20). That involved many thousands and now, without food and sustenance, still more could not pay their rents. Indeed, after two Famine years the number of tenants in that position could be counted in their millions. The landlords, who included very senior politicians in the British government and lesser members of Parliament, had a huge problem to deal with. It did not matter to the tax collectors whether a landlord's tenants were unable to pay their rents, the landlord was still required to pay the rates, a proportion of which maintained the local workhouses where the destitute were admitted when they had absolutely no other means of supporting themselves. Now even the workhouses were facing bankruptcy.

Fewer tenants meant a lower potential income but it also meant lower rates. The answer was to clear the estates landlord emigration. Paying the Atlantic fares for a few score, a few hundred or a few thousand tenants was far cheaper than paying too much towards the workhouse. And as already noted, the passage to Canada was far cheaper than to America, added to the fact that several of the older vessels could be chartered for a single voyage for a lot less than the newer and better equipped ships on the Atlantic routes.

Everything fitted in nicely, except for the unfortunate emi-grant.

Grosse Isle, an island 3 miles long and about a mile wide, lies 30 miles to the east, and down river, from Quebec. It was first used as a quarantine centre 15 years earlier when a cholera epidemic struck European emigrants. When it opened in the first week of May in 1847, the superintendent Dr George Douglas, had three medical staff, 50 beds and enough straw to accomodate a further 150 patients on the floor, if neces-sary.

They had ten days to prepare before the barque *Syria* arrived from Liverpool. Of the 241 passengers who had embarked, 9 had died at sea and one more on arrival, and 84 needed admitting with typhus. Eventually, a further 118 of the *Syria*'s passengers were reported as ill. The passenger who died on arrival, little Ellen Keane, only four years and three months old, was Grosse Isle's first victim of 1847.

Five days later, the *Wandsworth* arrived from Dublin, after 45 deaths at sea and with an unknown number suffering in the hold. Further supplies, more staff and 200 army tents to accommodate the sick were rushed to the island. By 28 May Dr Douglas reported he had 850 patients in his hospital with almost 500 awaiting admission, still on board their ships. Still more emigrants had been admitted to other hospitals around Quebec, and a further 13,000 were on another 36 ships, tied-up in the river, waiting for their medical inspection. All this had happened in the space of only two weeks, and the situation would grow worse.

June arrived and the ship *Looshtauk* finally reached Quebec after a voyage of seven weeks. The spread of fever on this vessel carrying nearly 500 passengers and crew was remarkable. First signs were witnessed after a week at sea when two men went sick, but the *Looshtauk* also had scarlet fever on board, as well as typhus, which soon killed all the small children. She was fortunate to make landfall: within 17 days of leaving Liverpool, practically the entire crew had gone sick with fever, leaving only the captain John Thain and his first mate to sail the ship with some assistance from their healthier passengers.

On May 28th, the very day Dr Douglas sat down to write his first report on the conditions at Grosse Isle, the ship *Virginius* was casting off in Liverpool and heading his way with 476 passengers. In early August he was forced to write yet another report, this time devoted entirely to the conditions on the *Virginius*:

> Fever and dysentry cases came on board this vessel in Liverpool, and deaths occurred before leaving the Mersey. On mustering the passengers for inspection yesterday, it was found that 106 were ill of fever, including nine of the crew, and the large number of 158 had died on the passage, including the first and second officers and seven of the crew, and the master and the steward dying, the few that were able to come on deck were ghastly yellow looking spectres, unshaven and hollow cheeked, and, without exception, the worst looking passengers I have ever seen; not more than six or eight were really healthy and able to exert themselves.

Dr Douglas added a poignant postscript:

> Since writing the above another plague ship has dropped in, the *Naomi* from Liverpool. This ship sailed on June 15th with 331 passengers, 78 have died on the voyage and 104 are now sick. The filth and dirt in this vessel's hold create such an effluvium as to make it difficult to breathe.

Perhaps the saddest statistic is the number of deaths among the staff at Grosse Isle. A total of 44 died: 22 nurses and medical orderlies, four doctors, four Catholic priests, three stewards, three policemen, two Protestant clergymen, and six more who carted the dead away, dug graves, carried supplies.

Marianna O'Gallagher, who wrote *Gateway to Canada*, the tragic story of Grosse Isle, traced a descendant of a passenger on the *Naomi*, six-year-old Daniel Kelly. His father Bernard Kelly died in Ireland shortly before his intended departure for Canada, so his wife Mary emigrated with his brother, Daniel's uncle, leaving their village of Lissenuffy in County Roscommon. Daniel's uncle died on the voyage and his mother in the island's quarantine centre.

Daniel was one of 600 orphans eventually adopted by local families living around Quebec, and genealogists and historical researchers have managed to trace the descendants of just two of them. Francis Tighe and his wife farmed outside the village of St Croix de Lotbinière, 30 miles west of Quebec City. They were a childless couple, French Canadians in their mid-50s, and they gave Daniel their family name, raising him as their son.

When Daniel Tighe was 18, his adoptive parents swore a will with the local notary and he was granted title to the farm where he grew up. In later years the family name was changed from Tighe to Tye, and Daniel married, raised a family, and eventually a grandson arrived . . . Leo Tye. The three generations lived together in the family farmhouse, and according to Marianna O'Gallagher, Leo, who is now well into his 80s and speaks only French, remembers his grandfather Daniel and a few of the stories he told with sketchy details of surviving as a Famine emigrant.

Only one out of four of these Kellys, including the father who died at home, survived, rather less than the overall average for the emigrants who set out to reach Canada that year when an estimated one out of six died. And so it went on at Grosse Isle. The *Sir Henry Pottinger* sailed from Cork with 399 passengers in steerage, 98 died at sea, and more than 100 were sick on arrival. The *Yorkshire* took on 392 at Liverpool, 45 died and 40 were sick. The *Larch* left Sligo with 440 aboard: 108 died at sea, 150 fever-ridden passengers were detained on the island. Also from Cork, the *Bic* buried 106 at sea, and the *Agnes* another 63 on the voyage, but this ship lost so many of her passengers during the two weeks that she was detained in quarantine. Of 427 passengers aboard when she first dropped anchor in the St Lawrence, only 150 remained alive when the ship was cleared to enter port.

From Limerick, New Ross, Dublin, Belfast, Waterford, Londonderry, Newry and Galway and virtually an armada from Liverpool came ships reporting burials on the way over and sick passengers and crew who were suffering severely from typhus as the voyage ended. A great many of these ships had been chartered by absentee landlords or by agents on their behalf, clearing hundreds and even thousands at a time from their Irish estates, from land given to these English earls, viscounts and barons by grateful political leaders, generals and monarchs.

Grosse Isle has been well documented over the years but there were hundreds more deaths in hospitals around Quebec and still more at Montreal, 180 miles further up river, and in just about every town or settlement where apparently fit emigrants arrived, only to go down with the fever or dysentery soon after becoming settled. More still had not recovered their strength by the time of the early snows in October and they were claimed by the cold, with the latest arrivals carrying on suffering and dying well into the first days and weeks of the following year.

Catholic persecution and the Penal Laws, the Famine and particularly the year 1847 with the clearings and the typhus, are at the root of today's strife surrounding Northern Ireland, and some of the feeling expressed in Gaelic by the Hibernian Order when they unveiled their memorial at Grosse Isle in 1909, still survives in America and Canada.

The Famine Emigration began slowly in 1846 and suffered a dreadful miscarriage in 1847. The stories of the coffin ships soon reached home, but the Irish were not deterred. How could they be? What else could they do, where else could they go? The flood across the Atlantic was set to continue for many years to come.

5

The Voyage of the *Jamestown* and Others

No fewer than 5,000 crossings are estimated to have carried the million Irish Famine emigrants westwards over the Atlantic. Yet a single passage in the opposite direction has achieved great significance historically. This was the voyage of the *Jamestown,* a well-armed man-of-war and one of only six sloops in the American navy, transformed overnight into a merchant vessel on a mission of mercy.

The winter months of 1846 right through to the following spring were bitterly cold, with unusually heavy snowfalls, and the full extent of the suffering in Ireland, especially during the early months of 1847, was never fully or widely appreciated around the world, especially in England where the plight of the Irish achieved neither recognition nor sympathy. The greatest help came from the United States: the recent emigrant arrivals carried the news with them and each one had a personal story which bore testimony to the hopeless situation in every corner of their homeland. Months before the first of the coffin ships sailed, a wave of relief organizations and meetings broke across America. Ships from Newark, Philadelphia and New York sailed before the spring arrived for Cork, Londonderry and Limerick, carrying some clothing but mostly food.

The Quakers Society of Friends were the first large-scale organizers of relief for Ireland, and when the American Vice-President chaired a huge public meeting in Washington on February 9th, they urged that every city, town and village should hold a meeting so that a large national contribution might be raised and forwarded with all practicable dispatch to the scenes of the suffering. Just before that meeting, the government in London announced they would pay the freight charges on all donations of foodstuffs to Ireland.

Washington matched this by stating that no tolls would be charged on roads or canals for goods on their way to Ireland, and several independent railway companies promised to carry suitably labelled packages for free. Cash came in from all sides, including a noteworthy contribution of US $170 dollars from the Choctaw Indian Tribe. Suddenly, available shipping for the eastern crossing of the Atlantic became scarce, and another crowded February meeting, this time in Boston, heard that Congress had been petitioned that one of the ships of war now lying in Boston Harbour, be released to sail for Ireland freighted with provisions.

Reaction in the capital was swift. We need to remember that at this time America was heavily engaged in war against Mexico. Congress voted on March 8th that the USS *Jamestown* in Boston and the USS *Macedonian* in New York be released from service, their armaments removed and assigned to the Irish Relief Committee in each city who would arrange for a civilian captain and crew to sail these ships to Ireland with relief supplies.

Three weeks later, the *Jamestown* set sail. The sloop, which was 157 feet long, 1,000 tons and normally carried 22 guns, was now commanded by Captain Robert Bennet Forbes, a well-known Bostonian. By May 16th he was back home, fully a month before the *Macedonian*, a frigate of 1,700 tons with 44 guns and buffeted by all sorts of political problems, could leave New York.

Loading had begun in Boston on St Patrick's Day; the Labourers' Aid Society composed almost entirely of native Irishmen, stowed all the cargo without drawing pay. If the departure of the *Jamestown* was seen as such a triumph in America, imagine how she was greeted as she dropped anchor after a voyage of only 15 days in the harbour of Cove, close to Cork City.

The *Cork Examiner* reported next day:

> Arrival of the *Jamestown*
> American sloop of war in Cove
> with provisions for the destitute Irish

> This event which has been looked forward to with such anxiety by the inhabitants of the South of Ireland in particular, and the whole of Ireland in general, took place at 5 o'clock on Monday evening, at which hour this noble ship was described entering the mouth of our harbour, majestically gliding in beneath a cloud of canvas.
> The town itself wore a most gay and exciting appearance, the quays and heights being thronged by anxious thousands desirous to see and greet the illustrious stranger.

The ship carried 400 barrels of pork, 100 large casks of ham, 655 barrels and 4,688 bags of cornmeal, 1,496 bags of corn, 1,375 barrels of bread, 353 barrels of beans and 84 barrels of peas supplied by the Boston Committee. From Charlestown had come 50 barrels of flour, 100 barrels of rice, 50 barrels of cornmeal, two barrels of bread, 60 barrels of beans, four barrels of peas and four boxes of clothing.

Other groups in America had sent ten barrels of oatmeal, 85 packages of potatoes, 547 bags of corn, a barrel of flour, 34 packages of rye, two packages of oats, three bags of wheat, a cask of dried apples, four packages of beans, six boxes of fish, 201 packages of meal and 28 parcels of clothing. The value of all these gifts and supplies was assessed at US $35,868 (£7,137) and the cost of the voyage around US $2,500 (£500).

Back home, Captain Robert Forbes reported:

I went with father Theobald Mathew only a few steps out of one of the principal streets of Cork into a lane; the Valley of the Shadow of Death, was it? Alas no, it was the valley of death and pestilence itself. I saw enough in five minutes to horrify me; hovels crowded with the sick and dying; without floors, without furniture, and with patches of dirty straw covered with still dirtier shreds and patches of humanity.

Some called for water to Father Mathew and others for a dying blessing. From this very small sample of the prevailing destitution, we proceeded to a public soup kitchen under a shed guarded by police officers. Here a long boiler containing rice, meal etc., was at work while hundreds of spectres stood without; begging for some of the soup which I can readily conceive would be refused by well-bred pigs in America. Every corner of the street is filled with pale, careworn creatures, the weak leading and supporting the weaker; women assail you at every turn with famished babies imploring alms.

Yet Mr Forbes was able to add this postscript: 'I shall ever look back on the voyage of the *Jamestown* as the happiest event of my life.'

In New York, the *Jamestown*'s sister-ship in the US navy was still moored with 2,000 barrels of meal and flour on board, the centre of a political controversy. Many years earlier, in 1812 when British forces burned much of Washington, a British ship named *Macedonian* was seized,

A soup kitchen in Cork – one of many in Ireland that kept thousands alive, at least for a few more weeks . . .

and although this vessel was a successor to the original, it was felt that a ship named after a prize of war should not be used to transport a relief cargo to Ireland, especially if the British government were going to pay the shipping costs.

The Irish Relief Committee refused to use her, even though the commander George Coleman de Kay promised not to accept a penny from the British and to pay all the costs of the 6,000-mile round-trip personally. The weeks of delay and frustration added to the bill and by the time he had paid the cargo-handlers and covered the wages for a crew and their supplies for the return-crossing, Mr de Kay was £3,000 out of pocket.

When he heard of the problems, Captain Forbes, now back in Boston, organized a *Macedonian* Committee. Supplies flowed in from many cities and on July 28th the navy frigate finally arrived in Cove where another ecstatic welcome awaited them. A member of the crew had been busy composing verse on the voyage and was allowed to reply in poetic rhyme.

> Brothers, although the ocean rolls between
> Our homes, no ocean rolls between our hearts
> With suffering soul Columbia has seen
> Pale Erin's wretchedness; and soon her marts
>
> Were crowded with her offerings of free,
> Full tearful aid; swart labour's horny hand
> Gave his last dollar, or sent over the sea
> Bread Stuffs, the staff of life in every land.
>
> Hence comes the *Macedonian* noble bark,
> The smile of heaven illuminates her sails,
> Which waves like Mercy's wings over famine stark
> And heals the wounds where pestilence prevails.
> Brothers in tongue, arts, bravery and blood,
> Let us be rivals strong, in doing good.

With today's ease of communications and information technology, the ability to incite world opinion would render the British government's exploitation of Ireland and the Irish people unthinkable. Of course, regularly throughout the period, newspapers reported on the Famine and its effects on the population, the London *Times* almost daily, and the *Illustrated London News* (*ILN*) weekly. But there was no radio or television or mass-media. There were no telephones, telexes or ticker-tapes to tell the rest of Europe and the world what was really going on, only limited telegraph lines used for vital commercial despatches. At that very moment in history, the German Paul Julius Reuter was founding the news agency which still carries his name. His original carrier-pigeon service was introduced in Germany, France and Belgium in 1850, and he moved to London to open his agency the following year.

The very moving accounts of the emigrant voyages and their arrival in the New World did nothing to change conditions during those six years. Passengers' Acts were amended but remained largely unenforced; the laws of supply and demand ruled the waves as well as determining market forces in Ireland.

One looks forward to the sea but does not expect to find a grave. Thus runs an old Irish proverb which proved so prophetic for many thousands of Irish emigrants in 1847, and in books, diaries, newspaper articles, official reports and Parliamentary papers dealing with the events of that year, the stories of those watery graves have been told and re-told.

The Ocean Plague was eventually published as a book but it was originally a daily chronicle kept by a man who sailed from Dublin on May 30th 1847, on an eight-week voyage to Quebec. Robert Whyte was a cabin passenger, although the book makes no mention of his ship's name. It carried an interesting quotation from Lord Sydenham as an introduction. 'To throw starving and diseased paupers under the rock at Quebec, ought to be punishable as murder.' These damning words came from a man who was formerly Governor General of Canada.

Ship owners and brokers cautioned passengers to bring on

board sea stock to supplement the official supply of food. Robert Whyte wrote that:

> . . . those of the emigrants who depended entirely for their sustenance on the 7lbs of provisions provided weekly under the Passenger Act, were starving.
> The captain and his wife were kindly enough, she dosed the sick with porridge containing drops of laudanam and a little girl, born during the voyage, was named after her. On June 15th ship fever broke out, 110 passengers are shut up in the unventilated hold of a small brig, without a doctor, medicines or even water.

He noted on July 9th that half the passengers and crew now had the fever. On July 25th they anchored off Grosse Isle: '. . . the river is a floating mass of filthy straw, refuse of foul beds, barrels containing the vilest matter, old rags, tattered clothes, thrown overboard from vessels cleaning their holds.' The sick were not taken off until August 1st, their 63rd day on board, and by then several had died. One was the wife of an emigrant from Meath whose funeral Robert Whyte attended, adding, 'After the grave was filled up her husband placed two shovels in the form of a cross and said . . . "By that cross Mary I swear to avenge your death. As soon as I earn the price of my passage home I'll go back and shoot the man that murdered you and that's the landlord." '

William Smith, an English cotton-worker, wrote *A Voice from the Steerage* as a record of his voyage on the *India*, filled with Irish passengers who began to succumb to the fever before the ship was a week out of Liverpool. The captain caught it and died, 26 of the passengers died, one threw himself overboard and three more became lunatics, according to the author, who also went down with the fever. On reaching New York after eight weeks at sea, 123 of the passengers were taken into quarantine on Staten Island. Mr Smith survived but he told a harrowing tale of his days spent in the hospital.

Another private log, this time of the voyage to Quebec, was kept by a passenger on the *Naparima*, a Sligo schoolteacher, Gerald Keegan, travelling with his wife Aileen. The Keegans had lived on the estate owned by Lord Palmerston. This account too was published as a book, *Famine Diary: Journey to a New World*. The first entry was for April 9th:

We sailed at daybreak this morning. Our barque the *Naparima* with estimated accommodation for 300 has over 500 on board. It will indeed be a prosperous voyage for the charterers and the captain who get £5 for each passenger. The *Naparima* is an ancient tub of a vessel that has reached a ripe old age. Her creaking timbers will be severely tested if we run into rough weather.

Three days rations of sea biscuits were served. They were tough and somewhat mouldy but the people were so famished that they ate them without complaint. Unfortunately, almost all of them were consumed the same day. About half of the passengers had no place to bed down for the night. They tried to rest on bundles and chests on the floor of the steerage quarters. There are no lights, no portholes and no ventilation except for what fresh air enters from the two hatchways.

The legal allowance is 33 inches in width, (bunk space) for each passenger but the overcrowding on the *Naparima* allows only about half of that. By noon hour today the air was already foul and if fever breaks out I fear for the worst. It is an ideal place for the disease to spread. I wonder what methods will be used to get rid of refuse of various sorts. One redeeming feature is the freedom to remain up on deck in fine weather. This afternoon the deck was crowded.

A month into the voyage, the schoolmaster felt compelled to intercede in an argument between his cousin and the ship's mate. They fought and the crewman was eventually overpowered. They arrived in St Lawrence on May 23rd, where they dropped anchor, and that evening when he went on deck, Gerald Keegan's view of the river was somewhat different to that of Robert Whyte's. I saw a shapeless heap move past our ship on the outgoing tide, he wrote. Presently there was another and another. Craning my head over the bulwark I watched. Another came and it caught in our cable and before the swish of the current washed it clear, I caught a glimpse of a white face. I understood it all. The ship ahead of us had emigrants and they were throwing overboard their dead.

That mid-ocean confrontation with the mate would cost the schoolteacher and his wife dearly. On June 2nd, as they ferried bodies to the dock by rowing boat, the *Naparima* sailed for Quebec City and the mate left them stranded on Grosse Isle. Both then went to work with the medical staff but within a few days Aileen had succumbed and Gerald soon followed.

This evening I asked Father O'Hare to look after this little book for I don't think I will be able to write any more . . . this writing looks very shaky. In reverent memory of all who have perished in this holocaust and of all who have suffered in any way, as well as to all those who have spent themselves in a heroic effort to help us, I dedicate the message in this little book. Farewell, Gerald Keegan.

That was penned on June 25th, only 77 days after he set out for this new life. A hungry man, but fit enough and strong enough to overcome a rugged seaman in a fist-fight, he was now one more wretched victim of ship fever.

The Perseverance. Her passengers embarked on St Patrick's Day 1846 in Dublin. Here she sets sail for New York.

Below decks. Three, four, maybe five thousand miles to go across the Atlantic.

South Street Seaport, New York. During the famine the Irish emigrants arrived at the rate of 300 every day for six years.

USS Jamestown. Congress in Washington loaned her to carry relief supplies to Cork in 1847.

The Ford family. Bound for the quays and Quebec . . . and Dearborn, Detroit.

The Harmony. All the way from Waterford, arriving in Boston to the welcome of a New England sunset.

Cushlamachree. From Galway, the 'Joy of My Heart' heads into the East River after eight winter weeks at sea.

The words of Stephen de Vere, a landowner in Limerick and a champion of the people, have been recorded many times. De Vere sailed in steerage among emigrants to Quebec in April 1847. His ship went from London but still served his purpose, which was to gather specific evidence on the sufferings of Irish emigrants at sea. Later that year his evidence was received in Parliament, by a House of Lords Select Committee on Colonization from Ireland. He wrote:

> Hundreds of poor people, men, women and children of all ages from the drivelling idiot of 90 to the babe just born, huddled together without light, without air, wallowing in filth and breathing a fetid atmosphere, sick in body, dispirited in heart . . . living without food or medicine except as administered by the hand of casual charity, dying without the voice of spiritual consolation and buried in the deep without the rites of the church.

Water was in short supply, food was usually uncooked because there were not sufficient fires, the captain sold liquor to the passengers, and though they were carrying a cargo of gunpowder for the British garrison in Quebec, pipes of tobacco were secretly lit below decks unchecked by the crew, according to de Vere's statement. The voyage took nearly three months and his account of the fever on board, the conditions in steerage, the hurried burials at sea and the captain's refusal to listen to his complaints, went to the Parliamentary committee who recorded his deposition but took no action.

By then, many an emigrant had found a watery grave and discovered the truth of the old Irish proverb. The year of the dreadful fever and hunger which claimed so many lives provides an appalling chapter in the history of the Famine

Emigration, and must never be forgotten. At the same time 1847 and the coffin ships must never cloud the triumph of the million who got there in those six years, who overcame the sickness and the hunger and walked off their ship, whether in Canada or America, and who continued to live and to thrive.

6

The Fords of Fairlane

Sixteen times the name FORD would have been written on
a ship's manifest in Cork but we do not know exactly
what ship or precisely when she set sail for Quebec, other
than the year. It was a name which would become famous
around the world at the turn of the century and a clear
example of the difficulty in maintaining records for that
dreadful year of 1847. What we do know is that Henry Ford,
inventor of the mass-produced motor car, was a direct
descendant of a Famine emigrant. His father William was
21 when he left home and the tenanted farm at Ballinascarty
with the rest of the family.

William's mother Thomasina failed to survive the journey
but we do not know whether she died at sea or soon after
arrival. She was almost certainly another victim of ship's
fever but there is no record of her burial. Despite the sadness
surrounding the departure and the voyage and the struggle
to create a new life, the Ford story is full of romance and
cherished memories of Ireland.

In the emigration party there were grandmother Rebecca,
a 71-year-old widow, her son John and his wife Thomasina,

with their seven children, of whom William was the eldest. They were joined by another of Rebecca's sons, Robert, his wife and four children, and their journey was continued immediately they arrived in Canada. For some years they had ignored the entreaties to leave Ireland from three older

Fair Lane in Cork, where the Ford family spent their last night in Ireland.

brothers, Samuel, Henry and George, who had gone to America in 1832, built homes and begun farming in Dearborn, near Detroit. That is where the remaining 15 members of the Ford family headed from Quebec.

Cork has a special place in the history of Ireland's emigrants to America, and not only from the Famine years. A dozen miles to the east of the city is the Cove of Cork, formerly called Queenstown and now reverting to the Gaelic name of Cobh, probably the largest and most natural harbour to be found anywhere in the world and intrinsically linked to the city of Cork itself. For more than a hundred years until the wide-bodied jet airliners arrived, thousands upon thousands sailed out of this port, taking their last look at Ireland, and for that reason it became known as the Harbour of Tears.

Back in the reign of Queen Elizabeth I, some 250 years earlier, the rape of Ireland by the English had already begun and in the south-west corner of the country 600,000 acres of land, confiscated from their owners, were graciously granted by the Queen to a few English gentlemen. They were probably among the first of the absentee landlords and the early Fords, a family of Protestant farmers, tenanted land on one of those estates, at Madame, near Ballinascarty. Just a few large stones from the tumbledown remains of their single-storey cottage lie on that spot today, beneath the wide branches of an old sycamore tree.

The Ford family had 30 miles to travel to reach Cork, and like many others they would have loaded their belongings on to a handcart along with the younger members of the family, while the older children and their parents walked alongside. On the rocky paths and what passed for roads at that time, it would have taken them two or three days. The railway link from nearby Bandon was then being planned but would not open until 1851.

In those days some ships loaded and sailed from Cork rather than the harbour at Cobh. The old city of Cork was built on an island created by the River Lee as it divides then joins again to flow into the Atlantic. Twenty different quays, each with its own name, lay around the island, and it was from one of those that the Ford's ship sailed. Not more than 300 yards away, the family spent their last night in Ireland, in a cottage in Fair Lane, off Fair Hill which climbs gradually away from the port and has since been renamed Wolfe Tone Street, after the Irish leader who tried to overthrow the English in the 1790s.

There were 97 one- and two-roomed cottages and small

stores listed in Fair Lane, and in one of those Thomasina Smith (her maiden name) had been born and raised. There were three families named Smith living in Fair Lane then. John, Daniel and Denis and all 16 Fords are said to have stayed the night in one of those cottages, with Thomasina's mother and father. The transfer to the ship would take only minutes. The fare would have been £2 or £2 5s, little more than US $10 each and half that for the smaller children.

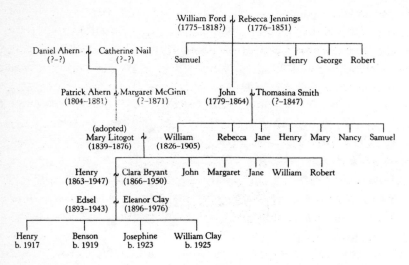

The Ford family tree. Thomasina did not survive the Atlantic crossing.

On the other side of the ocean, having lost his wife, John took his children William, Rebecca, Jane, Henry, Mary, Nancy and Samuel to Michigan and to Dearborn for a reunion with the brothers he had not seen for 15 years. The following year he bought an 80-acre farm from a man named Mayberry whom he had known at home in County Cork.

William could not settle on the farm. He moved around the country and spent some time working on the Michigan Central Railway, extending the line to Lake Michigan, but he eventually returned and found employment on a farm owned by Patrick Ahern. Although they had been in America for many years, the Aherns were originally from Cork and they may well have been close neighbours of William's late mother – a Terence Ahern was listed as owning a house, office and yard at No. 73 Fair Lane.

William Ford, Henry's father. At 21, he was the eldest of the 11 children in the emigration party.

The youngest child in the Ahern family had been adopted and retained the name Mary Litogot, and soon after they met William and Mary were married and moved on to a farm of their own, again at Dearborn. The first of their six children, Henry Ford, was born on July 30th 1863 and he would have three brothers and two sisters, all born and raised on the farm. Like his father during his 20s, Henry did not take easily to farming and later wrote, 'My earliest recollection was that, considering the results, there was too much work on the place.'

A fall from a horse at the age of 12 led Henry to tinkering with engines in a small machine shop he set up in one of the farm buildings and by the age of 15 he had constructed his first steam engine. Around about then he was out on a horse-drawn waggon with his father when they saw a traction engine for the first time: 'I was off that waggon and talking to the engineer before my father knew what I was up to, it was that engine which took me into automotive transportation . . .' Henry wrote.

Henry was soon off the farm and became a machinist's apprentice and an amateur watch repairer. Then he maintained and repaired steam engines, went to work as an engineer for the Edison Company, supplying electric light for Detroit, and had reached the age of 30 before he became involved with the internal combustion engine. He built his first car, the Quadricycle, in 1896, and the rest is history. Although his first involvement with a car company led to bankruptcy, Henry Ford, son of a Famine emigrant, went on to become the first mass-producer of the motor car, speedily revolutionizing American industry and doubling the wages of manual workers.

He was only a week off his 40th birthday when the first Ford motor car was sold, but he never forgot his origins. His father William had left Ireland in 1847, 16 years before his eldest child was born, and Henry was aged 49 when he made his first visit to the family home. He arrived in Cork in 1912, already a famous inventor and industrialist, and took the path many millions of Irish-Americans have taken before and since, to the farm his forefathers had worked for 250 years. And he went to the spot where his father, grandfather, great grandmother, uncles and aunts had spent their last hours in Ireland, in a cottage long since pulled down in Fair Lane.

Henry Ford took these memories back to America along with something more tangible. The hearthstone from the fireplace in the old cottage at Madame was installed in the wall of a mansion he was building in Dearborn which he subsequently named Fair Lane. But that was not enough. A housing estate in Dearborn where many of his workforce lived was also called Fair Lane, and appropriately, he used the name yet again for one of the most successful models his company ever produced, the Ford Fairlane. Henry Ford died aged 83 in 1947.

7

Absentee Landlords

L andlord emigration is more than a mere catchphrase. In two words it describes the monumental calamity in Ireland as the Famine took hold of the country. Looking at the economics existing on many of the great estates and the simple sums presented by their land agents to the owners of those estates, it cost a landlord half as much in one year to send his tenants abroad than it would cost to keep them at home. A dilemma many sort to overcome by landlord emigration.

Strokestown is a tiny community in County Roscommon, geographically close to the very centre of Ireland, and here a Famine Museum was opened by Mary Robinson, the President of Ireland, to mark the 150th anniversary of the year of 1845 when the Famine began. Strokestown Park House and the surrounding estate, which stretched for 9,000 acres, epitomized the problems Ireland faced as the Famine took hold of the country.

The land at Strokestown was granted to the Mahon family around 1680 by the English King Charles II, in return for their support during the Civil Wars. Fifty years later Thomas

Mahon, who had become a Member of Parliament, built the grand house in the Palladian style which can be traced back to the Romans. Even the stables where the museum is sited, had vaulted ceilings and a galleried kitchen which allowed the lady of the house to remain aloft and watch her cooks and servants at work below, without actually standing among them and absorbing the smells.

The date stone from the first Mahon house.

The estate passed down through generations of elder sons in the family and in July 1800 Maurice Mahon accepted a peerage to become the First Baron Hartland of Strokestown. But the last of the line, grandson of the original Lord Mahon, was declared insane, and when he died in 1845, without any children to follow him, the estate had suffered ten years of neglect. Ownership passed to a cousin Major Denis Mahon whose name became notorious two years later, at the height of the Famine.

Major Mahon was not entirely an absentee landlord, but he spent much of his time in England. Land agents ran the Irish estate for a fee, and at the new owner's command, unfortunately coinciding with the first season's failure of the potato crop, they prepared a plan for evicting tenants. Three years of rent arrears totalled £13,000 and several hundred of Denis Mahon's tenants became emigrants. Willingly or unwillingly, they took their place in the Landlord Emigration sweeping through the grand estates of Ireland.

Two of the ships which carried the majority of Major Mahon's former tenants to Canada were the infamous coffin ships the *Virginius* and the *Naomi,* condemned by Dr Douglas at Grosse Isle (see page 44–48), and suffered more than 200 deaths at sea with another 200 passengers critically sick with fever on arrival.

The physical condition of the passengers prior to the voyage was held to be partly responsible for so many deaths. Whatever the reasons, not six months after they left Ireland, on Monday, November 2nd 1847, Major Mahon was assassinated. He was shot in the chest as he drove his carriage home late in the afternoon to Strokestown Park House, and died instantly. He was not the first landlord to be murdered, but the controversy surrounding the estate clearings rumbled on for many months, with dozens of letters in Irish and English newspapers, and debates in the House of Commons and the House of Lords in London. Catholic priests and bishops were drawn into the row, which lasted until the last of the killers was hanged late in 1848. Whatever the rights and wrongs of 60-year-old Major Mahon's conduct, his death ensured that there were suddenly many more absentee landlords in Ireland, who fled the country in fear of their lives.

The politicians had a field day. Irish organizations agitating for a return to governing the country from Dublin instead of London, sided with the Roscommon peasantry who were accused of conspiring against their landlord. The *Freeman's Journal* wrote:

The people were said to be displeased at him for two reasons. The first was his refusal to continue the conacre system, the second was his clearing away what he deemed to be the surplus population. He chartered two vessels to America and freighted them with his evicted tenantry. In every other relation of his life Major Mahon was, we believe, much respected.

The newspaper referred to America rather than British North America, or Canada, but at this time the many newspapers engaged in the heated arguments, made no reference to the human tragedy on the voyage. How much, or how little, was known at that time in County Roscommon of the disasters aboard the *Virginius* and *Naomi*?

The poorest of those working the land were squatters without any legal claim whatever to the piece of ground they occupied. In a slightly better position were those working in the conacre system. Although tenants were not granted any rights, under conacre they would benefit from tending a stretch of farmland without any lease for a year at a time, the landlord maintaining and preparing the soil for sowing and taking a rent after the crop was harvested. Popular among the peasantry, conacre was less so with the landlords who too often found the rents difficult to raise, and after the first season's calamity with the potato, often impossible to collect at all.

Through the accumulation of poor rates paid by the landlords, it was hoped to support the really destitute population in the 130 workhouses originally planned in Ireland. In 1847 some of those had not opened, and some had not been built while others like that in Roscommon, faced bankruptcy. Denis Mahon sat on a local Relief Committee and shortly before his death he argued publicly with the chairman, the local priest Father Michael McDermott.

The day before his death the priest attacked Major Mahon from the pulpit.

Another report appeared in the local *Longford Journal*, in the week of the murder, and an excerpt of that was carried by *The Times* in London:

Major Mahon was a resident landlord and his exertions to alleviate the distress during the last distressing season were equal to any gentleman in the country possessing a similar income. Indeed it may be said that he had none, having to live on other resources, as he got little or no rent for the last 18 months.

The honourable gentleman, like many others, quarrelled with the priests in his neighbourhood about the relief of the poor, and although at an expense of £6,000 and £8,000 [US $30 and $40,000] he sent upwards of 700 poor people (who appeared thankful and expressed their thanks) to America . . . this season he has been from the chapel altars, even on this very last Sunday, reprobated and abused as a tyrant, oppressor of the poor etc., and now we behold the result.

We believe at the present moment letters of thanks to Major Mahon for sending them out, and thanking God that they went out of poverty, could be shown by friends of the emigrants in the neighbourhood of Strokestown. But what signifies it, if they were taken out of poverty and placed beyond the reach of want?

The Bishop of Elphin was being pressured to discipline the priest, and a Catholic conspiracy was also blamed for the Major's murder. But the Bishop's public reply came in April the following year when he wrote a leading article, also in the *Freeman's Journal*, headlined:

ABSENTEE LANDLORDS

EXTERMINATION BY THOUSANDS! THE STROKESTOWN MASSACRE DEVELOPED

By now the news of the typhus and the horrors of Grosse Isle had reached Ireland, and the Bishop wrote a report on the evictions at Strokestown, attacking Denis Mahon and holding him accountable for the deaths of 3,006 men, women, including 84 widows, and children. And the Bishop listed every one of their names:

> We call on all Christian men to examine these proscription lists, worse than those of the Roman tyrants. Perhaps the fact has no parallel in history . . . three thousand men, women and children swept from their homes and firesides, and exposed to almost certain death, simply because one man, acting under a British law, willed their expulsion! Except in crowded cities, visited by war or pestilence, we know of no waste of life to be compared with that on Major Mahon's property within the same period of time.
>
> Major Mahon willed the annihilation, the law confirmed it, and the 28 townlands [villages] were reduced to solitude and three thousand, only imagine the number, THREE THOUSAND! driven forth in misery and mourning, one huge mass of penury and suffering, the old and the young, the widow and the orphan, the able-bodied and crippled, fathers, mothers, wives, children, all in one confused and ghastly crowd, for to the seashore to seek a new home beyond the waters, but destined to divide their bodies between the sea and pestilence. Scarce a fragment of those three thousand exiles now survives.

County Roscommon has a curious mixture of land and water. Bordered by the River Shannon, it has many lakes and four huge loughs, a fisherman's paradise. A third of the land is bog, but much of the remainder provides superb grazing for sheep and cattle, with little acreage given over to crops. Undoubtedly, Major Mahon's position as owner of 9,000 acres and landlord to so many hundreds of families, was very strained. A letter from his agent the previous year illustrated his situation very clearly as the first plan to emigrate many of his tenants was laid out. This affected 479 families, a total of 2,444 people living off just 2,105 acres.

Nearly half of all the farms in Ireland were under 5 acres. These Strokestown families being lined up for emigration were of average size, two parents and three children. And they occupied roughly four acres per family. By comparison to millions of others they were fortunate, but there is no material difference between half an acre of rotten potatoes and 4 acres of rotten potatoes.

The agent pointed out that if the potatoes were replaced by oats to provide the staple diet for the tenant population, each family would need 12 acres to grow a crop large enough for them to exist for a year, following a good harvest. 'It would seem, if this calculation be correct, the population on this land exceeds what it can support by two-thirds at present,' the agent wrote, containing:

The cost of keeping a pauper in the Roscommon Poor House averages about 2s. 9d. a week [68 cents], that is £7 3s. a year [US $36]. The cost of emigration to Quebec averages £3 12s [US $18]. The cost of clearing this surplus population would be £5,865, the cost of supporting them in the workhouse £11,634, so the difference in favour of emigration is £5,769 [US $28,245].

I think the facts are sufficient without any further remarks of mine, to show the impossibility of collecting poor rates or rents, or of affecting any change in the condition of the people or prevent[ing] any expenditure while the land remains in such small divisions in the hands of paupers, unable to support themselves much less to till it to advantage.

There were many exchanges of letters between the local agent and Major Mahon who went away for long periods to Manchester, a minimum four-day journey from Roscommon, and London, which was probably a week away. The Major wrote that he could not afford £5,000 and urged the agent to find a cheaper passage out of Sligo or through the port of Liverpool. He argued that he had to borrow money to pay those tenants who wanted to travel independently a small remuneration for their livestock and crops, and he needed to borrow more to pay the fares of others plus the cost of extra food for the voyage – rice, salt, oatmeal and salted herrings – to provide one pound of food per day above the government ration.

Nearly 1,000 emigrated, costing him £2,400, on the *John Nunn* and the *Erin's Queen* as well as the *Virginius* and *Naomi*. A great many tragically failed to complete the journey and many more died soon after setting foot in Canada. They were dying at home too from typhus and dysentry. Fever sheds had been raised on the estate in the village of Dysart, and in June that year it was reported from there that the amount of mortality averaged four or five every day. Many victims had received some compensation for giving up their land and were then found to be too ill to travel abroad.

The murder of Major Mahon had a dramatic effect, not least on his former neighbouring landlords. Four days after his death 288 acres of prime land and a lovely farmhouse were put up for auction with a reserve of £20,000, said to be half the estimated, true value of the property. The sale was cancelled when the highest bid reached only £2,500. Within a matter of weeks four more landlords in Ireland were shot and land agents and rate collectors were being threatened and assaulted. Nearly a full year passed before two men, Patrick Hasty and James Cummins, were tried and publicly hanged for killing Major Denis Mahon.

Further west in Ireland in the summer of 1847, 2,000 of Lord Palmerston's tenants were sailing from Sligo and others being routed through Liverpool, all bound for Canada. Henry John Temple, the Third Viscount Palmerston, was very much an absentee landlord. As a career politician he was forced to spend all his time in London. He became a cabinet minister in the British government as early as 1809, serving 15 years as Foreign Secretary, and later still, served two periods as Prime Minister.

The nine vessels carrying his former tenants were destined to join the ranks of the coffin ships. When the first, the *Eliza Liddell*, arrived at Saint John, New Brunswick in July, the Canadian authorities were enraged. There were few men of employable age on board, mainly widows with young children and elderly men and women who were unfit or too old to work.

Worse was to follow. Late sailings to Canada were always dangerous; ports on the St Lawrence were forced to close as soon as the ice built up in the autumn, and as the weather declined, new arrivals were bound to suffer. Yet one of Palmerston's vessels, the *Lord Ashburton*, arrived at Saint John on October 30th. On the voyage 107 had died and 60 were seriously ill along with many of the crew which had to be supplemented by passengers to complete the crossing.

Three days later the *Aeolus* arrived with more of Lord Palmerston's tenants; more deaths, more sickness and even more poverty accompanied them. The captain was forced to pay £1-a-head bond to allow his passengers to land at Saint

John. They were so ill and so poorly prepared for the voyage that the chief surgeon at the quarantine station reported, '. . . many are almost in a state of nudity; 99 per cent of the passengers on this ship must become a public charge immediately.'

Later still the *Richard Watson* arrived. Although fewer deaths had occurred at sea the account of this voyage was none the less horrifying. The passengers were kept waiting for several days in Sligo and finally went on board on August 10th, but differences between Emigration officials and the ship's broker kept her at the quayside until the 26th. Contrary winds were blamed for her remaining in Sligo Bay until September 8th when the brig put to sea. But adverse weather forced her back into Sligo and her final departure was delayed until the 22nd. After 43 days the passengers were no nearer to their destination. The voyage ended on November 8th, fully 90 days, three months since they had gone on board. Not surprisingly, they too were in a very poor state.

There was an uproar in Canada. Protests flowed to the Colonial Secretary in London, and despite his lofty position in government, Lord Palmerston was officially asked for an explanation. Though ignorance should not be accepted as a defence, he deftly switched the blame to his Irish agents Messrs Kincaid and Stewart, and their response, in a letter dated February 1st 1848, concluded:

The emigrants were unfortunately poor and without any means of support except what they could obtain by their labour, but that was their misfortune not their fault, and they were both able and willing to work for their bread and for the support of their families.

Notwithstanding the reports from the authorities in Saint John and Quebec . . . very favourable accounts

EMIGRATION.

PAPERS

RELATIVE TO

EMIGRATION

TO THE

BRITISH PROVINCES IN NORTH AMERICA.

(In continuation of the Papers presented December 1847).

Presented to both Houses of Parliament by Command of Her Majesty.
APRIL 1848.

LONDON:
PRINTED BY WILLIAM CLOWES AND SONS, STAMFORD STREET,
FOR HER MAJESTY'S STATIONERY OFFICE.
1848.

The alarming cholera statistics from Dr Douglas at Grosse Isle were debated by politicians in Quebec, Montreal, London and Dublin, with little result.

" I have the honour to report, for the information of his Excellency the Governor-General, the arrival since my last report of 22 passenger vessels, having on board on leaving port an aggregate of 7629 souls; among these three were vessels from Bremen, three from Scotland, having no sick on board, or deaths on the voyage. All the others being from Liverpool and ports in Ireland have more or less sick and deaths, and among the number were six having on board on leaving port 2500 passengers. These have arrived in a very sickly condition, the few that remain healthy I have ordered to land at the tents at the East End.

" Three of these sailed from Great Britain in the month of May, having had nine weeks' passage. The 'Sir Henry Pottinger' sailed from Cork, May 29, with 399 steerage passengers. Fever appeared almost on leaving the port, 98 died on the voyage, and upwards of 100 were found sick yesterday when inspected.

" The Virginius sailed from Liverpool, May 28, with 476 passengers. Fever and dysentery cases came on board this vessel in Liverpool, and deaths occurred before leaving the Mersey. On mustering the passengers for inspection yesterday, it was found that 106 were ill of fever, including nine of the crew, and the large number of 158 had died on the passage, including the first and second officers and seven of the crew, and the master and the steward dying, the few that were able to come on deck were ghastly yellow looking spectres, unshaven and hollow cheeked, and, without exception, the worst looking passengers I have ever seen; not more than six or eight were really healthy and able to exert themselves.

" The third vessel was the 'Yorkshire,' sailed from Liverpool 9th June, with 392 passengers; of these, 45 have died and 40 were found ill. I am convinced that six days after the healthy passengers of these last three vessels are landed at the tents, and when they have eaten of fresh bread and meat, from 25 to 30 will die, and from 150 to 180 require to be admitted to hospital.

" The exposure to atmospheric changes in the tents is very trying to weak and debilitated people, especially young children and aged people.

" Since writing the above, another plague-ship has just dropped in, the 'Naomi,' from Liverpool; this vessel sailed on the 15th June with 331 passengers, 78 have died on the voyage, and 104 are now sick. The filth and dirt in this vessel's hold creates such an effluvium as to make it difficult to breathe.

(Signed)   " G. M. DOUGLAS,
" Medical Superintendent."

The following statements received from authentic sources establish the true character of the year's emigration, and the consequent necessity for incurring an immediate expenditure which could not be refused to the call of humanity, but which the Provincial Revenue could not afford, and should not be required to bear:—

Of the whole number of British emigrants embarked	89,738
Died on the passage	5,293
Leaving for arrival here	84,145

Of these there died,

At the Quarantine	3,452
At the Quebec Emigrant Hospital	1,041
At the Montreal Emigrant Hospital	3,579
At other places in the two Canadas, at which Boards of Health have been formed, and of which no less than twenty-six were established in Upper Canada, from two of which alone, the cities of Kingston and Toronto, the number of deaths amount to	1,965
	10,037
Leaving	74,108

The numbers admitted into hospital for medical treatment,

At Quarantine	8,563
At Quebec	2,500
At Montreal	11,000
At Toronto	3,876
At Kingston	4,326
Total of sick	30,265

The returns from the other 24 Boards not having been received.

It will thus be seen that more than one-seventh of the total embarkations have died; more than one-eighth of the total arrivals have died; and more than one-third of those arrivals have been received into hospital.

The authentic returns also show that, up to the 12th November last, the number of destitute emigrants forwarded from the agency at Montreal to Upper Canada was,

Male adults	12,932
Female adults	12,153
Children under 12	10,616
Infants	3,080
Total forwarded	38,781

arrive almost daily to their friends in this country from those who emigrated last year from Lord Palmerston's estate, and that already some of them have been able to send home money to their friends out of their earnings in the Colonies.

Palmerston was one of many who acted in much the same way. No one sought to deny that landlord emigration meant sending out of Ireland the tenants who were not wanted because they were too old for work or unfit or lazy or bad characters. Good tenants who were young and healthy, who gave no trouble, who worked the land and paid their rents, were welcome to stay. There were many edges to the sword wielded by the absentee landlords.

8

In Widow McCormack's Cabbage Patch

M ention the year 1848 to any lawyer in the English-speaking world and he will almost certainly reply, 'That was the year in which habeas corpus was suspended in Ireland.' As old as the common law itself in England, a writ of habeas corpus requires a jailer to produce his prisoner before a court and to state the reason for his detention. The suspension of habeas corpus implied arrest and imprisonment without trial – the last move of a desperate government in a free society. In the same year, revolution was sweeping across Europe and the British Parliament was in constant fear of an uprising in Ireland. But there was only one uprising – it lasted all of one Saturday afternoon in July, 1848. By this time, the flow of emigrants had subsided as news spread of the emigrant death toll from the previous year. But two events soon restored the numbers of Irish anxious to get away. First, the potato crop failed, once again. Second, tougher rules and higher fares were anticipated. America had already tightened her immigration controls in an effort to exclude the pauper and fever-ridden Irish and now the British planned to introduce new Passengers' Acts, again reducing the numbers allowed on board ships and, inevitably, forcing up the cost of the Atlantic passage. As a result, many emigrants were keen to sail before the new rules and fares came into force.

The government in London still declined to recognise the state of Ireland's rapidly diminishing population. There was little fight left in the people, little strength to fight the hunger and none at all to fight the British who mistook the mood of the people and remained insensitive to the reality of their situation: even peasant armies cannot fight on empty bellies. Tenants on some of the larger estates banded together to avoid paying rents, current or arrears, and formed combinations while in the towns and cities Confederate Clubs were set up; but that was as far as they went – there is no evidence of well-organised conspiracies to murder landlords or agents, however much they were hated. But the apprehension of an Irish uprising had been growing steadily for more than two years among Britain's leaders. Elsewhere in Europe, uprisings were rife: in January 1848 the people in Sicily forced concessions from their King; in February a bloodless revolution overthrew the French Parliament; in early March the army in Vienna was routed by the city's people; then the Austrian rulers were driven out of Milan by the Italians. These winter insurrections encouraged radical leaders of the Young Ireland Party to rebel. As a result, in March three men, William Smith O'Brien, Thomas Meagher and John Mitchel, were arrested and charged with sedition. After the first two were acquitted, the third, Mitchel, a journalist, was tried in May under another act and convicted. The Attorney General in London had just drafted a new Treason Felony Act, decreeing, '. . . any person who, by open and advised speaking, compassed the intimidation of the Crown or of Parliament,' was made guilty of felony. And in the current climate any person found guilty under this Act would be sure to face a heavy sentence – transportation to an overseas colony possibly for life. Within an hour of the jury returning their verdict, and sentencing Mitchel to 14 years' transportation, he was on his way out of the country, not on an emigrant ship but aboard a British warship, bound for Tasmania on the other side of the world.

Fear is often fuelled by rumour, which was rife at the time. Misleading stories spread of great protest gatherings, 10,000-strong, and marches of 20,000 militants were reported to London. It was rumoured than an Irish Brigade was being raised in America, and that the Confederate Clubs were arming their members. As a result, the British Government determined to quash the threat of a peasant uprising. More English troops and weapons poured into Dublin and spread around the country. Additional English warships were despatched to strengthen the fleet at Cove, near Cork.

The British decided that further examples should be made among the would-be leaders and early in July, Thomas Meagher, son of the Mayor of Waterford, was re-arrested. His speeches in previous years, urging armed rebellion, had earned him the title Meagher of the Sword. He was detained by the police right outside the offices of the *Waterford Chronicle* whose editorial that day, on July 12th, cautioned against immediate rebellion, urging instead, 'Wait until England is engaged in a major European war. The *Chronicle* will equip 200,000 men to fight against England.'

Earlier copies of the *Chronicle* had carried notices of forth-coming auctions:

ARMS   ARMS   ARMS
Mr L P O'Neil, auctioneer,
will offer for sale

by Public Auction
at the Quay of Waterford
on Tuesday, the 2nd day of May, instant
upwards of three hundred GUNS and
two hundred PISTOLS, all warranted,
and will be sold without Reserve.
Full particulars will appear in future advertisements.

A front-page story in the *Chronicle* prompted:

It will be seen by advertisements in this day's paper, an opportunity will be afforded to the public of arming themselves with guns, pistols, rifles etc. The coming opportunity might be found most favourable for some of our artizans to get rid of their stock of pikes. At all events the people have just as good right to arm as the government officials, in fact better. The former in most instances having property to protect, the latter nothing but themselves. We hope the sale will be well attended, and the purchasers numerous.

This was real fighting talk and when Meagher was again accused of treason, another journalist was arrested with him, not the editor of the combative *Chronicle* but Gavan Duffy, editor of *The Nation*. Martial law was imposed in the cities of Dublin, Cork, Drogheda and Waterford where a week later no fewer than six British Naval sloops, frigates and troop ships were moored in mid-river. And on July 22nd, the British politicians went one better – suspending habeas corpus. One week later came the uprising they had feared.

William Smith O'Brien, another leader of the Young Irelanders, was a well-known and well-respected patriot. A Protestant politician and himself a landlord, he was descended from the legendary Brian Boru, the last King of

Ireland. Brian had died at the age of 88 in 1014, fighting and overcoming earlier overseas rulers, the Norse invaders from Denmark at the famous Battle of Clontarf. In 1848, O'Brien was virtually the only leader of the Young Irelanders who remained at liberty, though Meagher was on bail awaiting trial. At the end of July O'Brien toured the south, addressing a series of rallies and meetings, encouraging hope and positive action. He spent a week trying to rally armed supporters but, unable to feed his starving followers, made little headway. Rumours of mounting support from his 'thousands of followers' were sadly false, based on fear and ignorance. The British still lacked any real awareness of the widespread and weakening effects of the Famine on the Irish rebels.

On the last Saturday of July the remnants of O'Brien's force gathered in a field at Ballingarry, in County Tipperary; there were not more than 40 men, only half with firearms. The rest were armed with home-made pikes or farmers' pitchforks while others, possibly 80, were prepared to throw stones. Hearing of this gathering, the police intended to break it up, but took fright at the final moment of confrontation and fled for the cover of the nearest building, a stone-built cottage belonging to Widow McCormack. Though she was out shopping, her six children had remained at home in the charge of her eldest, aged ten.

Pursued by the rebel force, the police, numbering 30 constables and an inspector, barricaded themselves inside the cottage which stood in the centre of a cabbage patch. The rebels decided to smoke them out and stacked hay, from nearby stables, against the front door. This was the scene which greeted the widow on her return – she was separated from her children by a small rebel force laying seige to her home where her children were trapped along with the police. As much as anyone, the widow McCormack was responsible for ending the showdown with just a few shots fired, one death, some injuries and many a bruised ego.

The constables emerged as the peasant army dispersed, O'Brien allegedly escaping on a captured police horse. Five days after the brief uprising, O'Brien was arrested, and later wrote this sad epitaph:

> It matters little whether the blame of failure lies upon me or upon others; but the fact is recorded that the people preferred to die of starvation at home, or to flee as voluntary exiles to other lands, rather than to fight for their lives and liberties.

At their trials, Meagher, who was only 25, and 45-year-old O'Brien were sentenced to be hanged, drawn and quartered for their acts of high treason. Queen Victoria intervened and the sentences were commuted to emigration. Soon they were aboard a convict ship, bound for Tasmania, off Australia. Within very few years Mitchel and Meagher escaped and found their way to America where they were welcomed as heroes and continued their political fight for the Irish cause. Thomas Meagher enjoyed a particularly distinguished career in the United States, until his premature death in 1867. During the Civil War he became a general in the Federal Army and organised the famous Irish Brigade. His heroic service in the war was rewarded by an appointment as Governor of Montana, but soon after, he drowned in a tragic accident. In his absence John Mitchel was elected to Parliament for Tipperary but, as a convicted felon, was not allowed to take his seat. O'Brien had suffered ill-health in exile and, when eventually pardoned, he returned to live in England where he died in 1864.

The Battle of Ballingarry had proved a desperate disappointment for the Irish cause but, within a few days, news of even greater calamity broke upon the country: the potato crop failed again. Though the previous year, 1847, had produced a reasonable crop of sound potatoes, only a relatively small acreage had been planted as, with so much blight in earlier seasons there was a constant shortage of decent seed potatoes for planting. Then in the summer of 1848 the potato blight was worse than ever: practically the entire crop had failed. Elsewhere in Europe and America, 1848 was an eventful year. America finally overcame Mexico which led to the formation of California, the 31st State of the Union. Though the white population of California was originally little more than 5,000, the Gold Rush in 1848 quickly swelled their numbers. Many a famine emigrant, fit enough after the crossing and a few months living and working in America, joined the stampede heading for Sacramento. Most Irish emigrants knew how to wield a shovel, and for many, digging for gold seemed more appealing than digging canals or building railroads.

Waterford, the site of the Irish rebellion, has a colourful maritime history. The early Viking invaders gave the town its original name, Vradaford, recalling its network of watery inlets, reminiscent of their own homeland in Scandinavia. By the 1400s, Waterford's maritime trade had become so extensive that the town was nick-named Rich Waterford. The River Suir widens to more than a mile as it flows ten miles from the city centre out to the Atlantic, and the fame of its boatyards spread far. In the early 1500s Henry VIII, one of the strongest of the English Monarchs, commissioned the boatyards of Waterford to build two ships for the Royal household. Legend has it that, a century later at Waterford, Oliver Cromwell coined the phrase, 'by hook or by crook'. Hook Head lies on one side of the estuary, a crook-shaped promontory at Brownstone Head. Just before landing with his troops, Cromwell allegedly vowed: 'By the Hook or by the Crook we will be victorious by tonight.' He meant that no matter on which side they went ashore or how they carried out their attack, a rapid conquest was assured.

Waterford's appearance had changed little over the past 150 years. The lively quays beside the Suir in Waterford remain the very heart of this attractive town. One much-loved feature, Reginald's Tower, has survived 1,000 years, having been built by the Vikings in the year 1003. The old tower saw the Normans invade in the 11th century, followed by the English armies in the 16th century, and later witnessed the departure of countless emigrants during the Famine years.

During the Famine, Waterford was the home port for nearly 250 ships. A great number were named after owners' or captains' wives, mothers, daughters and sisters, such as *Juliet, Louise, Catherine, Margaret, Ann Henry, Ann Carr, Ann Kenny, Victoria, Eliza, Ellen, Lavinia* and *Sophia* – all vessels of the 40-strong fleet which sailed with the Famine emigrants from Waterford to America.

'Day after day our quays are crowded with people seeking for American ships, and no sooner is a ship's departure for that prosperous land announced than she is filled,' reported the *Chronicle* as the Famine took hold. In one week in the spring of 1846 ten ships sailed with passengers for Canada. The rate slowed down during the following year, with around three ships leaving every week through the summer months. But the pace of departures picked up in 1848 as the potato-failure and the reality of the doomed insurrection were recognised.

The busiest of the famine ships operating from Waterford that year was the *Harmony* which took passengers to New York sometimes, though more often to New Orleans and

Boston. After one spring voyage, she tied up at Boston on May 27th in 1848. On that day in the space of two tides there arrived at Boston three emigrant ships from Liverpool, plus the *Gulane* from Limerick; the *General Scott* from Cork; the *Princess* from Donegal and the *Lord Fitzroy* from Galway. The armada from Ireland was in full flow.

Waterford's famous, hand-made Waterford Crystal, admired all over the world, was first produced in 1783 when George and William Penrose opened their glass factory. Recognising the profits to be made in ship-building, the Penrose family opened a shipyard too. The shipping movements are now few, but the hotels, busy shops and converted warehouses, look out on the ancient cobble-stones and weather-beaten bollards, the view across the wide river unbroken by any buildings. Reginald's Tower, the walls as robust as ever, has been converted to a small museum, an ancient witness to so much history and bloodshed, heartache and grief.

9

A Noble Rescue

On the emigrant voyages to America around 50 emigrant ships foundered during the six Famine years. This is a remarkable figure, given the condition and age of many of the vessels, the lack of provision for winter weather and the great number of crossings. The mortality rate rises if account is taken of the shipwrecks on the perilous journey to Canada, on which ships encountered icebergs even in the spring. Emigrant death also occurred on the odd cargo ships carrying only a dozen or so emigrants, and on the hulks lying in the port of Liverpool; these were used as temporary accommodation when the lodging houses were overflowing or beyond the meagre finances of the hundreds arriving every day from Ireland. But the overall mortality figure is still relatively low.

Fire was a constant threat on these old wooden ships, with inadequate equipment to fight the flames fanned by the wind. Fire drill consisted of forming a line and passing buckets of water to douse the flames. If the order to abandon ship was issued, too often there were nowhere near enough lifeboats for everyone. The burning of the *Ocean Monarch* in 1848 became a cause celebre, and the tragic event was illustrated by several oil paintings. Though cameras had only recently been invented, in *c.* 1830, they were rarely used outside a studio, and journals relied on lithographic drawings for illustration.

Throughout the Famine period the *Illustrated London News* (*ILN*) caught the mood and despair of the Irish people. This news-magazine was a weekly publication and in its heyday was highly influential and powerful, regularly reminding Queen Victoria and her government of Ireland's plight. With its full page drawings, pictorial layouts and lively reportage, it offered the Victorian equivalent of today's visual news media. One *ILN* artist, James Mahoney, who lived in Cork and toured the country, produced illustrations which undoubtedly helped highlight the dreadful fate over-taking the country. As no other visual news medium existed, the *ILN* could publish world-exclusive pictures of such historic events as a fire aboard the blazing *Ocean Monarch* on August 24th, 1848.

A huge triple-decked ship of 1,300 tons, built in 1847, the *Ocean Monarch* belonged to Boston ship-owner Enoch Train. He was justifiably proud of his fleet of packet ships, many of them recently designed and built specifically for the emigrant trade. But his White Diamond line suffered one of the greatest marine catastrophes of the period when the *Ocean Monarch* caught fire, while still within sight of the coast, just 25 miles out of Liverpool. Just before the alarm was raised, the scene on board was calm and cheerful as crew and passengers relaxed, unaware of impending disaster. Captain James Murdoch unwound, and ordered tobacco to be passed among the crew. The passengers were especially excited as, guided by southerly winds, the ship was sailing close to the Irish coast, allowing the emigrants a last glimpse of their homeland. As their ship tacked south in the Irish Sea, they continually crossed paths with another Boston packet, the *New World*, the largest sailing ship in the world. Passengers and crew anticipated the thrill of a race home across the Atlantic Ocean. The last thing anyone expected was fire sweeping its way through the lower decks and soon to engulf the ship. The steward who discovered the smoke and the initial flames on a lower deck, did not panic. The dreaded cry, 'fire down below' died on his lips and he dashed aloft to inform the captain personally.

He sent a mate and another crew member below where they found the fire had surrounded the aftermost cabin on the port side, near to a metal ventilator, but they could not trace the seat of the fire. The captain went to investigate himself and quickly realised that the blaze was out of control and spreading rapidly. His first thought was for the passengers and the 42-strong crew, and he tried to make for the coast of Wales, only 4 miles away. Though the tide was in their favour carrying the ship to shore, Captain Murdoch soon realised that there was no time to force her aground. Instead, he brought the *Ocean Monarch* round into the wind and dropped both anchors, trying to halt the spread of flames and contain the fire to the stern of his ship. The bewildered passengers, 332 poor emigrants and 32 cabin-class passengers, crowded on to the upper deck where 'to their shouts and screams were added the noise of distressed cattle and sheep', according to a surviving witness. Livestock was often kept aboard the larger vessels, especially the multi-decked American packets, and slaughtered en route to provide fresh meat for the wealthier cabin passengers.

Within minutes the blaze had gained control. The noise on deck made it impossible for orders to be passed among the crew and in all this confusion only two lifeboats could be unlashed and launched. As the passengers were forced off the ship, some jumping into the sea, crewmen tossed spars, oars, and anything that would float over the side to help people stay afloat, but many drifted away on the flooding tide out of sight. Then the burning mizzen mast, at the stern of the ship, crashed overboard and the captain, trying to direct rescue operations on the after-deck, was himself forced to jump into the sea. A few passengers remained on board, hoping to escape the perils of both fire and sea by clinging to the bowsprit and jib-boom beyond the bows of the ship and farthest from the flames.

By great good fortune, two other ships were close enough to help. First to the rescue was the yacht *Queen of the Ocean*, returning to Liverpool from a summer regatta in North Wales. The skipper lowered a small boat which picked up 32 survivors from the sea, transferring small groups to the yacht which sailed to and fro, supervising the rescue mission until she was forced to leave, unable to take any more on board.

The *Affonso*, a steam-frigate in the Brazilian navy, was on a courtesy visit to England and enjoying an afternoon cruise when she joined in the rescue. She was a paddle-steamer and, though wooden-built, her 300 horse-power engines enabled the 180-feet frigate to manoeuvre easily around the stricken ship. Manned by a crew of professional, disciplined sailors, she carried some distinguished guests including the Prince and Princess de Joinville, the Duke and Duchess d'Aumale and Admiral Grenfell of the British Royal Navy. Both crew and passengers joined in the rescue operation though the presence of the more illustrious passengers was not apparent until much later. Five boats were lowered and a cable, attached from the frigate's stern to the bows of the blazing packet ship, encouraged emigrants still clinging on to the *Ocean Monarch* to jump clear. A final act of bravery was required to rescue 16 stranded women and young children silhouetted against the flames too terrified to leap or too young to understand their dilemma. More ships had tacked close by to lend assistance, including the American *New World*. On board, a New York seaman, Frederick Jerome, himself a former emigrant from Portsmouth, stripped off his clothes and dived overboard. He swam with a line to the blazing wreck and clambered up a trailing section of rigging to reach the desperate women and children. Jerome lowered each one to a boat waiting below and ensured that no one remained on board before joining the last of the survivors. Jerome was hailed as a hero by all those watching from the *Affonso,* and rewarded with gifts of gold. Subsequently, he also received £50 from Queen Victoria and, when he returned home a month later, was presented with a gold casket and the freedom of the City of New York.

The *Ocean Monarch* burned for 12 hours, right down to the waterline, and finally sank in 60 feet of water. The captain was picked up after spending an hour clinging to a section of timber. In the forthcoming weeks 170 bodies were washed ashore. Though many more remained missing, 203 passengers had been saved plus 13 of the crew, out of a total complement of 396. The following week, many of the survivors bravely sailed out of Liverpool again, on another ship to reach their new homes in America.

The full story was vividly described in the *ILN*'s immediate and extended report, appearing in late August, 1848:

Early on Thursday morning, 24th of August, the *Ocean Monarch* sailed from Liverpool for the United States with 396 souls on board. She had not proceeded many miles ere the fire was discovered. A brief unavailing endeavour was made to save the ship but the flames were unconquerable and the vast multitude on board surrendered themselves to despair.

The burning element progressed from stern to stem;

spars and masts, wrapped one by one in the living flame, fell, crushing in their descent the shrieking masses on the deck and numbers, in desperate frenzy, sought safety but to find death in the waves around.

The yacht *Queen of the Ocean* and the Brazilian steam-frigate *Affonso*, which were in the vicinity, hastened to render assistance, and by their boats rescued numbers. Other vessels also rendered assistance; but yet the lamentable fact must be recorded, that of the vast multitude on board, a large proportion perished. The *Queen of the Ocean* (a private yacht) succeeded in saving 32 persons. Several pounds were collected on board the yacht for the relief of the sufferers.

The flames were bursting with immense fury from the stern and centre of the vessel. So great was the heat in these parts, that the passengers crowded to the fore part of the vessel. In their maddened despair women jumped overboard with their off-spring in their arms, and sunk to rise no more. Men followed their wives in frenzy and were lost. Groups of men, women, and children also precipitated themselves into the water, in the vain hope of self-preservation. But the waters closed over many of them forever. The heat was very intense, sufficient to make them jump into the water, seeking escape from one element by taking shelter in another, equally as destructive, but far less agonising in its effect and many met with a watery grave.

No pen can describe this awful scene. The flames continued to rage with increased fury.

As the fire was making its way to the fore part of the vessel the passengers, and crew, of course, crowded still further forward. To the jib-boom they clung in clusters as thick as they could pack even one lying over another. At length the foremast went overboard, snapping the fastening of the jib-boom which, with its load of human beings, dropped into the water amidst the most heart-rending screams, both from those on board and those who were falling into the water. Some of the poor creatures were enabled again to reach the vessel, others floated away on spars, but many met with a watery grave.

The *Affonso* was out on a pleasure excursion, commanded by Captain J.M. Lisboa. There were also on board the Prince de Joinville, his lady and suite; the Duke and Duchess d'Aumale; the Brazilian minister the Chavalier de Lisboa; Admiral Grenfell and daughters; and other distinguished persons.

When the *Affonso* discovered the *Ocean Monarch*, no time was lost in bearing down to her. Four boats were at once lowered and were soon followed by the large paddle-box boat. Captain Lisboa jumped into one and Admiral Grenfell into the another.

The rescuers were untiring in their exertions to save the poor people. The Prince de Joinville was particularly assiduous in assisting the passengers on board the frigate.

From the crowd of human beings in the water, clinging to the spars etc., the boats were unable to get as close to the vessel as they otherwise would have done, and of course considerable time was unavoidably consumed in rescuing the poor unfortunates.

The *Affonso* rescued in all about 160 persons, including 13 seamen. Admiral Grenfell, Captain Lisboa and the officers and crew of the Brazilian frigate are beyond praise. All exerted themselves in a most energetic and humane manner; and Admiral Grenfell has been most untiring procuring clothes, money, and provisions for the survivors.

London's *ILN* report was followed by newspaper coverage in Ireland, Liverpool, Boston and New York. Nine days after the disaster the *ILN* displayed a dramatic drawing, from the Prince's sketch-book, with the caption:

> This dreadful calamity was briefly reported last week. We now accompany our illustration of the sad catastrophe with a full statement of the details. The scene presented in the engraving is from a sketch made by the Prince de Joinville who so distinguished himself by his humane exertions on this lamentable occasion. This sketch was placed in the hands of Monsieur Morel Fatio, the celebrated marine painter, to make whatever use he pleased of it, either as a painting or an engraving.

An official inquiry was held after some weeks of amassing evidence, but the outcome was inconclusive, as none of the survivors could identify the actual cause of the outbreak.

Though nothing could be done for the unfortunate victims, the *Affonso*'s celebrities immediately raised funds for the survivors. Initial collections produced an assortment of clothes, gold sovereigns and jewellery. Later, successful appeals prompted further gifts and support: Queen Victoria donated £100, and a larger, unknown sum was generated by the lottery sale of a dramatic sketch of the rescue by the Prince de Joinville.

Of the many heroes of the day, Francois-Ferdinand-Philippe-Louis-Marie d'Orleans, Prince de Joinville, was the most celebrated. The third son of Louis-Philippe, a former king of France, he had been forced into exile with his family after his father had been deported in 1848, following the July Revolution of 1830. Joinville was married to the daughter of Pedro I, the Emperor of Brazil, which explains his presence on the *Affonso*. An adventurous and courageous man, he enjoyed a dramatic career in the French Navy, with considerable spells of active service and speedy promotion to Vice Admiral. After some years spent writing books on naval and military strategies, he went to America in 1861, offered his services to President Lincoln, and fought in the Civil War. Nine years later he returned to France from where he was expelled, only to return again under the pseudonym Colonel Lutherod. Joinville was soon on the battlefield again, fighting alongside his fellow countrymen in the final stages of the Franco-Prussian War. After the war, he revealed his true identity and was elected to the French National Assembly. After retiring from political life, he lived quietly in Paris until he died at the turn of the century. Coincidentally, an emigrant ship named the Prince of Joinville had successfully crossed the Atlantic from Belfast to New York during the year before the fire.

Though the burning of the *Ocean Monarch* was a major catastrophe, many more unfortunate passengers might have drowned and failed in their quest to find a new life, without the direction and courage of the Prince, the generosity of his friends and the bravery of Seaman Jerome and countless unsung heroes.

10

Comfort for the Convicts

B y 1848 ship owners had started to build ships specifically for the emigrant trade, sometimes converting old
vessels, such as the huge packet ships of the American
running fleet. The worst of the famine had just been
reached: the ruin of the potato crop in the summer of
1848 was almost universal throughout the country with
the result that virtually an armada crossed the Irish Sea
to Liverpool every day. Though the recent tightening of the
Passengers' Acts served their purpose in preventing captains
and shipowners from taking too many liberties with their
passengers, yet emigrants sailing under British rule were still
very much at risk. The mandatory examinations for masters
and mates had yet to be introduced, and, up until 1850,
masters achieved their status by climbing up through the
ranks, by dint of age, experience and capability. In September 1850, the Board of Trade in London finally introduced the Mercantile Marine Act, forcing masters and
mates to sit a formal examination for their Master's or
Mate's Tiquet. But the backlog of examinees was so great
that many masters and mates were allowed to remain in

their commands until an opportunity arose to sit the tests at one of the major ports.

Rules were also imposed on passengers by the Board of Trade and, rather ironically, were introduced a year earlier that those for seamen. The Rules for Passengers of October 6th 1849 stipulated that all passengers must rise by 7 am,

Certficates of Competence for a ship's captain were not needed at the time of the Famine sailings.

unless excused by the surgeon, and be in bed by 10 pm. Breakfast could not commence until the decks, including the space beneath the berths, had been swept, the bedding stowed away; the long list of edicts even included religious behaviour on Sundays. Many hundreds of thousands of emigrants would have appreciated these rules for preserving order and securing cleanliness and ventilation on board passenger ships proceeding from the United Kingdom to any of Her Majesty's possessions abroad. Ship's captains were expected to enforce the rules as a general principle on any and all passenger ships, whatever their destination.

The vessels themselves were covered by the flimsiest regulations. For a ship to be listed in Lloyd's Register, it had to be surveyed and judged first-, second-, or even less, third-class, according to its age, condition and general seaworthiness. Second-class status covered ships that were unfit to carry dry cargoes but perfectly fit for the conveyance on any voyage of cargoes not in their nature subject to sea-damage. Emigrants were allowed on second-class ships as it did not matter if they got wet. A third-class status prohibited any but short voyages; not out of Europe but, with the pressure of the emigrant trade, such regulations were sometimes broken. Lloyd's classification was introduced primarily for insurance purposes but there were still countless ships sailing the seven seas and all the five oceans, which had never been either surveyed or listed. While no unlisted ship could be chartered by the government to transport convicts to the colonies, such restrictions failed to protect innocent emigrant passengers. The only requirement for emigrant ships was that the appointed Local Inspector of Emigrant Ships satisfy himself as to the fitness of the vessel. But that inspector was not always an experienced sailor or ship-builder and frequently lacked the competence to make such judgments. Masts, sails, halyards, decks, cabin fittings and superstructures can be examined easily enough but it takes an expert to pass decent verdict on the soundness of a ship's hull, particularly the bottom. Among the coffin ships, especially those chartered by the agents organising the landlord emigration (see pp 43–44), were several unlisted by Lloyd's, including: the *Syria*; *Wandsworth*; *Virginius*; *Lord Ashburton*; *Richard Watson*; *Naomi*; *BIC*; *Eliza Liddell*; *John*

Nunn and the *Sir Henry Pottinger*. Presumably the owners were either careless or feared their vessels unfit to pass Lloyd's survey.

The convict ships, like the slave ships before them, were properly provisioned with food and water for the voyage. Dietary regulations for the convicted felons directed that they should have meat on three days a week, as well as on Sundays, alternating with meat-broth on other days. No such basic necessities formed part of the statutory provisions for emigrants. The stipulation of space on board for the emigrant passengers soon turned the minimum allowance into the maximum allowance. A convict ship was not allowed to carry cargo, for a variety of reasons, in case it should cramp the conditions or accommodation on board and endanger the ship in bad weather. Emigrant ships carried whatever cargo pleased the captain or the owner, even iron which had a habit of shifting in the hold, sometimes in mid-ocean. The ship could carry as much as two-thirds of its registered tonnage in this dangerous cargo, and overladen vessels with either too much cargo or too many passengers or perhaps both were not as rare as they should have been. Nearly 30 years would pass before the introduction of the Plimsoll Line.

Devised by the politician, Samuel Plimsoll, the Plimsoll Line was a load line painted along a ship's hull to indicate the ship's maximum load-bearing capacity in water. If a ship's Plimsoll Line sank below the surface of the water, then the ship was deemed to be overloaded and from 1876 could be detained in port.

During the height of the famine, a parliamentary committee examined contemporary regulations and proposed increasing crews. On convict ships and all other ships chartered by the government, there were to be four seamen for every 100 tons of registered burthen. For emigrant ships, however, the proposed increase was less – only three seamen for every 100 tons, and even this modest measure was quashed by the powerful Liverpool shipping lobby.

Convicts had a rigorous medical inspection at both ends of a voyage and most of these ships actually carried a doctor on board. While emigrants, were usually thoroughly inspected on arrival, they were rarely checked seriously on embarkation, and doctors were only found on the very largest emigrant vessels, usually the American packet ships. Dublin's politicians protested to the British government about conditions aboard emigrant ships, stating in *c.* 1848: 'We would recommend that free emigrants should be treated at least as well as convicts in transport ships.' But their plea met with little response.

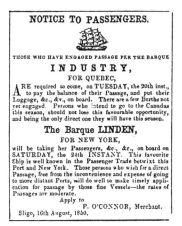

Throughout the Famine every newspaper in Ireland carried similar notices.

The port of Sligo on Ireland's north-west coast achieved infamy as an emigrant point a year earlier. Sligo was the embarkation point for many of the coffin ships and for the poorest passengers, usually the victims of landlord emigration. Three broad inlets reach into the Atlantic coastline, doubling the size of Sligo Bay, with the town's quays magnificently sited in the narrows of the Garavogue River beyond the bay. The port had a long tradition of sending her ships to all corners of the world and Peter O'Connor, a leading Sligo merchant, ordered the 276-ton barque *Industry* to be built in 1839 with a light draft to carry a regular cargo of Canadian timber through the shallow channel in the bay, and up the river to his saw mills, at all levels of the tide.

At the start of the Famine, *Industry* had valuable two-way cargoes and we can only imagine the effects of the shallow draft on the ship and her cargo, carried west-bound out of Sligo across the heaving ocean. The voyage home was nearly always faster with the favourable westerly winds but in June 1845 *Industry*'s owners proudly proclaimed that she had journeyed from Sligo to Quebec, under Captain Thomas Barrett, her regular master, in 29 days. It is not known whether she was carrying passengers on that trip, but 18 months later she conveyed 184 Famine emigrants from Sligo to New York, embarking on December 26th 1846, under the command of Captain Michael Kelly. Though the late crossing was unusual at the time, winter voyages would become common during the Famine years.

During the crossing, *Industry* ran into a succession of storms which allowed little progress. Over three long winter months the ship floundered at sea; food and water ran low; and, even with the introduction of strict rationing, two seamen and 15 passengers died from malnutrition. *Industry* arrived in America on April 11th 1847, after 106 days at sea. The round trip took almost six months, with the *Industry* returning to Sligo on June 16th 1847. The following year *Industry* narrowly escaped disaster as she tried to enter port in a fierce December gale, on passage from Liverpool with a mixed cargo of Indian meal, flour and coal. She was driven on to the beach at Bowmore where she stuck fast and, during the following weeks, took a fearful battering. The cargo was recovered but the ship could not be re-floated and Peter O'Connor decided to sell the wrecked vessel. The auction of *Industry* as she lay was announced in Sligo but withdrawn when O'Connor discovered she was not as badly damaged as had first been first thought and she was immediately renovated. The local newspaper, the *Sligo Champion*, announced on February 19th, 1848, more than seven weeks after *Industry* went aground:

> Strong hopes are entertained that the barque *Industry*, which lies upon Bowmore Strand, will be got off in the course of time. She appears to have suffered no material damage during the late storm. She won back her listing as a first-class vessel in Lloyd's Register of Shipping after large-scale repairs to her hull and the total renovation of the deck.

Industry ran aground on a beautiful stretch of Irish coastland: there are many, many miles of wonderful scenery the length and breadth of Ireland, both none more so than in the west where the abundance of water, the sea mists and loughs, the rivers, streams and the ultra-reliable rainfall endows the surrounding countryside with the green cloak for which it is justly famous. Sligo is no exception and the majestic sweep of its broad bay is dominated by Benbulben, by the dramatic rise of this angular, flat-topped mountain. This is Yeats' country, where William Butler Yeats, born in 1865, found the inspiration for so much of his poetry and where he chose to be buried, in the shadow of Benbulben, in the churchyard at Drumcliffe. All around, from the wide strands of sand to the valleys and mountains and glens, the landscape evokes some of his best-known lines:

> Go gather by the humming sea
> Some twisted echo-harbouring shell,
> And to its lips thy story tell . . .

Out in the bay lie many islands, including Coney Island, which is so close to the shore that it can be reached on foot at low tide. Legend has it that Coney Island in New York was named after the Irish isle by a Sligo sea captain who was reminded of the mud flats outside his home port.

On these same mud flats and the gently sloping beaches, *Industry* ran aground. But after her successful renovation in February 1848, she once again embarked on emigrant voyages to America, returning with cargoes of timber. Under a new skipper Edward Fawcett, she made an emigrant voyage in May, from Cork, and then again in September from Dublin, bound for New York in both cases. Despite news of her earlier grounding, she continued to attract passengers and for some years made an average of two round-trips from Sligo to Quebec once a year, as well as emigrant crossings from Sligo direct to New York. A newspaper advertisement, for *Industry* and a sister-ship, the *Linden* announced on March 7th 1851:

> The above fortunate passenger ships are well known in the passenger trade; they will be fitted up in the most comfortable manner and the passengers will be supplied with good provisions, water, fuel etc., agreeable to the Passengers' Act.

Though such vessels could accommodate as many as 140 to 150 in steerage, they were not, strictly speaking, passenger ships, and spent more than half their sea-going lives carrying all kinds of cargoes on journeys both long and short. The term, 'fitted up in the most comfortable manner' usually referred to the speedy erection of wooden bunks which were fitted in the cargo holds by the ship's carpenter as fast as he could saw lengths of wood and hammer home his nails, and as soon as the ship discharged her inward cargo. Fresh bunks were raised on each passenger trip. But the ship owner, O'Connor, was probably no worse and possibly a lot better than many of his competitors for he remained in the passenger trade for many years. After her early disasters in 1846 and 1847, *Industry* could certainly be described as fortunate, surviving some narrow escapes as in 1854, when, 500 miles out in the Atlantic, she sprang a leak with nearly 200 passengers aboard; but put about and reached home safely after three weeks at sea. The last advertised sailing of *Industry* with emigrants to Canada came the following year, in 1856, after which she was sold, and cut down to a brig, with her third and stern-most mast removed. On a cargo trip, carrying coal to Kronstadt in Russia, she went down in a gale in 1876 in extremely cold waters in the Gulf of Finland. Luckily, her eight-man crew survived.

Dromahair is a village lying close to Sligo, on the far side of Lough Gill, another source of inspiration for Yeats. The lough's Isle of Innisfree formed the subject of Yeats' poem *The Lake of Innisfree.*

I will arise and go now, and go to Innisfree,
And a small cabin build there, of clay and wattles made;
Nine bean-rows will I have there, a hive for the honey-bee,
And live alone in the bee-loud glade . . .

Where the wandering water gushes
From the hills above Glen-Car,
In pools among the rushes
That scarce could bathe a star,
We seek for slumbering trout . . .

Yeats not only described the atmospheric homeland of the emigrants, but in his play *The Land of Heart's Desire* he dramatised the plight of the hungry emigrants:

> Of a land where even the old are fair
> And even the wise are merry of tongue . . .

> Where beauty has no ebb, decay no flood,
> But joy is wisdom, time and endless song.

The Irish emigrants fled a land of stunning beauty, which could no longer support their meagre lives, to seek refuge in an unknown country across the perilous seas. Another Sligo vessel, the *Dromahair,* was named after the village, and her comforting name probably made her a popular ship with the emigrants, evoking happier memories on their journey to the New World. She was owned by her master, Captain Peter Pyne, who made many a voyage during the famine years to both Canada and America in the 353-ton barque. Pyne's popularity was boosted by a famous crossing in 1844, when the *Dromahair* voyaged from Quebec to Sligo in just 18 days. Pyne first sailed to New York with emigrants in the late autumn of 1848 and made six similar voyages in the next three years with an average of around 150 passengers each time. Twice in 1851 the *Dromahair* received good publicity on either side of the Atlantic. When she arrived in New York on May 1st, an advertisement in *The Irish-American* newspaper announced:

> Those who desire to visit the Emerald Isle can do so economically and pleasantly by booking passage on the first-class barque the *Dromahair* for Sligo. The captain P. Pyne is a gentlemanly and agreeable companion and an able seaman. Parties desirous of bringing out their friends

have now an opportunity as this well known and fortunate ship will leave Sligo for New York in July.

On her second crossing to New York, much later that year, she arrived on October 15th. When she returned to Ireland once again, via Glasgow, in Scotland, six of her crew decided to desert ship as soon as she berthed back in Sligo. As they were still under contract, they were arrested and tried when caught. Irish newspapers carried reports of their trial, during which they accused Captain Pyne of violence and cruel food rationing but the magistrates accepted the master's version of events, found the seamen guilty of unlawful desertion and sentenced them to two weeks' imprisonment. On their release, they were put back on board the *Dromahair* which sailed at once for America.

Like many ships of the period, the *Dromahair* came to a sad end. On her last voyage, in 1858, under a new master, she again carried Canadian timber from Quebec. Her captain, Hutchinson, decided to heave-to in a strong gale while still far out in the Atlantic. The ship was struck by a heavy sea which washed away most of her equipment including the wheel. She was almost a complete wreck, water-logged and with depleted provisions; six of the crew were either swept away or died of starvation but the other seven hung on for 21 days until they were rescued by a passing American ship, and eventually arrived safely back in Sligo.

11

Joy of My Heart

T he country and the millions still suffering in Ireland in 1848 were not to know that the worst effects of the Famine would continue to be felt for another three or four years. Throughout 1848 the shape and pattern of the emigration changed: the desperate paupers of the previous year were no longer the main emigrants. Vast tracts of land were untenanted and the farms were unworked. Scores of villages were uninhabited. Landlords who wanted to sell could find no buyers. Many landowners were quite prepared to give their farms away, rather than face increased debts as their Poor Law rates mounted up. Ireland was rapidly heading for a standstill, so the better-off farmers, retailers and tradesmen were now thronging the quays.

The winter sailings, by now a regular feature of the emigrant trade, were horrendous. Short days and long nights were spent in cold, tortuous conditions on board; and when darkness fell, the British sea-captains, unlike their American counterparts, rarely kept all their canvas aloft; instead they reduced the number and size of their sails for safety which slowed progress and prolonged the voyage. Many a vessel was beaten back into port, particularly into Londonderry when the strong winds would not allow a ship to round Mallin Head at the very northerly tip of Ireland. Sometimes a ship was one week, two and even three weeks into its voyage, with supplies greatly depleted, and yet the coastline of Ireland was still in sight. In such cases, ships were often forced to return to the home port, re-provision and set sail again. Imagine the horrors of braving days, even weeks, at sea in these perilous conditions only to arrive back in Ireland again. The passengers aboard the *Creole* suffered just such an experience. A barque of 456 tons and the veteran of 40 Atlantic crossings, the *Creole* was a well-known ship on both sides of the Atlantic – easily identified in port with the unusual figurehead of a Creole Indian in full head-dress and war-livery. In December 1848 she was bound for Philadelphia out of Londonderry under the command of Captain James Clarke. When she was well out in the Atlantic, a vicious electric storm surrounded her and she was hit full on by a streak of lightning. The *Creole* lost two-thirds of her sails, her main and mizzen masts, but under one remaining mast she limped back into Cork, on December 7th 1848, after three weeks at sea. Fortunately, all the crew and 221 emigrant passengers were safe.

Londonderry, the most northerly port in Ireland, had built up a successful trade with the smaller American ports as well as with Canada where most of the ships owned in Derry were built, usually in Saint John and New Brunswick and Halifax. A sturdy little barque of under 200 tons was actually named the *Londonderry* and carried emigrant-passengers to Quebec, Montreal and Savannah. On one trip home from this cotton stronghold in Georgia, Captain Samuel Hatrick reported, 'I have been 57 times across the Atlantic and never encountered such severe gales. For 24 hours at a time I was forced to run under bare poles.' The winds were so bad that he was compelled to lower all his sails, and trust to God. In direct contrast in size, the huge 875-ton *Marchioness of Abercorn*, was at one time the largest in the Irish-owned fleet. Commanded by Captain John Hegarty, she regularly carried upwards of 500 Famine emigrants to Quebec during the summer, and to New Orleans in the winter. She was fast and registered a round-trip to Canada of 44 days – 25 out and 19 home. But size is not everything – a rival in this northern port was the much smaller 260-ton brig *Unicorn* which unloaded her passengers in Quebec, took on a cargo of timber and sailed home, under Captain William Allen – land-to-land in 15 days in the summer of 1848.

Another Londonderry ship owner was William McCorkell who allowed his son Bartholomew to name their 408-ton barque *Fanny* after his new wife, but the ship almost had a very short career. In a winter crossing from New Orleans, after disembarking her passengers and reloading with American grain, she lost her bowsprit and mizzen (rear) mast in a storm. The crew had to throw much of the cargo overboard to remain afloat but she made it back to Cork in February. Repairs never took very long as trade was too important, and by the spring the *Fanny* was carrying emigrants once more to Quebec. Later, in August 1848, under Captain John Quinn, she had an astonishingly brisk passage, leaving Londonderry on the 4th and arriving in New York on the 26th. Such a short westward crossing of only 22 days was a real exception, and though the wind must have blown hard to afford such speed, it was mercifully mid-summer. The *Fanny* could carry as many as 158 emigrants, but on this voyage conveyed just 69, with only 12 children in total. Thomas McKeever and his wife, Jane, travelled with their three; Bridget McHue, with six and Betty Conrery with three. Were the husbands and fathers of these two families waiting on the other side?

Some years after the Irish potato Famine, a former ship's

surgeon, Dr Custis from Dublin, wrote a newspaper series relating his experience on six emigrant ships in the late 1840s: 'The torments of hell might, in some degree, resemble the sufferings of the emigrants on board . . . Take all the stews in Liverpool, concentrate in a given space the acts and deeds done in all for one year, and they would scarcely equal in atrocity the amount of crime committed in one emigrant ship during a single voyage.' While the good doctor undoubtedly exaggerated, there was no shortage of reports of brutality to passengers. On the other hand, though many sailors were hard men and may have been unkind, the percentage of ships constantly engaged in the emigrant trade was small, and those sailing out of the Irish ports would hardly have courted bad publicity. The worst atrocities appear instead to have been committed on the shorter voyages, from Ireland to Liverpool, often undertaken by fairly new steamships.

There was another ship with the name *Londonderry*, a paddle-steamer which berthed at the quayside in Derry one Sunday in the winter of 1848. She was only seven years old, big for a ship of her kind, weighing 222 tons. Manned by a crew of 26, she sailed regularly between Sligo and Liverpool. On this winter trip, while hugging the coast of Donegal, she hit bad weather. She was carrying general cargo down below, a deck cargo of cattle, three cabin passengers and 174 passengers in steerage. This was a fairly average-sized manifest for the relatively short journey to Liverpool – not much more than 300 miles. Many of the passengers were undoubtedly seeking onward passages on arrival in Liverpool. The majority of the steerage passengers would expect to complete most, if not all the voyage on deck but when a storm broke one evening, the master ordered his crew to drive all passengers into the after cabin, though it was far too small to hold all 174 of them. They struggled for space and fought for air to breathe: some were crushed and others

113

suffocated. When the cabin door was opened the following morning, shortly before the ship tied up at Derry, 31 women, 23 men and 18 children had died. After the tragic voyage, the master and two mates were arrested. During an inquest, survivors accused the Scottish crew of being cruel and savage. The captain protested he had given orders for the decks to be cleared for the passengers' safety while the storm raged. The coroner's jury returned a verdict of manslaughter, commenting that more consideration was shown to the cattle than to the passengers entrusted to their care.

Drogheda was another busy town in the north just inland from the coast, lying 70 miles north of Dublin, 4 miles from the mouth of the River Boyne, famous for its salmon fishing and infamous for the battle in 1690 to which it gave its name. The site was established as a stronghold by the invading Norsemen more than a thousand years ago and two towns, full of rivalries and with strong and separate identities, grew up on either side of the river. The name Drogheda means Bridge of the Ford, and during the 15th and 17th centuries, the town grew to be one of the most important in Ireland. Its demise came in 1649 when the protestant ruler, Oliver Cromwell, who had deposed the king in London, arrived with 12,000 troops, crushed the Catholic forces defending Drogheda and then ordered his army to slay all the inhabitants. Though the population was massacred by the army, Cromwell declared: 'It is a judgment of God on those who have embrued their hands in so much innocent blood.'

While the Ulster ports of Newry, Belfast and Londonderry enjoyed the lion's share of the shipping trade, the short passage across the Irish Sea to Liverpool made Drogheda a favourite port for those seeking passage on the bigger and more frequent vessels. During 1848, Drogheda sent emigrants directly to New York, aboard the *Ann*, *Adeline Cann*, *Janet* and *Warrior*. This was unusual for nearly 2,000 of the

Famine emigrant ships made only one voyage into New York. Perhaps ship owners and captains found the new Passengers' Acts, recently passed in Washington (see page 29–30), too restrictive. If the emigrant sailings had slackened in the early part of 1848, they increased later on, principally from the Irish ports of Dublin, Cork, Sligo, Limerick and Belfast while Liverpool continued to take the biggest share of the trade.

One of the most graphic accounts of life on board an emigrant ship is contained in a letter by Henry Johnson, dated September 18th 1848. After an eight-week voyage aboard an unnamed ship, he arrived in New York, but unable to find a job, he moved on to Hamilton, Canada, from where he wrote to his wife Jane at home in Dungonnell, County Antrim:

I have had rather a rough time of it. I was a week in Liverpool before the ship sailed on July 7th. We started with a fine, fair breeze and got along well until the third day when it came on to blow very hard. I was lying in my berth sleeping when I was wakened with a cry, 'ship's lost, the ship's sinking'.

I started up, and such a sight. Men, women and children rushing to the upper deck, some praying and crossing themselves, others with faces as white as a corpse. On deck they were gathered like sheep in a pen, crying on the captain to save them. I seen sailors rushing down to the lower deck and I followed, determined to know for myself, and there sure enough the water was coming in through one of the portholes at the bow as thick as a large barrel.

For a long time all the efforts of the sailors and two mates was unavailing to stop it and they gave it up in despair and came and told the captain to lower the boats. He cursed them and told them to try it again but the first mate refused and told him to go himself which he did telling the man at the helm at the same time, to put the ship before the wind, a very dangerous experiment at the time as we were near some rocks on the Irish Coast. However, he went down and got it partially stopped which partly quieted the fears of the passengers although some of them didn't get over it until the end of the voyage.

Johnson noted that he was one of about 40 Protestants on the ship, among some 450 Catholics who, in the time of danger did nothing but sprinkle holy water, cry, pray, cross themselves and all sorts of tomfoolery instead of giving hand to pump the ship. Of his own reactions, he commented:

I took the matter cooly enough. I knew if we were to go down I might as well take it kindly as not, as crying wouldn't help me. Under this impression I enjoyed the scene about me well. We got all right again and went on our right course.

Up to this time I had not opened my provision box as it was lowered into the hold but when I did get at it I found the ham alive with maggots and was obliged to throw it overboard. The remainder of the stuff I eat as sparingly of as possible but could not spin them out longer than four weeks at the end of which time I was obliged to subsist on the ship's allowance which was 2lbs of meal or flour and 5lbs of. biscuit in the week. The pigs wouldn't eat the biscuit so that for the remainder of the passage I got a right good starving.

There was not a soul on board I knew of I might have got a little assistance but it was every man for himself. Altogether it was nearly eight weeks from the time when we started from Liverpool until we got to New York, the longest passage the captain said ever he had. Six days before we got in a regular storm came on with the wind in our favour and anything I had read or imagined of a storm at sea was nothing to this.

We had some very hard gales before but this surpassed anything I ever thought of. Although there was some danger yet the wind being with us and going at the rate of 13 miles an hour through mountains of sea, I enjoyed it well. In the six days the storm lasted we made more than we had done for six weeks before. This was the pleasantest time I had though not for some others. One poor family in the next berth to me whose father had been ill all the time of a bowel complaint I thought great pity of, he died the first night of the storm and was laid outside of his berth.

The ship began to roll and pitch dreadfully. After a while the boxes, barrels etc. began to roll from one side to the other, the men at the helm were thrown from the wheel and the ship became almost unmanageable. At this time I was pitched right into the corpse, and there, corpse, boxes, barrel, women and children, all in one mess, were knocked from side to side for about 15 minutes. Pleasant that, wasn't it Jane dear? Shortly after the ship got righted and the captain came down, we sewed the body up, took it on deck, and amid the raging of the storm he read the funeral service for the dead and pitched him overboard.

Though Johnson intended his wife and children, Mary and Alexander, to join him in America, sadly, they never saw each other again. While Mrs Johnson and the children sailed for Quebec on the *Riverdale*, Johnson unaccountedly travelled to New York where he died of cholera.

On the last day of 1848, the *Cushlamachree* was berthed in Galway, prepared to sail for America; she rocked gently at the quayside as some of her 119 passengers boarded, while others milled around the harbour in a tearful mood. It was

117

N°. *3*   **Certificate of British Registry.**   N°. **2.**

England Ninth
THIS is to Certify, that in pursuance of an Act passed in the ~~Fourth~~ Year of the Reign of
Queen Victoria
~~King WILLIAM the Fourth~~, intituled, " An Act for the Registering of British Vessels," —

Joseph Evans of the Town of Galway Ship Broker —

having made and subscribed the Declaration required by the said Act, and having declared that *He* ~~together with~~

Jane and Registered as
of March 1848 N° 6 —

— (sole Owner — (in the proportions specified on the Back hereof) of the Ship or Vessel called the
"*Cushlamachree*" of *Galway* — which is of the Burthen of
Two hundred ninety four 95/3500 Tons, and whereof *John Thomas*
is Master; and that the said Ship or Vessel was *Built at Weymouth in Nova Scotia in the*
Year One Thousand Eight Hundred and forty five as appears by a Certificate of
of Registe granted at the New Brunswick dated 13th June 1846 & now delivered up and
cancelled & properly being Transfered to this Port —

and *W James Dawson Surveying Officer at this Port* — having certified to us that
the said Ship or Vessel has *Certain rooms for a* } Deck and *Three* — Masts, that her length from
Second
the inner part of the Main Stem to the fore part of the Stern Post aloft is *One Hundred* —

— feet *Three* — tenths, her breadth in Midships is *Twenty four* —

— feet — tenths, her depth in hold at Midships is *Fifteen* —

— feet — tenths, that she is *Ship* — rigged, with a *Standing* — Bowsprit;
is *Square* — sterned *Carvel* — built; has *no* — Galleries, and a *Woman's figure*
Head; and the said subscribing Owners having consented and agreed to the above Description, and having
caused sufficient Security to be given, as is required by the said Act, the said Ship or Vessel called the
Cushlamachree" — has been duly registered at the Port of *Galway* —

Certified under our Hands, at the Custom-House, in the said Port of *Galway* — this
Eight — Day of *March* — in the Year One Thousand Eight Hundred and *Forty Seven*

(Signed) { *J Richardson* Collector.
{ *R.D. Clague* Comptroller.

Admeasured under the Act ~~5 & 6 Will. IV. cap. 56~~ *8 & 9 Victoria cap 89*

No. 267.
Certificate of British Registry, (Copy) 2 new Act.

*The Certificate of British Registry shows that the
Cushlamachree was only 100 feet long and 24 feet wide.*

not the first time this ship had carried emigrants across the Atlantic but this was a special day, a Sunday, and who knows what special prayers for their journey were offered at Mass on board. Among the emigrants, the bachelors, easily out-numbering the 30 spinsters, were nearly all in their 20s. Matthew Kain and his wife arrived with their young family, Catherine and Biddy, and the seven-year-old twins Patrick and Ann. There were only ten more children aboard, including the four Sweenys (Thomas aged seven, Penny, five, Ellen, three, and nine-month-old Mary) apparently in the charge of their 18-year-old brother John, according to the ship's manifest. As the year of 1849 dawned, the day passed with further preparations directed by the master, John Thomas from Cardigan in Wales. The crew comprised two mates – who would both desert the ship on arrival in New York – five seamen, a cook and three apprentices. The youngest seaman, William Kelly was only 16: he was leaving his starving hometown for yet another voyage in his young life, but he would be well-fed on board. With such a small crew, steerage tickets at £3 10s (US $17.50), and ample cargoes to be picked up at either end of the trip, this would be a profitable round-trip. The owner, Patrick Lynch, a Galway merchant, had bought the 294-ton, 100-feet long ship two years earlier, specifically for the emigrant trade, for only £808 7s 7d, hardly more than US $4,000. The Lynchs, one of the famed Fourteen Tribes of Galway, were the most powerful of the ancient tribes. In the city, itself dating back to 1270, a grand, stone-built townhouse in Shop Street is known as Lynch's Castle, the site of a tragic legend: in 1493 a jealous teenage Lynch killed a 19-year-old Spanish nobleman, named Gomez, for making eyes at his girl-friend, Agnes. Gomez, from Cadiz, had been a guest at the house of Judge James Lynch, the magistrate and Mayor of Galway. After the murder, investigation disclosed a stiletto and several other

Names of the several Owners within-mentioned.	Number of Sixty-fourth Shares held by each Owner.	Form of Endorsement for Change of Master.	
		Custom-House,	Dated
Joseph Evans	*Sixty four* 64		has now become Master.
			Collector.
Signed *J Richardson Col*			Comptroller.
R D Clague Compr			

The following endorsement appears on the former Certificate of Registi. Custom House Galway 15th January 184? Joseph Evans of Galway Ship Builder hasby Deed of Mortgage dated 31 December 1846 transferred the Ship to Patrick Mass-Lynch of the same place Esquire for securing the payment of Eight Hundred and Eight Pounds Seven Shillings and Seven pence together with Interest thereon

J Richardson Col

Signed R D Clague Compr

18th March 1848. The above Deed of Mortgage Cancelled this day

Patrick Lynch bought the Cushlamachree *for only £808 7s 7d.*

clues implicating the Judge's son, Walter Lynch. He was arrested and detained in the prison next door to his fathers house. Judge Lynch dutifully tried his son, and finding him guilty was obliged to carry out sentence – death by hanging – as no one else could be persuaded to hang the Judge's son.

As the ship's owner, Mr Patrick Lynch was obliged to provide 7lbs of food each week and a gallon of water each day, for all the passengers on board. The crew fared rather better, according to the rations set out in the crew's agreements for the voyage:

1lb of bread/biscuits per man per day; 1½lbs of beef four days a week; 1¼lbs of pork on the other three days; flour, peas; ½oz of coffee, ⅛oz of tea and 1 gallon of water per day; and 1lb of sugar a week.

During the Famine years, no ship could carry sufficient supplies to last the long journey to America. The wind was the emigrants' only ally, speeding them on their way from a certain death in Ireland to a new life in America, yet there were times when the voyagers would hate the wind with every fibre of their frail bodies.

The *Cushlamachree* left on the early morning tide on Tuesday, January 2nd, as a reluctant wintry sun began to light the crown of the Connemara Mountains and slowly reveal the majestic sweep of Galway Bay. Who could be afraid in a ship with a name meaning *Joy Of My Heart*, but there would never be a moment on the voyage when the 119 brave people would feel at peace. Though all eventually landed safely, the voyage was hampered by bad weather and it would take eight bitterly cold weeks, 57 dreadful days and nights, before the *Cushlamachree* tied up in New York on March 1st 1849.

121

NAMES OF PASSENGERS	AGE	SEX	OCCUPATIONS	DATE PORT SHIP	NAMES OF PASSENGERS	AGE	SEX	OCCUPATIONS
					GLYNN, Michael	27	M	Laborer
					WALSH, John	23	M	Laborer
					QUINN, Ann	29	F	Wife
					Dominick	35	M	Laborer
CUSHLAMACREE 01 MARCH 1849					Patt.	32	M	Laborer
					GLYNN, James	18	M	Laborer
From Galway					John	38	M	Laborer
					SUMMERVILLE, Ceila	22	F	Spinster
					CAMIDEL, Daniel	31	M	Laborer
					ODONNELL, John	25	M	Laborer
CRUSIDINE, Ann	22	F	Spinster	01Mr14Gv	CONNORS, Hugh	25	M	Laborer
KILLELEA, William	26	M	Laborer	01Mr14Gv	KENNY, John	20	M	Laborer
CONAN, Margaret	22	F	Spinster	01Mr14Gv	GILMORE, John	30	M	Laborer
NELLY, Connor	27	M	Husband	01Mr14Gv	SHEEHAN, Mary	30	F	Spinster
Winny	23	F	Spinster	01Mr14Gv	John	08	M	Child
LARGHY, Margret	21	F	Laborer	01Mr14Gv	DEVANY, Mary	18	F	Spinster
WALTER, Patt.	24	M	Laborer	01Mr14Gv	QUIRK, Honor.	23	F	Spinster
BUTLER, Patt.	26	M	Laborer	01Mr14Gv	LYNSKY, Larry	20	M	Laborer
KEEHAN, Fergus	25	M	Laborer	01Mr14Gv	MITCHELL, John	36	M	Laborer
WALKER, Mathew	31	M	Matron	01Mr14Gv	KELLY, Edward	11	M	Laborer
SWEENEY, Mary	28	F	Laborer	01Mr14Gv	BEHANY, Bridget	20	F	Spinster
BROUN, Michael	24	M	Laborer	01Mr14Gv	HANLEN, Bridget	18	F	Spinster
HART, Thomas	20	M	Laborer	01Mr14Gv	KENEDY, Patt.	45	M	Laborer
CREVAN, John	21	M	Laborer	01Mr14Gv	MCDONOGH, Val.	31	M	Laborer
FYNN, John	20	M	Laborer	01Mr14Gv	CONNELLY, Michael	40	M	Laborer
HEALY, Patt.	20	M	Laborer	01Mr14Gv	James	38	M	Laborer
Julia	30	F	Matron	01Mr14Gv	KAIN, Mathew	30	M	Laborer
Ann	07	F	Child	01Mr14Gv	Catherine	12	F	None
Margret	04	F	Child	01Mr14Gv	Biddy	10	F	None
COMMANE, Bridget	18	F	None	01Mr14Gv	Patt.	07	M	Child
MCMAHON, Bridget	18	F	Spinster	01Mr14Gv	Ann	40	F	Matron
SWEENY, Thomas	07	M	Child	01Mr14Gv	Ann	07	F	Child
Penny	05	M	Child	01Mr14Gv	POWER, Martin	30	M	Laborer
Ellen	03	F	Child	01Mr14Gv	EGAN, Michael	25	M	Laborer
Mary	.09	F	Infant	01Mr14Gv	FEENEY, Martin	34	M	Laborer
KILKELLY, Malachy	20	F	Laborer	01Mr14Gv	FAHY, Ellen	26	F	Spinster
KAIN, Thomas	19	M	Laborer	01Mr14Gv	MUNANE, John	27	M	Laborer
MORRIS, Martin	21	M	Laborer	01Mr14Gv	TONLEY, Martin	16	M	Laborer
NOON, Frank	18	M	Laborer	01Mr14Gv	HANLY, Peggy	20	F	Spinster
SWEENY, John	18	M	Laborer	01Mr14Gv	COSTELLO, Patt.	25	M	Laborer
TANEL, John	21	M	Laborer	01Mr14Gv	COUGHLAN, John	24	M	Laborer
FAHY, Martin	17	M	Laborer	01Mr14Gv	FLOOD, Mary-Ann	20	F	Spinster
MCMAHON, Biddy	10	F	None	01Mr14Gv	RUANE, John	03	M	Child
RUANE, B.	17	F	Laborer	01Mr14Gv	TRACY, Patt.	12	M	Laborer
MOLLOY, Thomas	30	M	Spinster	01Mr14Gv	KELLY, Margaret	00	F	Spinster
RUANE, Nea	26	F	Laborer	01Mr14Gv	Honor.	00	F	Spinster
Catherine	24	F	Laborer	01Mr14Gv	BURKE, Bridget	00	F	Spinster
KELLY, Patt.	21	M	Spinster	01Mr14Gv	KENNY, Sally	00	F	Spinster
FITZPATRICK, Patt.	18	M	Laborer	01Mr14Gv	MULLIN, Patt.	00	M	Laborer
CARROLL, Nancy	16	F	Spinster	01Mr14Gv	WADE, Henry	00	M	Laborer
MONOHON, Mary	24	F	Spinster	01Mr14Gv	MCMAHON, Biddy	00	F	Spinster
COYE, Patt.	24	M	Laborer	01Mr14Gv	COILE, Margaret	00	F	Wife
ALLEN, Michael	20	M	Laborer	01Mr14Gv	Stephen	00	M	Merchant
MILAN, Michael	20	M	Laborer	01Mr14Gv	MCCARTHY, Denis	00	M	Child
WHEELAN, John	20	M	Laborer	01Mr14Gv				
MCHUGO, Lawrence	20	M	Laborer	01Mr14Gv				
MOONEY, Michael	30	M	Laborer	01Mr14Gv				
Patt.	26	M	Laborer	01Mr14Gv				
CORMICAN, Judy	24	F	Spinster	01Mr14Gv	**PAGEANT 02 MARCH 1849**			
KELLY, Michael	24	M	Laborer	01Mr14Gv				
Nappy (W)	24	F	Wife	01Mr14Gv	*From Galway*			
MARION, William	35	M	Laborer	01Mr14Gv				
NOWLAN, Winny	20	F	Spinster	01Mr14Gv				
HEALY, Thomas	20	M	Laborer	01Mr14Gv				
Mary	50	F	Matron	01Mr14Gv	KUGGOON, Hnor.	26	F	Matron
DONNELLY, Bryan	27	M	Laborer	01Mr14Gv	HANNIFFY, Francis	33	M	Carpenter
FAHEY, John	30	M	Laborer	01Mr14Gv	DIVINODY, Patt.	20	M	None
BROWN, Kitty	24	F	Spinster	01Mr14Gv	BRANDURK, Edward	13	M	None
WARD, Daniel	24	M	Laborer	01Mr14Gv	Laurence	12	M	None
TRACEY, John	30	M	Laborer	01Mr14Gv	NAUGHTON, Patt.	40	M	Hatter
CORBETT, Thomas	30	M	Laborer	01Mr14Gv	JOYCE, John	30	M	Laborer
DOHERTY, Antony	23	M	Laborer	01Mr14Gv	Honor (W)	25	F	Wife
CASEY, Thomas	21	M	Laborer	01Mr14Gv	Catherine	06	F	Child
Nancy (W)	20	F	Wife	01Mr14Gv	Bridget	04	F	Child
Biddy	.09	F	Infant	01Mr14Gv				

463

The passenger list for the Cushlamachree, *presented to US Immigration officials in March 1849.*

Two other ships, the *America* and the *Enterprise*, sailing on the same tide, arrived a day later on March 2nd. Both had suffered a particularly long voyage from Liverpool. Similarly, sailing just behind the *Cushlamachree*, the *Pageant*, under Captain Dawkin carrying 61 passengers, at least half her load, arrived on March 2nd. The *Clarence*, who had begun the same passage almost a month earlier, had fared even worse, battling for 74 days on the Atlantic before she arrived safely in port. The *Cushlamachree* had made the voyage twice before in much less time and, on the next trip, with 143 passengers aboard, the same captain would force her across the ocean in the summer breezes and into New York in only 27 days.

12

Surviving the Icebergs

It is difficult to imagine how, in the middle of the last century, any passengers on board a ship built of wood, propelled by sails, and guided by only the most rudimentary navigational aids, could survive a collision with an iceberg. Even assuming that some survived the immediate impact and the freezing waters, their only hope of rescue lay in a chance encounter with another ship, for there were no radios to send out distress calls. Though the American Samuel Morse had developed his dot-and-dash code in 1838, and the electric telegraph had been invented in 1846, sailing ships were not equipped with anything so sophisticated and were unable to send out SOS signals until much later, during the second half of the century.

With limited navigational aids, it was hard to foresee or steer clear of danger. On a clear day the icebergs might be sighted through a telescope, but at other times the only safeguard was a cautious look-out. Other guides consisted of Atlantic sea charts, a magnetic compass, a simple chronometer for measuring time and longitude and a sextant for checking position. The captain would seldom miss an opportunity in rough weather to use his sextant to determine his ship's position; if the clouds cleared, he would shoot the angle between the horizon and the sun by day or a specific star at dawn or dusk. Essentially the captain was reliant on his seaman's instinct for predicting storms, though a simple weather glass – an open-necked bottle half-filled with coloured water – indicating pressure changes, might help him gauge the weather. The first barometer was not invented until 1844 and another ten years passed before Admiral Fitzroy devised a method to predict storms and forecast the weather. Proximity to land, again, was often gauged by natural signs and means, by watching the flight of birds overhead and the flotsam floating in the water. News of such hopeful portends often raised the spirits of crew and passengers alike, and sometimes led to the lifting of food rations – on the assumption that land was close at hand.

Many a captain had a favourite route across the ocean, but the prevailing wind, on embarkation and during the early days of the voyage, was usually the determining factor. If the captain were forced by the winds to steer north, the journey would be shorter, but the weather worse and the danger increased. A weather expert, Brian Oatway, from London's Meteorological Office explains:

> For ships out of Ireland in the mid-19th century I would think the course they took largely depended on the winds they found at the start of a voyage. It was a far longer voyage going south and their difficulty with provisions would make that a less popular route. They were used to sailing into and out of Canada with timber and various cargoes so if they were in the northerly latitudes, especially between April and June, they would always be on the lookout for ice. Look at the *Titanic*. This was many years later with a lot more navigational aids available, yet the

biggest liner in the world on her maiden voyage from New York, sank after colliding with an iceberg. Weather satellites now photograph these ice-masses regularly and plot their journey southwards so that navigators today steer accordingly. Prevailing weather, approaching gales and storms, and their personal preference still make a ship's captain decide on going north or south in the Atlantic. Our ability to photograph the icebergs from above is an enormous benefit.

Four ships are known to have gone down after hitting the ice in 1849, and a large number of emigrants lost their lives, either drowned or crushed by the ice. But two amazing rescue missions are recorded, both involving very small, Irish-owned ships. The first, *Hannah*, a 175-ton brig, was wrecked on the 26th day of a voyage from Newry, in Ulster. Their ship went aground on the leading edge of the iceberg in darkness at four in the morning. The captain, first and second mates, expecting the ship to capsize instantly, apparently abandoned their passengers, seized a lifeboat and made their escape. In fact, 40 minutes elapsed before the ship sank, allowing many passengers and crew to clamber onto the ice. They huddled together clad only in their night-shirts for over 15 hours until miraculously, later that evening, a ship appeared in the gloaming and the brave captain of the *Nicaragua* made an inspired rescue mission. Over 129 were saved and conveyed to safety, eventually reaching Canada. Many suffered severe frostbite. For his part in the rescue, the heroic Captain Marshall of the *Nicaragua* was awarded £43 13s ($218.25).

The incident was reported to Lloyd's of London, where shipping movements around the world are collated, and several newspapers covered the dramatic rescue in the stilted but evocative language of the period, as in the *ILN*'s report:

126

Wreck of an Emigrant Ship
and Loss of Life

Intelligence of the total wreck of the *Hannah*, freighted with nearly two hundred emigrants bound to Quebec from Newry, was reported during the week at Lloyd's, the particulars having been received by an American mail-steamer at Liverpool.

The Hannah was a brig of between 150 and 200 tons and manned by a crew, it is said, of 12 seamen under the command of Mr Shaw, the master. On the 3rd of April last she sailed from Newry with the above number of emigrants on board, having been previously overhauled and examined by Her Majesty's emigration agent at that port. The emigrants chiefly consisted of agricultural labourers and their wives and children.

The passage up to the 27th, considering the season of the year, was favourable. The vessel then encountered heavy winds and a quantity of floating ice. On the morning of the 29th [of April] the unfortunate ship struck on a reef of ice; it was about four oclock when she struck.

A charge is brought against the master and first and second officers, of their having been guilty of one of the most revolting acts of inhumanity possible to be conceived. They had got the lifeboat out and the moment they found the vessel would inevitably go down, they jumped into it and abandoned the wreck with the emigrants on board.

Their screams for help rent the air and it was with difficulty that the remainder of the crew could induce the frantic creatures to comprehend the only chance left of saving their lives. Fortunately, the ice was firm under the ship's bows and the seamen convincing them as to its security, many got on it. Its solidity being then apparent, a desperate struggle took place among the emigrants to leave the wreck.

Men, women and children, with nothing on but their night attire, were scrambling over the mass of ice. Many of the poor creatures slipped between the huge masses and were either crushed to death or met with a watery grave. The last to leave the wreck were some of the crew who contrived to save a small portion of spirits and a few blankets.

Soon after they had got clear, the ship's stern rose as it were above the water and she went down head foremost just 40 minutes after the collision with the ice. The sufferings of the wretched creatures were most harrowing.

The seamen who were among them humanely gave up what covering they had to the women, some of whom had been shockingly wounded and bruised. Thus were they exposed the whole of that day until five o'clock in the afternoon, when a vessel hove in sight and bore down to the edge of the field of ice. It proved to be the barque *Nicaragua*, also bound for Quebec, under Captain Marshall.

He got the ship's ice-fender down and prepared to take to the ice. By seven o'clock he had got so close in, that in the course of two hours he and his crew succeeded in getting hold of about 50 of the poor creatures and placing them on board his vessel.

The remainder stood crouched together in another part of the ice some distance off, inaccessible from the position of the ship. Captain Marshall had all sails clewed up and got a rope fastened to a piece of ice, and with the long-boat pushed off with his men to the spot. After considerable difficulty he succeeded in getting to the edge, where they remained huddled together.

The whole were saved. The number got on board the *Nicaragua* were 129 passengers and seamen, the greater part of whom were frost-bitten. As far as Captain Marshall could ascertain from the survivors, the number that perished by being crushed to death between the ice and being frozen to death, were between 50 and 60.

As soon as he succeeded in getting all on board, the ship was got underway and proceeded in the direction of Cape Ray. Every comfort that his means afforded was placed at the sufferers' disposal. The next day, meeting with the barque *Broom*, of Glasgow, 27 of the poor creatures were transferred to that vessel; and in the course of the following day 49 of the survivors were placed on three other vessels.

The *Nicaragua* reached Quebec on the 10th of last month [May]. The fate of the master and the others who took to the life-boat and abandoned the emigrants, is not known.

A later issue revealed further news of the renegade crew:

It has been ascertained that the master and part of the crew of the emigrant ship *Hannah*, who left the ship when she was foundering with 200 passengers, many of whom were subsequently rescued, were picked up four days after the melancholy event and landed at Quebec.

Though the editor called for the deserters to be charged, they seemed to have escaped unpunished as no official record exists of any disciplinary action.

The second record of an amazing escape relates how the *Maria*, sailing from Limerick to Quebec, hit an iceberg at night, just 50 miles from the Canadian coast. She sank rapidly. Nine passengers jumped on to the ice as she went down and three crew members grabbed a lifeboat as it floated free, but the remaining 109 died. The *Armagh Guardian* reported the tragedy in May 1849:

Foundering of Another Emigrant Ship
One Hundred Lives Lost

Scarcely has the melancholy intelligence of the loss of the *Hannah*, Irish Emigrant ship and 200 lives subsided, ere it falls to our painful duty to announce another similar catastrophe, the foundering of the ship *Maria* from Limerick in a field of ice and the sacrifice of a vast amount of human life.

The particulars contained in the advices of the shocking event, as received on Wednesday from Quebec, state that the ship's destruction took place at midnight, on the 10th of last month [May] so suddenly that she almost instantaneously, on striking, went down, carrying no less than 109 unhappy human beings, all of whom perished.

The *Maria*, it appears was an old vessel, manned by a crew of ten hands, including the master Mr Hesligeau. Whether she underwent the necessary inspection by the officers of the Emigrant Commission on her leaving Limerick has not yet been ascertained.

She sailed from that port on the 2nd April last with 111 passengers, about 80 men, and women, and the remainder their families for Quebec, the emigrants intending to settle in Canada.

About 40 days' sailing brought the vessel to within 50 miles of St Pauls. Here severe weather was encountered and a large field of ice sighted. The ship hove to with a view of clearing the huge frozen mass. Unfortunately, however, the manoeuvre had but little effect for late that night, 10th of May, she ran into a berg with terrific force.

The whole of her bows were stove in and the next moment the sea was rushing into the hold with the violence almost of a cataract. A piercing shriek was heard from below but it was only for a few moments' duration, as the ship went down almost immediately.

It was the mate's watch who, with one seaman and a cabin boy, succeeded in saving three lives by one of the boats, which floated from the wreck as she foundered. About 20 of the passengers managed to reach the deck just before she went down, some of whom jumped on to the ice, while others clung to the floating spars.

Nine only, however, could be preserved – six men, two women and a boy, who had got on to the ice. Nothing was seen of the master or the rest of the crew. They all perished with the remainder of the passengers. Exposed in the boat to the most inclement weather, the helpless survivors remained for the whole of the following day.

Eventually, a barque named *Roslin Castle* and the *Falcon*, a brig, approached and took them on board. The poor creatures had suffered severely from the cold, and their condition was the most heart-rending. Their names are given as follows –

Michael Cusack, Joseph Lynch, Bridget O'Gorman, spinster; Connors, William Brew, John Hogan and Pat McTogue. The survivors of the *Maria*s crew are –

William Collins, mate; John Pickering, seaman; and Michael Tague, cabin boy; making in all, out of one hundred and twenty one souls on board, only twelve saved.

In consequence of the brig *Falcon* being short of water, those who were picked up by her were transferred on board the *Roslin Castle*, which proceeded to Quebec and arrived there last Saturday fortnight.

The daily shipping newspaper, *Lloyd's List*, recording departures, arrivals, sightings, weather and cargo information for the shipping and insurance industries, reported in July 1849:

The immense field of ice that has been encountered in and near the Gulf of St. Lawrence this season has not been equalled for many years. In addition to the melancholy loss of the *Maria*, as also the *Hannah*, which foundered near the same bearing, two other vessels were lost, the *Gleaner*, a large barque, 500 tons burthen, and the ship *Torrence*, out of Glasgow. (Neither of these carried emigrants.)

In both instances scarcely five minutes elapsed from the moment of their striking the ice to their foundering. The crews were providentially saved. Those of the *Torrence*, however, were exposed seven days in the ship's boat before they were picked up. The loss of these vessels is reported to be little short of £40,000.

Many an emigrant ship came in sight of these icebergs and every crew in the Atlantic knew how menacing they were. Ice is still a hazard for North Atlantic shipping. The greatest danger occurs in the spring when ice-floes and icebergs float down from the Arctic. Though voyages to Quebec proved particularly hazardous, ships heading for Boston and New York during the spring months were also at risk. According to today's meteorologists, icebergs travel a long way south in the western reaches of the ocean. A cold current coming down from Labrador, through the Greenland-Canadian gap, prevents the ice melting in the warm Gulf Stream flowing northwards. Icebergs have frequently travelled as far out as latitude 40° North (on a line with Philadelphia), decreasing in size on the way. Even so, marine documents record an iceberg of 30 feet in diameter and 2 feet high, sited at 33.5° North/71° West – far out in the ocean but just about level with Savannah, Georgia.

The North Atlantic's icebergs, not to be confused with ice-floes, are formed from huge chunks of fresh-water glaciers which have slipped into the sea off the Greenland icecap. Icebergs can easily measure a mile long and reach more than 200 feet above the waves, as high as a 20-storey apartment block, with very deep basements, as generally only one-seventh of an iceberg shows above water. The ice itself may be 5,000 years old by the time it breaks off the glacier. Blown by moderate Atlantic winds, the iceberg might travel for around three months, covering up to 1,500 miles. Icebergs move at one nautical mile an hour. When the wind abates, they spin slowly in the water, following the rotation of the earth. Even in mid-July, ships passing through the St Lawrence River in Canada need to beware iceberg remnants, known as growlers because of the noise they make moving in the waves. Icebergs are always a terrifying sight for a look-out at night. Even a moderate iceberg may be similar in size to a cathedral or a white palace, with blue and grey tints on its jagged peak and huge, melting teardrops flowing down its face. Icebergs vary in shape from towers to pyramids, and are sometimes sculpted by the wind into saddles. When the wind was slack it might take a ship hours to slide past these pearly monsters. The iceberg itself was sometimes obscured by clouds formed on its face by the chill temperatures. Terrifying though they were, icebergs represented just one more hazard to be faced by the intrepid emigrants on their way to forge a new life in America.

13

Flags for Convenience

During the 19th century, thousands of ships plied the seaways, rivers and canals, loaded with cargoes and passengers. Sea transport was a haphazard and ill-regulated trade until the latter half of the last century. At any one time, ten or 20 ships, often very similar in size and design, and sometimes bearing the same name or ensign, might cross the ocean. Certain much-loved names abounded, such as *Eliza*, a popular Christian name for a girl. *Constitution* was also common; at least three ships of that name sailed between Liverpool and New York during the Famine years; and two *Hannah*'s, registered to ports in Ireland, carried Famine emigrants. Though a ship could be identified by its owner's pennant, this was normally only hoisted when entering or leaving port.

At the time of the Famine, however, Lloyd's Register introduced a series of identification flags which corresponded to ships' identification numbers in the Register. Captain Joseph Marryatt, an officer in the Royal Navy, suggested this system of identifying ships in the 1830s and by the following decade it was accepted throughout the world. Ten coloured flags represented numbers from zero to nine, and each ship flew the four flags corresponding to the number by which she was known in the Register. One was signified by the colours white with a blue square; five by a red flag; eight by blue with a yellow square; and nine by blue and yellow quarters. But configurations involving double numbers, such as 2102, 3103 or 9109, were avoided. As a result, far fewer than 9,999 ships could be identified by the use of the four flags. To overcome the problem, ships introduced later in the century flew a First Distinguishing Pennant either from a different mast or above their own signal flags. This was a long, triangular flag in white with a red spot near the hoist. Later, Second and Third Distinguishing Pennants were added and, by the time *Marryatt's Code of Signals* was published in 1856, some 30,000 separate identities were established

Possibly these identities were not of such great consequence once a ship was at sea, but if lost or wrecked, a ship's position and identity was of paramount importance – to the owners and especially to the insurers and Lloyd's officials. To help keep track of ships' movements, all vessels were logged on entering and leaving port, and when sighted by another vessel at sea, such sightings being reported to Lloyd's local agents. As all sea-faring nations, especially America, began to increase their tonnage on the high seas, these new identification systems and enforced regulations became essential for the smooth running of an expanding shipping trade. There were other flags in the system which conveyed a particular message when flown alone, such as 'I have lost my anchor chain – request assistance'. Lighthouses and coastguards also flew special flags signifying various warnings for ships at sea.

There were also time-honoured distress signals: the Red Ensign, a red flag with the Union Jack in one corner, identifying the British merchant fleet, was flown upside down on a halyard at the stern to signal distress. Two ships in distress were forced to fly the signal in 1849. First, the 460-ton barque *Atlantic* left Liverpool in January bound for New Orleans with more than 300 Irish emigrants. On their second day at sea they were hit by severe gales which blew the ship miles off course and ripped the sails to shreds as the captain, William Rose, tried to maintain some sort of headway. Rose plotted a course to take his ship north around Ireland, into the ocean, heading much further north than was ideal, especially for such a southerly destination, but the fierce south westerly winds gave him no choice. With such little canvas left, the *Atlantic* drifted towards the Pladda Lighthouse, positioned to warn ships to keep clear. The west coast of Scotland is wild but luckily the *Atlantic* was in the vicinity of the mouth of the Clyde, leading up to the docks at Glasgow where the steam-tug *Conqueror* circled, waiting to tow ships into port. The *Conqueror*'s captain spotted the upside-down ensign flying from the *Atlantic*, and on closer inspection saw the tangled mass of spars where the sails had been attached and the battered state of the ship. The master of the tug exchanged signals with his opposite number on the *Atlantic* and both agreed that the sea was too rough and the weather too unpredictable to attempt any transfer of passengers. With the *Conqueror* steaming close by, Captain Rose headed slowly towards the nearest harbour at Ardrossan. The few sails remaining allowed him little opportunity to manoeuvre and as they sailed over the bar, with the harbour in sight, the barque went aground and stuck fast in the sand. To add to their problems the ship started to leak; now there was no choice but to abandon ship. By using the long-boat, the passengers were ferried in small batches to the tug. The *Atlantic* was fortunate both in being so close to land when disaster struck, and in being sighted within three days by a steam vessel, powered independently of the prevailing winds.

By no means so fortunate was the *Caleb Grimshaw* (named after its owner) which left Liverpool later in the year, bound for New York with 425 passengers aboard. Misfortune fell early on in the voyage when the ship was becalmed despite the late season, but the Atlantic Ocean and its weather are fickle and often unfriendly. The ship drifted for 19 days at sea before a decent breeze blew up. Just as Captain James Hoxie set about making up for lost time, fire in the forward hold was reported. The passengers were naturally terrified, as there was not another ship nor land in sight. The ship was reasonably equipped, and its crew of 30 managed to pump water on to the seat of the blaze; but the flames were fanned by the fresh winds. While the crew battled with the fire, some passengers took matters into their own hands and lowered one of the ship's boats but it crashed into the water, and swamped the passengers. Twelve of them were swept away and drowned while the rest clambered back on board. On deck, the scene became chaotic. Another boat was lowered but this time by the crew, equipped with a compass, a chart and supplies of food and water. They escaped the burning ship and raised a sail to remain safely in the lea of the *Caleb Grimshaw*.

The fire raged all night and during the early morning another boat was lowered – with the captain's wife and daughter safely aboard, later to be joined by some of the cabin passengers. The unfortunate men, women and children in steerage had to fend for themselves. In the afternoon of the second day, when the captain himself abandoned ship, the poor emigrants felt certain they were heading for a watery grave. From his long-boat, Captain Hoxie tried to reassure them, promising to sail alongside and direct the rescue efforts from his boat. There were no more boats left aboard the ship:

one was wrecked and two were at sea, attached to the mother-ship by tow-lines. The remaining crew decided to build rafts. The first raft, launched with a tow line, was quickly overloaded with 30 passengers, some of whom cast themselves adrift – never to be seen again. A salutary lesson was learned and fewer crowded onto the second raft; both rafts were kept in tow, forming a flotilla with the two boats.

Though water-logged holds prevented the fire from spreading, it had taken a firm grip amidships and experienced seamen knew that the *Caleb Grimshaw* was doomed. But as big ships can be seen from distant horizons (unlike small boats riding low in the waves), the victims' best chance of rescue was to remain close to the burning barque. The ship's course was set to sail towards the busy shipping lanes leaving from England and Ireland. On the fourth day of the fire, the ship seemed to revive, at least momentarily, and the crew put her before a freshening wind while everyone prayed for help. Their prayers were answered at midday when the look-out spotted the barque *Sarah*, sailing from London to Halifax in Canada. Within two hours, the *Sarah* had drawn alongside the *Caleb Grimshaw*. Her captain, David Cooke, first rescued the passengers on the boats and rafts which, once cast adrift, sank immediately. By midnight, a storm arose, the sky darkened and the flames devoured the *Caleb Grimshaw*, while over 250 passengers still on board clung to the burning wreckage. With dawn on the fifth day, the weather turned, and half the survivors on the stricken ship were transferred to the *Sarah* until there was literally no more space aboard the rescue barque.

For three more days and nights the two ships moved slowly through the water, the *Sarah*'s sails reefed in to slow her down. There was little canvas aloft on the *Caleb Grimshaw* and she was lying very low in the water. The coastline of Europe was closer than America or Canada but not close enough, about 750 miles according to the sea charts. Over 100 stricken passengers still clung to the burning ship. Weakened, without water and subject to freezing nights on deck, they began to sicken and die. Though eight days had passed since the fire broke out, their ordeal was far from over. Two more days passed before land was at last sighted, when the peak of a 3,000-feet volcano broke the horizon, and gradually the island of Flores in the Portuguese Azores came into view. But the burning ship could not go on much further, nor could her stricken passengers. Forty had already died. As the *Caleb Grimshaw* keeled over and sank, the *Sarah* was forced to take on board the last of the survivors. With all the extra passengers and an unkind wind, it took the *Sarah* another four days to make port in Flores. There she remained, tied-up for five days in quarantine while fresh fruit and water were ferried daily to the survivors aboard.

Altogether, 90 passengers were lost. When the survivors eventually went ashore, they found that, though 40 days out of Liverpool, they were still 2,000 miles from their destination, and with their ship on the ocean floor. A few continued their journey aboard the trusty *Sarah* while others waited to take passage on the small ships which called by the Azores regularly, to re-provision. There was praise indeed for gallant Captain Cooke and his crew, praise for some of the *Caleb Grimshaw*'s crew, but a great deal of scorn was heaped on Captain Hoxie.

When his ship reached New York and news of the two-week episode spread, Captain Cooke was granted the Freedom of the City and he and his crew shared a reward of US $8,000 dollars for their bravery. What happened to Captain Hoxie? He was lambasted in the editorial columns back home but he escaped official censure for leaving his ship when she was still ablaze. Once again the Board of Trade seems to have been fairly inactive. Questions were raised in

Parliament as to the cause of the fire, and letters exchanged in the Colonial Office denying responsibility for the outbreak of the fire: 'It is denied there was anything on board capable of spontaneous combustion . . . it is suggested ships be forced to carry means of making signals at night.'

Returning to Liverpool where one version of events was preferred to many others, Cooke showed great courtesy to Hoxie and wrote a letter to the editor of the *Liverpool Mercury* defending his fellow officer. He emphasised that the wild behaviour of the passengers, who clambered aboard a lifeboat immediately the fire was discovered, had led Captain Hoxie to believe that he could direct rescue operations better from a boat at sea, than combat the pandemonium on board. Thereafter he did all he could to save as many as possible and secure onward passage from the port of Fayal, reported Captain Cooke. Captain Hoxie kept quiet.

14

On the Way to the White House

The roll-call of Irish emigrants who made their fame and fortune in America is unending, especially when we include their descendants. The names Ford and Kennedy are prominent from the Famine era. Both families succeeded for very different reasons, but both share a strange coincidence in that little is known about their departure from Ireland. Henry Ford's father sailed in 1847 but the details of his family's passage from Cork through Quebec and on to Detroit remain obscure (see page 61–65). Patrick Kennedy sailed in 1849. His arrival in Boston is well chronicled, as is the later family history and the celebrated accession of his great-grandson, John F Kennedy, to the highest office of all when he became the 35th President of the United States of America. But we know nothing of Patrick's journey prior to the day he took passage on an American packet ship in Liverpool.

Though the potato blight had been less severe in the south-east corner of Ireland where Patrick's family lived, they were losing the struggle to maintain their whitewashed cottage and the 25 acres at Dunganstown in County Wexford, where they grew vegetables and cereal crops. The farm, big as it was by comparison with neighbouring plots, commanded a high rent and could not support Patrick, his brother James, and a sister Mary, as well as their parents. An older brother had

The original 1849 advertisement for Patrick Kennedy's ship.

already died and it seemed imperative to reduce the number of mouths to feed. Emigration to America seemed one way of easing the burden on farm and family. Soon after Patrick left, his family was evicted and forbidden to return until many years had elapsed and the laws had changed. Generations of Kennedys have continued to farm the land. Today, a distant cousin of the American family, Mrs Mary Kennedy Ryan lives in the same cottage. Her grandmother was the daughter of Patrick's brother James.

Several American biographers of the Kennedys refer to the death of Patrick's older brother, John, at the Battle of Vinegar Hill in 1798. Vinegar Hill was the last serious uprising by the Irish against the English for more than a century. The battle site at Enniscorthy, where 15,000 rebels were overcome by a Royalist protestant army, is close to the Kennedy home. Yet if John died in 1798, over 40 years seem to lie between the brothers, for Patrick was born in 1823, and, assuming that John was just 14 when he died fighting the English, then he would have been born around 1784.

At the time of the Famine it was not at all rare for the youngest in the family to leave the homestead and emigrate. By doing so, he or she might be better able to raise enough money to bring over the rest of the family. More often, departure meant total separation, and the youngest left amid sad and heart-wringing farewells. Sometimes, even, a wake of a kind was held for the departing son, though there were few enough wakes of the conventional kind during the Famine years when mourning was a luxury. Patrick was 26 when he left his homestead, probably setting off early one morning in late winter on the road to New Ross. He knew the way as his family usually sold their barley crop to the local breweries, and their vegetables at New Ross market. The journey down the long hill to the busy quays at New Ross would take an hour by foot. The town was only 3 miles from home, but 17 miles inland on the River Barrow. On the quays, agents were always selling tickets for ships leaving for America and Canada, from Dublin, Cork and Waterford, even from New Ross itself later in 1849. Just a short trip away lay Liverpool, where even bigger and faster Atlantic ships set sail for America and Canada. Coasters, cutters and small schooners left for Liverpool daily, charging a modest fare of a few shillings, under a dollar.

As Patrick was young and strong, he may have chosen to take a longer route by foot, to Ballyhack wharf 8 miles and two hours away – further down river and closer to the sea, Ballyhack was nearer to America. Though historians have no idea exactly when or how Patrick travelled to Liverpool, it has been established that he arrived at the English port early in the year and boarded the *Washington Irving,* bound for Boston. This fact was discovered by an amateur American genealogist, Katherine O'Brien, who found Patrick's birth certificate, on the reverse side of which were pencilled the words: 'SSWI Train Passenger 198'. The clue led her through the passenger manifests lodged by ships' captains and held by the US Immigration Service, to discover that Patrick had arrived in Boston on April 22nd aboard the Sailing Ship *Washington Irving*, owned by Enoch Train's White Diamond shipping line.

The *Washington Irving* was a splendid ship named after one of America's first literary giants, author of *The Legend of Sleepy Hollow*, and creator of the memorable characters, Rip van Winkle, Ichabod Crane and Diedrich Knickerbocker. The ship was the product of a famous shipbuilder, Donald McKay, who built five such fast ships for Enoch Train in the East Boston yards between 1845 and 1850. According to *Western Ocean Packets,* a history written by Basil Lubbock in the 19th century:

> McKay's ships were celebrated for their strength; they were designed to carry a tremendous press of sail in heavy weather without straining. In light winds they were not fast, but then packet ships did not sail in the latitudes of light winds.

Like all Train's packet ships, the *Washington Irving* was strongly built, with smooth and regular lines. Launched in

1845, she weighed 776 tons, measured 151 feet and was well-equipped with three square-rigged masts and single top-sails. She was sister-ship to the *Anglo Saxon*, the *Anglo American*, the *Daniel Webster*, a monster of 1,187 tons, and the *Ocean Monarch* which burned so tragically in 1848. All these ships were engaged on the Atlantic emigrant-run and the unique company flag – a bright red square with a white diamond in the middle – was carried by a fleet of 24 packet ships sailing bi-monthly from Boston and weekly from Liverpool.

The scene aboard the *Washington Irving* is dramatically brought to life in *Some Famous Sailing Ships*, written in 1928 by Richard C McKay, grandson of the boat-builder:

> One cannot help admiring the daring that impelled Enoch Train to start his celebrated line of sailing packets and to commission Donald McKay to build them expressly for the trans-Atlantic passenger, freight and mail service. He had to contend not only with the keen rivalry of the New York packet lines, but the Lords of the Admiralty (in London) had charge of the Royal mails and sometime previously had contracted for the conveyance of these with Mr Samuel Cunard.
>
> He then brought into existence buildings required to house the live-stock for supplying the cabin table, the most important being the cow house where, after a short run ashore on the marshes at the end of each voyage, a well-seasoned animal of the snug-made Alderney breed, chewed the cud in sweet content.

An animal farm might be a practical option aboard one of Cunard's early steamships, which could proceed with reasonably level decks, but keeping livestock aboard a sailing ship was a tricky business. However, as Enoch Train was forced to compete with Cunard's steamships, live animals were kept aboard his packet ships to supplement supplies. As McKay points out:

> Preserved milk was unknown in those times; and the officers of a passenger ship would rather have gone to sea without a doctor, to say nothing of a parson, than without a cow and some nanny-goats. The ship's cow and her health was always a most important matter and it is related that on one occasion, after a long spell of very bad weather, one of these creatures fell off in her supply of milk and was brought around again by a liberal supply of nourishing stout, wisely prescribed for her by the ship's doctor.
>
> Pigs always proved a thriving stock on a ship farm. Next to the pig, goats were the most useful stock. These animals soon made themselves at home on shipboard; they had good sea legs and were blessed with an appetite that nothing in the way of tough fibre was too much for, from an armful of shavings to an old newspaper or log-book. It was not, however, always practical to turn in sheep to feed with pigs at sea, for the last-named animals were apt to develop a taste for a good live leg of mutton after a few weeks afloat.
>
> Truly in those days a ship was more like a small bit of the world afloat than it is now. One can imagine the noisy confusion that must have reigned aboard one of these packets on sailing day. Ducks, geese and poultry in general always sympathised with excitement near them while pigs and even sheep, thrown together for the first time, had a noisy way of their own. At intervals, even the old cow bemoaned her lot in life.

McKay's account really only describes the diet of the cabin-class who enjoyed a grand lifestyle of white linen, fine china and silver cutlery laid out in the saloon and exchanged tales of wonderful adventures on the high seas. Down below in steerage, life was vastly different: on a good day, an emigrant's meal might consist of a salt herring, a piece of mouldy cheese and a stale biscuit.

Another cameo of life aboard in the mid-19th century is drawn by George Francis Train in *Young America Abroad*. The Boston ship-owner Enoch Train employed his nephew, George Francis Train, as a freight clerk. In one passage, he confesses to the dismal failure of a business opportunity:

> I can well remember the fatal result of my first shipment of onions to Great Britain. I saw everybody shipping them and believed a fortune was to be made, and I worked days, thought at my meals and dreamed nights until the bills of lading were signed at 2s 6d [12.5 p or 62 cents]. Twenty-five barrels of silver-skin onions, marked T in a diamond were loaded on board the good ship *Washington Irving*. They were picked by hand and packed in the cleanest of barrels, and coopered with scrupulous exactness and paid for from my clerkship salary. I went without a new suit for Sundays all that summer. It was an awful suspense; my letter of instructions was carefully written, not a word too many, simply advising the quality and using the words Prompt Sales and Prompt Remittances. Four months went past and I was about to order the aforesaid suit when a letter came.
>
> It was sealed and bore that well-remembered stamp B.B. & Co. – Baring Brothers and Company. I broke the seal, I saw the words 'dull market' and 'regret' and 'perishable article' and 'debit of £3 17s 9d' [$19.44]. That was my first and last shipment of onions to Liverpool. I stopped the order with the tailor and practised economy until all was right once more.

Train does not reveal whether he paid the debit note of £3 17s 9d to Baring Brothers who were bankers to the Queen and the Royal Family in London, and many other notables, until 1995 when they went bust in a blaze of publicity, engulfed by billion-dollar debts incurred by a rogue commodities dealer in Singapore.

Aboard the *Washington Irving* in 1849, Captain George Upton, in the tradition of American masters, kept his canvas busy through the hours of darkness. The journey across the Atlantic to Boston took 31 days and nights. During the trip a romance blossomed between Patrick Kennedy and a 27-year-old colleen named Bridget Murphy. Bridget had also lived in County Wexford, at Barron's Farm in Gusserane. Though Barron's Farm lay just under ten miles from Dunganstown, their homes were separated by Sliebh Coillte, a densely wooded hillside, forming a physical barrier between the communities on either side. Yet on this ship bound for the other side of the world, the two young people met and fell in love. Bridget's own parents had also enjoyed an unusual courtship. Her mother, Mary Barron, had been sent to the local fair at Nash to sell two of the farm's pigs on a leash. She found both a buyer and a husband at the same time when she met Phillip Murphy who bought her pigs and married her soon after. Many years later, the couple received news from Boston in a series of letters written by Mary Kennedy, their eldest granddaughter, who they would never set eyes on. Today, on the slopes below Sliebh Coillte, an arboretum of trees grows in commemoration of an even younger Kennedy, John F Kennedy, the American President who was assassinated in 1963. Patrick and Bridget continued their courting through the month-long voyage and when they arrived in America, two among nearly 64,000 famine emigrants who had sailed to Boston, they did not move far from the docks on Noddles Island. After their wedding on September 26th, they set up home in Sumner Street, in East Boston, close enough to Enoch Train's yards where the *Washington Irving* had been built. Patrick earned his living as a cooper, shaping wood into barrels for waggons bound for the Gold Trail out west, and for transporting whiskey sold at the waterfront saloons.

The first generation of American Kennedys raised a family of three girls and PJ, the first politician in the Kennedy clan. He was only ten months old when his father died, at the age of 35, from cholera. Patrick's widow did odd jobs to keep the family going and finally became a hairdresser in a Boston store. When PJ left school he, too, did odd jobs until he found work as a dock-hand. He saved his money and bought a saloon in Haymarket Square and years later, became a partner in two more saloons, then a wholesale liquor distributor. In 1886 the barkeep became a politician when he was elected to the Massachussets State House of Representatives and later to the State Senate. PJs son, Joe, began his career in similar fashion. After rapid promotion to dockyard manager, he later made a fortune on the stock market and, according to many sources, from bootlegging during the 1920s prohibition. In the 1930s Joe became an advisor to President Franklin Roosevelt who appointed him to be the American Ambassador in London in 1938. Joe had married Rose Fitzgerald in 1914, the daughter of Honey Fitz, Boston's mayor. Of their nine children, three sons went into politics – John F Kennedy went to the White House; Bobby was assassinated as he campaigned to become President and Senator Teddy continues the political lineage, with their sister, Jean Kennedy Smith, now America's Ambassador in Dublin. As the great grandchildren of an Irish Famine emigrant, all remain keenly aware of their Irish heritage.

15

The Famine Ships Sail Again

In 1849, shortly before Patrick Kennedy left for America, the first three ships to sail directly from his home port of New Ross to America, cast off with their quotas of Famine emigrants. The *Lady Constable*, the *Boreas* and the *Dunbrody* were all bound for New York, and crossed the Atlantic at the same time as the *Washington Irving*, carrying Patrick Kennedy to his new life in America.

The *Dunbrody* was named after Dunbrody Abbey standing high on the east bank of the River Barrow, just beyond the point where the Barrow joins the Suir flowing down from Waterford. Further down the river where the calmer waters emerge into the swell of the Atlantic, stands another Catholic landmark, St Dubhan's Monastery close to Hook Point. For centuries the monks took a vow to warn mariners of the dangers of the rocks below and maintained a lighthouse near the monastery. Caligula, the Roman Emperor who ruled at the beginning of the first century AD, built the world's first lighthouses as his legions spread across Europe. Some 400 years later, St Dubhan established the oldest lighthouse in Ireland on Hook Point. The monks kept the beacon alight in those early days by burning coal, pitch, charcoal and tar each night. Later, the Canons of St Augustine took over and built an 80-foot-high tower for the light with a small fortress below. The monks continued to preserve the light until 1657 when the lighthouse passed into public ownership. The original tower, coated in white lime to stand out by day, is now 700 years old, and 'in such good repair it will probably last another millennium', comments the Irish coastguard service. The tower performed an essential service for all ships entering the delta on their way to Waterford, Wexford, New Ross, or any other harbour en route. For the emigrants on a ship sailing from Ireland on a southerly course, the ancient lighthouse served as the last memorable monument to their homeland. The kindlier captains allowed emigrants up on deck, to catch a last glimpse of their beloved homeland before she disappeared beyond the horizon. With dry mouths, damp eyes and hands clasping the rail, the tearful emigrants gazed in silence at the disappearing coastline. Eventually the silence would give way to the exciting hiss of the bow wave and the roaring seas and the sad men and women would be shepherded down below.

The Dunbrody, a barque of 458 tons, was built in 1845 at Quebec for a small shipping line in New Ross – William Graves and Son. She did not often sail in the passenger trade. Her usual destination was Canada to pick up timber for her owner's saw mills. The 1849 voyage was her one and only venture to America throughout the Famine. Under Captain John Williams, she arrived in New York on May 4th with 176 passengers. The *Boreas* was not so fortunate, arriving five days later with 157, eight having died at sea.

A replica of the *Dunbrody* is soon to be built in New Ross as part of a project developed by the Kennedy Memorial Trust and Museum, led by the Trust's director, Sean Reidy. Supported by the Irish government, the European Union has granted £1.6 million (US $3,250,000) towards the project. The Trust's headquarters are situated in New Ross in a disused warehouse on the quayside close to the town's only bridge.

A 1996 drawing for the reconstruction of the Dunbrody.

New Ross has in fact become closely associated with the Kennedy home over the last few decades. During his term of office, President Kennedy visited New Ross, made a famous speech and took tea with his third cousin, Mary Ryan, at her cottage in Dunganstown. When the new *Dunbrody* is finished, the museum will be transferred to her lower deck. The trust is building up a huge database of passenger manifests of Irish emigrants who sailed on ships bound for Canada, America, Australia, New Zealand, South America and elsewhere in the world. Visitors will be offered a chance to trace their forefathers. The new *Dunbrody* will be carefully reconstructed to evoke a sense of life aboard a Famine ship, though a clean and modern sailing ship riding at anchor can never truly depict the terrors of the ocean.

In the south-west corner of Ireland, at Tralee Bay, another distinguished Famine ship, the *Jeanie Johnson* will soon be recreated, commemorating the Famine emigrants who voyaged from Tralee to Canada. Tralee typically experiences a great deal of weather, 'but not much climate' with even temperatures throughout the year and ceaseless heavy squalls of rain sweeping in from the ocean. The Kerry bogs give way to the beautiful lakes around Killarney, guarded by the highest mountain peaks in Ireland, the famous Macgillicuddy Reeks. But all along this western coast, the potato blight took its heaviest toll. The destination for nearly all the Famine ships out of Tralee was Canada. During the Famine years, the population of Tralee, already sparse and scattered, was reduced by half. As an emigrant port, Tralee was not as busy as Limerick or Cork, which drew many of Tralee's more determined emigrants.

The original *Jeanie Johnson* was built for a Tralee merchant, Nicholas Donovan. He commissioned the ship in Quebec City in 1847 at the height of the coffin ship episode in Canada (see pp 36–41). Originally intended as a cargo ship she was an ideal size to convert for other crossings, and she carried passengers from Tralee, returning with timber from Canada. At just over 100 feet long, she accommodated up to 220 passengers in steerage. During the Famine she concentrated on the Canadian emigrant runs, making voyages to America only after the Famine years. Throughout her long career, she never lost a passenger while at sea. On her maiden voyage from Tralee in April 1849, a son was born to Daniel and Margaret Ryal and he was named after the owner as well as the ship, and the last line on the passenger manifest reads: 'Nicholas Johnston Ryal .0 months.' There were many births in mid-ocean, but few would carry such an unusual name, bestowed with such sound judgment. The young man would never be allowed to forget his unusual start in life.

The plan to build a replica of the *Jeanie Johnston* is part of a £4.5 million project (US $6,750,000) employing a group of American and Irish youngsters as boat-builders, guided by a team of experts from North Europe. The replica will be perfectly reconstructed in oak and pine. At the millennium, she will embark on a commemorative voyage from Ireland to Canada and America, calling at all the emigrant ports: Saint John, Halifax, Quebec and Montreal, Boston, New York, Baltimore, Philadelphia, Washington, Charleston, Savannah and New Orleans.

For those who stayed in Ireland throughout the Famine, either by force of circumstance or by personal good fortune, the most significant event of 1849 was the visit of the British monarch, Queen Victoria, who enjoyed a great welcome despite Anglo-Irish hostilities. Cheering crowds turned out in August to greet the Queen and her husband, Prince Albert, son of the German Duke of Saxe-Coburg. The royal couple visited Dublin and Cove, the magnificent harbour town 13 miles to the east of Cork. Though Ireland's political leaders were opposed to the royal visit, the Queen was aware of Ireland's suffering and was intent on judging the situation for herself. It is, of course, doubtful that she was able to witness the full horrors of the Famine, the starving beggars and overcrowded workhouses. Instead, she was honoured with lively and expensive festivities. At Cove, the royal yacht was greeted by rockets launched from her naval ships stationed in port; and local residents lit huge bonfires. The servants of one country house were so enthusiastic with their firework display that they set fire to 14 acres of woodland. The next day, at the official welcoming ceremony, the Queen surprisingly announced, 'I have much pleasure in giving my sanction to the change of name which has been sought by the inhabitants and direct that this town shall in future be called Queenstown.' The port had been known as the Cove of Cork, or Cove for short, but it retained its royal name until 1922 when Ireland achieved her independence, and Queenstown was re-named Cobh, which is the Gaelic for cove. Cove is probably the largest and most natural harbour in the world. Its share of maritime tragedies are by no means confined to the Irish Famine and Emigration. Cove was the last port of call for the Titanic, the safest liner afloat, on her fateful maiden voyage, ending in disaster. Nearby, in 1915, the Lusitania was sunk by a German submarine – an act which precipitated America's participation in the First World War. As the years rolled by there can have been little comfort for the local population of Queenstown.

16

A Miraculous Escape

Among the many hazards faced by ships at sea were fog and slack winds which often accompanied each other. Extra look-outs could be posted but were often of little avail in the dense mists. The fog was specially hazardous when nearing port and entering the busy shipping lanes where crashes were a constant potential danger. Close to port meant close to land, where lack of a decent breeze further endangered the ship, for the force of a tide flowing to shore might be too strong to counter the ship's rudder, trying to steer without any way on the ship. The despairing flutter of redundant sails was never a welcome sound to the crew – more alarming even than the bellowing roar of strong gusts bouncing off stretched canvas. For a mariner the worst sound of all was the unmistakable grind of the ship's hull, as she scraped the sea bed, followed by an anxious cry from the look-out, inevitably too late, 'Going aground sir, going aground!' A shudder would run through the ship as her masts leaned forward momentarily and her rigging crackled in protest. The deck would vibrate with the impact and the ship's keel would screech louder as it wedged more firmly into the ocean bed. There would be a period when the decks remained more or less level before the ship started to settle and list to one side. Running aground was common enough and rarely created any great panic among an experienced crew, though passengers were often petrified.

Such hazards were faced by the *Constitution*, a 1,500-ton vessel built in Quebec in 1846. With 160 passengers aboard, she left Belfast on November 28th in 1849; her passengers well-pleased with the ship and the passage they had chosen. Two other ships left on the same tide, the *California* and the *Amoy*, bound for New Orleans, 2,000 miles further on. *The Belfast Newsletter* had advertised earlier in the month:

> The well known and favourite coppered and copper-fastened ship *Constitution* of Belfast, 1,500 tons burthen, Robert Martin commander. This well known and fortunate ship has just arrived after a remarkably quick passage of 19 days from Quebec, and will be punctually dispatched from Belfast for the City of New York on the 26th of November.
>
> The *Constitution* will as usual be fitted up in a most superior style for the accommodation of cabin, second cabin and steerage passengers under the immediate inspection of Lt Starke, the Government Emigration Officer; and will be provided with the full scale of provisions, free of charge, which is included in the rate of Passage Money. For terms of passage which will be very moderate apply to Samuel McRea, General Emigration Office, 37 Waring St, Belfast.

The weekly food rations were listed as 2½lbs Navy biscuit; 1lb wheat flour; 5lbs oatmeal; 2lbs rice; 2ozs tea; half-pound each of sugar and molasses; 1lb beef or pork; 1 pint vinegar and 3 quarts of pure water daily. These provisions seem generous, but they might not last the whole voyage at sea. The reference to coppering was persuasive language indicating that the hull was covered, its timber sound, protected from any hungry oceanic creatures. But the agents had lied about her size, though the *Constitution* was undoubtedly a very large, square-rigged vessel carrying abundant canvas on her three masts, and over the past two years she had sailed on three successful and uneventful emigrant voyages from Belfast to New York.

The ship's captain, Robert Martin, a 29 year-old from Bangor, County Down, was relatively young. Though he had sailed regularly aboard the *Constitution* as first mate, he had commanded on only two previous trips since his promotion in 1840. As captain, he would earn £10 (US $50) for the round-trip, from Belfast-to-Belfast, instead of £4 10s as first mate. Martin and his first mate, Thomas Johnston, along with four young apprentices were the only members of the 22-strong crew to have served aboard the *Constitution* before. The rest of the crew comprised a second mate, a steward for the cabin passengers, a carpenter, a cook, ten seamen and two other apprentices. Martin was one among many young officers of the period who were inadequately qualified for their positions. Though the Board of Trade in London had initiated a system of voluntary examinations of competence for masters and mates of foreign-going British merchant ships in 1845, the examination did not become compulsory until late in 1850 (see pp 99–100). It was not until the following year on September 11th 1851, that Martin finally obtained his Masters Ticket, No. 51,297, before a local marine board at Liverpool.

Shortly after midnight on January 9th, 1850, the *Constitution* eased through the waters beside Long Island on the approach to New York. The still air persistently refused to support the sails and the mist hung cold and damp on the faces of the uneasy crew. Most of the passengers huddled together in the hold below, while a few sheltered in the poop deck cabins. During the long choppy voyage, the passengers had grown accustomed to the sounds of the ship's motion as she reared and plunged in the waves, the creaking and complaining timbers, the never-ending waterfall of sea-spray and the deafening winds. But for the first time on this voyage, on this cold winter night, they now experienced an eerie silence, broken only by an awful grating, rasping sound below, while the ship wallowed on the still waters. The dark night and thick fog blinded Captain Martin, and the bitter cold numbed his mind, yet he realised that his ship, his crew, his cargo and, worse still, his passengers were in grave danger. For the *Constitution* to go aground so near its destination was such a bitter, bitter blow. Were the hapless passengers to die on the very day they might have set foot on the Promised Land? After 42 days at sea, land had at last been sighted. Just a few hours earlier, the captain had optimistically forecast: 'If the breeze picks up we shall be in port tomorrow.' But as the ship passed Mantauk Point, fog drifted in with nightfall, and gradually thickened as the wind dropped and the sea calmed. Too late, the captain realised that the strong swell running from the south-east had taken him too close to land. As the ship started to settle, her stern swung with the tidal race and she swivelled to face the open sea, pointing towards Ireland again as she keeled on to her port side. The captain was well aware of the dangers of abandoning ship in darkness, and decided to wait for dawn – to wait and hope and pray. Little did he know, that on that very day, the *New York Tribune* had reported heavy masses of ice floes threatening to close the river below the city's harbour:

Western Navigation – The river yesterday [Wednesday] was filled with heavy masses of floating ice and there were no arrivals from below. The weather for two or three days past has been intensely cold and appearances are now in favour of an entire close of the river.

In the darkness the crew struggled against the unusual angle of the deck to take in all the canvas, while First Mate Johnston reversed the red ensign flag at the stern, as a signal of distress to any passing ship. Yet no ship could ease their plight unless the sea and the flood tide could boost them upright again. As first light lifted the grey strands of mist, the tide turned and began to run on to the starboard sides of the stricken ship. The early shafts of a wintry sun beckoned and the masts were bared and dipped in defeat. Only the mizzen topsail remained aloft. Then, miraculously, as the mists cleared, the outlines of the town of Southampton became evident, and everyone's hopes surged. The sloping port sides of the ship were just within reach of the deserted beach below and the crew hastily rigged their ropes and lines into an escape web for the passengers. A sturdy trunk, roped boxes of tools and a few pathetic bundles were dropped from the deck – all their worldly goods, their mementoes of home and of Ireland. Together, cabin and steerage passengers clambered to shore. They were followed by the crew and finally, as decreed by tradition, the master, Robert Martin, was the last to abandon ship. A hundred paces further up the beach, and all the survivors joyfully realised that they were safe at last. Their dream had come true and they had finally arrived unscathed if shaken on the shores of America at the start of a new life – not the best start to a new life but it could have been so much worse. On the following day, Captain Duval of the steam tug *Samson*, hoping to share in the rewards of salvaging the *Constitution* reported: 'She went aground at Southampton, Long Island, midnight Jan 9th 1850 . . . she lies in a bad position, listing, masts standing, mizzen topsail flying, decks broken up, starboard sides stove in.'

The ship's owner, John Dunn, was a leading merchant in the Ulster province, well-regarded in shipping circles. Though he was already busy in the emigrant trade, he collaborated with a group of ambitious Belfast ship owners who made their fortune on the other side of the world, by transporting indentured Chinese from Hong Kong to California, principally to San Francisco, and so establishing the first Chinatowns in America. The 'Coolie Business' was indeed risky as the Coolies were usually criminals who had volunteered to be indentured to evade a gaol sentence, and would mutiny at the slightest provocation. At least two of Dunn's emigrant ships, the *Hibernia* and the *Gulnare*, sailed to the China Sea. When the *Gulnare* rounded the Cape of Good Hope off South Africa, the Chinese set fire to her and attacked the crew. In quashing the mutiny, the Irish crew killed ten Coolies, three more were thrown overboard and drowned, and another 14 were injured. John Dunn went bankrupt in 1857, owing £43,000, (US $215,000), and only able to pay 1s 4d in the pound – 6.5 cents in the dollar.

Seventy years later, with the ship's logs, and the owner's papers at his disposal, Ernest B Anderson wrote in his well-respected book *Sailing Ships of Ireland*:

This Quebec-built ship of 558 tons was built for the emigrant trade. For ten years she was considered one of the fastest and most fortunate vessels sailing out of Belfast. After running aground at Long Island, the *Constitution* was a total loss, its solitary cargo of salt ironically returned to the ocean. All that we know of her passengers and crew is recorded in the bleak but official reports of the shipwreck . . . they were all safely landed.

N°. _59_ — Certificate of British Registry. N°. 2.

THIS is to Certify, that in pursuance of an Act passed in the Fourth Year of the Reign of King WILLIAM the Fourth, intituled, " An Act for the Registering of British Vessels,"

John Dunn of Belfast in the County of Antrim, Merchant,

having made and subscribed the Declaration required by the said Act, and having declared that *he is*
together with

Certificate Cancel.ᵈ April 1850

Vessel Lost.

sole Owner (in the proportions specified on the Back hereof) of the Ship or Vessel called the *Constitution* of *Belfast* which is of the Burthen of *six hundred and fifty eight 3500* Tons, and whereof *Robert Neill* is Master, and that the said Ship or Vessel was *built at Quebec in the Province of Lower Canada in the year one thousand eight hundred and forty as appears by a certificate under the hand and seal of the Collector at Quebec dated 12ᵗʰ June 1840 granted by him pursuant to the 11ᵗʰ Section of Act 3 & 4 William 4 chapter 55*

and *Maurice Leyne, Tide Surveyor,* having certified to us that the said Ship or Vessel *has one within four main* Decks and *three* Masts, that her length from the inner part of the Main Stem to the fore part of the Stern Post aloft is *one hundred and twenty* feet *five* tenths, her breadth in Midships is *twenty six* feet *one* tenth, her depth in hold at Midships is *twenty* feet tenths, that she is *Square* rigged, with a *standing* Bowsprit; is *Square* sterned *Carvel* built; has *no* Galleries, and *a scroll* Head; and the said subscribing Owners having consented and agreed to the above Description, and having caused sufficient Security to be given, as is required by the said Act, the said Ship or Vessel called the *Constitution* has been duly registered at the Port of *Belfast*

Certified under our Hands, at the Custom-House, in the said Port of *Belfast* this *Fifth* Day of *August* in the Year One Thousand Eight Hundred and *Forty*

Collector.

Comptroller.

Tonnage ascertained under act 3 & 4 W.ᵐ 4 Cap 55 — 502 ⁴²⁄₇₄ Tons
Admeasured under the Act 5 & 6 Will. IV. cap. 56.

No. 267.
Certificate of British Registry, (Copy). 2 new Act.

Certificate Cancelled April 1850, Vessel Lost. A sad end for the Constitution.

17

Life in America

When the new Americans stepped ashore to sample at last the opportunities in the Land of the Free, what did they find? The majority were of course fleeing hardship, but also looking forward hopefully to the promise of a better life. But for many, their first encounters and experiences were trying: they ran the gauntlet of thieves and pickpockets on the dockside, ticket sharks and ruthless boarding house runners, and countless, colourful confidence tricksters, clad in lively green waistcoats – all with a recognisable line of blarney. By 1855, however, emigrants were formally processed at Castle Garden in New York, where they were advised about onward journeys, accommodation and even job prospects.

In Liverpool the Commissioners for Emigration handed out a small pamphlet warning passengers embarking for America of what they might expect:

As may be supposed there are many people engaged in the business of forwarding emigrants, and the individuals and companies thus engaged employ a host of clerks or servants called runners who try to meet the newcomer on board the ship that brings him or immediately after he has put foot on shore, for the purpose of carrying him to the forwarding offices for which they act.

The tricks resorted to in order to forestall a competitor and secure the emigrant would be amusing, if they were not at the cost of the inexperienced and unsuspecting stranger. It is but too true that an enormous sum of money is annually lost to the emigrants by the wiles and false statements of the emigrant runners, many of them originally from their own country and speaking their native language.

Of course, runners operated in Liverpool itself. There were proven cases of runners who, having spotted a particularly susceptible traveller with more money than usual in Liverpool, had boarded an earlier ship bound for New York, there to await the victim and fleece him again, sometimes aided by fellow crooks. The ticket-scam was particularly rife. Bogus tickets, promising onward journeys through America, were sold either in England or on arrival in America. There were similar and impressively printed tickets for non-existent ships apparently sailing from British ports. Two men who posed as a ship's master accompanied by the agent chartering his vessel, were trapped by Emigration officials in London in 1851. Tried and sentenced to be transported for seven years, they soon found themselves on a real ship – as convict passengers bound for Australia. Newly arrived emigrants were also often fooled by false exchange rates.

The emigrants would find America very different from Canada. Both were young countries where life was rough in the cities and raw out on the plains. Yet life was changing fast and, even as early as 1850 in New York, the Emigrant Industrial Savings Bank opened and *The Shamrock* newspaper started publishing job vacancies. In Boston, the Irish Emigrant Society reported finding 'a hundred jobs a day' for Irish girls. American Immigration records report that in 1850, 43 per cent of the foreign-born population resident in America were Irish.

Few personal letters or diaries, chronicling the lives of individual emigrants have survived, partly due to the lack of literacy among emigrants. A letter home from Famine emigrant Samuel Laird has survived. Soon after arriving in Philadelphia, he wrote on May 4th 1850 to his mother living near Limavady, 12 miles from Londonderry. Laird had travelled on the *Creole*, famous for its dramatic misfortune 18 months earlier when it had been dis-masted out on the ocean by a lightning-strike. Yet Laird arrived safely and earlier than many of his friends who had sailed on the *Provincialist* and *Superior* at the same time:

I am safely arrived after a passage of 28 days, nothing transpired worth noticing on the passage only one great blessing, that we all enjoyed good health. When we got to the wharf we made inquiry for the place where Robert Barnett lived which we found without any great difficulty and we remain there as yet.

I have been engaged with a gentleman to drive his carriage and I have $10 for the first month, $12 for the second month and $14 afterwards. Also Elisa is engaged [employed] and is to live in the house with Martha Barnett, she has $5½ a month and we are all happy and well. I have seen all my friends in general and there seems to be nothing the matter with any of them. The ships *Superior* and *Provincialist* have arrived but the *Creole* was first in the race.

I am not long enough in this country to form any notion of what it is but although I am in a strange country, I am not among strange people. We are all well, we will unite very soon.

Laird came from a very large family in Ireland and much of his letter was taken up mentioning his many relations, his brothers and sisters, their wives and husbands, his aunts, uncles, cousins and friends at home. Assuming that his letter was passed among his many contacts it is a small miracle that it has survived. Another emigrant's letter was written by Andrew Greenlees. In the last of a series of 12 letters, sent to his brother during the 1850s, Greenlees wrote from Plattsburg, New York:

There is a mistake in your last letter which I wish to correct, that is your opinion about the usage of farm servants. The customs of this country are quite different from the old and strangers coming here think it quite odd until they get initiated into the rules of the Yankees, but after they get civilised and know how to take right hold to any piece of work and do it up in Yankee fashion, then they get along well and feel quite at home.

To be sure there are some bad masters in all countries but these are exceptions, and I believe my first master was one of them. In this country Jack's as good as his master, if he don't like one then go to another, plenty of work and plenty of wages, plenty to eat and no landlords, that's enough, what more does a man want?

Farming operations are going on quite brisk, here the ground is quite rich and easier laboured than in the old country. For instance, planting potatoes, two men will plant two acres per day . . . the bigger the better, put them three feet asunder. No use for manure, just scratch a hole, drop the potato in and cover it up. Three of these holes where the potatoes are put, yield a bushel as an average crop.

Greenlees had found work as a blacksmith and metal worker, and wrote about his new trade:

> As respects my health, it never was better and my trade, I am getting master of it quite fast and I am very comfortably fixed in other respects. I don't have so long hours to work as on a farm, we commence in the morning at half-past-six. As for quitting we can't be regular, if we have a heavy smelt we're later and a light smelt, half-past-five. The furnace I'm in runs all year, not as good a chance to make money . . . but the wages are $1½ a day

In closing he quoted at length from the Bible, as did many emigrants when writing home.

Many famine emigrants went to work with a shovel in their hands, even before they recovered their health and strength after the strenuous crossing. By 1850, New York had more Irish-born citizens than Dublin. In the main, they formed the nation's labouring work force. The men spread across the country in work-gangs digging the canals, the railways and the roads. Others were low-grade artisans – carpenters and builder's mates, bartenders, boat-builders, dockers and waiters. In later life they might become policemen or firemen. The women often found work as house-servants or seamstresses. The emigrants were forced to consider almost any work available, and even then, were often barred by prejudice – many advertisements being accompanied by the proviso NINA (No Irish Need Apply). When supply exceeded demand, they worked for as little as 50 cents a day and rarely for much more than a dollar. Conditions were often dangerous, as related by *The Irish in America* written in 1868 by John Francis Maguire. One of its stories recounts the building of the Erie Railroad through difficult terrain in New York State. Irish drilling crews were lowered down the mountain sides in baskets; after setting their charges and lighting the fuses, they were hurriedly dragged back up the mountain before the explosion.

As the new emigrants laboured across the United States, their mobile living quarters sometimes took on a degree of permanency, increasing in size over the years to form villages with Irish names, such as the nine communities named Dublin.

Many Irish emigrants were drafted into the army during the Civil War when former neighbours or fellow passengers sometimes found themselves unwittingly fighting on opposite sides of the war. The Union Army had no fewer than 144,000 Irish-born troops. But the Irish formed their own fighting force in 1850 – the Ninth New York State Militia, with their distinctive light green uniforms; the Militia included units of Irish Dragoons, the Carroll Light Guard, Erina Guard and the Saarsfield Guard.

One aspect of life on the other side of the Atlantic, long known to the man-in-the-street, began to concern the governments of both Canada and Australia. Increasingly, it was felt that the massive Irish emigration, consisting mainly of men, had unbalanced the population. The men who far outnumbered the women had little prospect of marrying and producing native-born citizens. The shortage in women was partly made up by recruiting workhouse girls, as recorded in the minutes of a meeting of the Board of Guardians at Dungarven workhouse. Dungarven, an excessively pretty coastal town near Waterford, on the road to Cork, was then a fishing village and a feeder-port for the Famine years. A few coasters ferried local produce up to Dublin or across to Liverpool. In 1849, 34 young women, that is to say teenagers, mostly orphans, had been sent to

Australia. In May 1850, local newspapers advertised for 200 'able-bodied women, single or married without families, who have been inmates of the workhouse for at least one year'. The girls, it seems, had little choice as the minutes of May 16th, 1850 record that, when two girls refused to comply, they were discharged from the workhouse: Mary Snow and Mary Shea had refused to go to British North America - and both were discharged from the workhouse at once. Fifty girls were selected for the trip. As many were young, a matron, Julia Keane, accompanied them on the voyage. At least 36 girls lacked any suitable clothing, but the workhouse supplied various items, logged in the minutes: 'shawl, calico dress and wrapper, a flannel and a calico petticoat, two pairs of stockings, one pair of shoes, handkerchieves, a trimmed bonnet, two caps and a clothes bag'; plus soap, thread, tape, needles and a promise of 15s (US $3.75) on arrival.

Their destinations were Quebec, Montreal, Saint John or New Brunswick.The party left Dungarven for Liverpool, where they boarded the *Colonist*, but their plans went much awry, and they left instead on July 15th aboard the *Essex*. After a week at sea, the ship sprung a leak and spent another seven days returning to port – to Cork, not many miles from the spot where the young women had spent much of their recent life in safety, if not in comfort. Forty-three decided that they preferred their former life – they had been scared stiff on board the leaky ship. Once in port, they escaped and returned to Dungarven. When an ultimatum was issued, the majority handed back their clothes but remained in Dungarven, while 17 hurriedly returned to Cork where they rejoined their ship. The minutes do not record the rest of their story.

18

From Wexford to Wexford

As the Famine entered its sixth year the farewell and funeral ceremonies had become a regular feature of life in Ireland, virtually a daily happening even in the smallest communities. All over the country, churches had increased the size of their graveyards to cope with the burials. In his parish straddling the county borders of Wexford and Wicklow, Father Thomas Hore decided to take positive action. An extraordinary 54-year-old priest, Hore refused to stand aside and watch his parishioners suffer. Believing that America offered the only chance of survival for many of his flock, he set out to lead them to safety.

Hore was raised in Wexford, close to Tacumshane, birthplace of another hero, Commodore John Barry, himself commemorated by a statue in Wexford's Crescent Quay. Honoured as the Father of the American Navy, Barry was born in 1745 and, it is thought that, when his family was evicted, he was raised by his aunt, living in Port Rosslare. According to legend, John Barry first went to sea as an 11-year-old cabin boy on an Irish barque owned by his uncle, and bound for Jamaica in the West Indies. By the age of 21, he had become master of a Philadelphia merchantman and went on to fight with distinction in the War of Independence, against the British. His statue in Wexford was an inspiration to emigrants and in 1850 there were many who would follow the Commodore's course out of Wexford, led by Father Hore.

Ecclesiastical records state that in 1841 Father Hore was appointed priest to the parish of Annacurra and Killaveney in the diocese of Ferns, about 30 miles south of Dublin. Within three years, he had built the Church of St Kevin. He would never have dreamed that one day, on June 2nd, 1850, he would preach to a huge congregation in St Kevin, encouraging his flock to take refuge in America. Many would embark on a journey lasting nearly six months, and covering over 6,000 miles before they were all settled in America. The story of the memorable voyage is narrated in St Kevin's parish records, compiled from emigrants' letters home and from the testimony of Father Hore himself who eventually returned to Ireland seven years after the voyage:

> The misery and poverty in which the majority of the people of rural Ireland lived during the first half of the nineteenth century is hard to imagine. When Father Hore became parish priest nearly half of all the families in Ireland lived in one-roomed mud-walled cabins, roofed with sods of earth. Many families slept on the floor and bed-clothes were practically non-existent.
>
> It was during this terrible period that Father Hore was ministering to the people of his parish. Conditions were so desperate that he saw the only way to alleviate the people's distress was to follow after those who had emigrated earlier. During the autumn of 1849 he discussed the prospects with his parishioners and told them of his own experiences in America. It was resolved to start preparations at once for the momentous step they were about to take.

171

It was certainly a momentous step for the dedicated clergyman who had spent 11 years of his early priesthood in
Richmond, Virginia, where he was ordained. He faced the
possibility of arrest, trial and a prison sentence if he was
deemed guilty of sedition or inciting a rebellion. Word spread
through the parish and beyond. The people waited patiently
while the priest carefully laid his plans. After inspiring a
congregation of 2,000 with the vision of a new life in
America, Hore watched his excited parishioners spill outside
St Kevin, and overflow into the churchyard with its many
freshly-dug graves.

In Dublin Castle the civil servants who administered
Ireland on behalf of Britain's rulers, had also heard about
Father Hore's planned pilgrimage. The Royal Irish Consta-
bulary was more of a militia force at that time and Police
Constable David Lynch was despatched as a spy to infiltrate
and attend the assembly, and gather information. Constable
Lynch's long, hand-written and often misspelt report provides the only record of Hore's encouraging words when he
addressed his 2,000-strong congregation:

Tinahely, June 3rd 1850

I beg to state that I attended Divine Service on yesterday at
the RC Chapel at Whitefield [the parish on the opposite
side of the road to Killaveney]. After Service the Rev
Thomas Hore addressed a numerous and mixed congregation who had assembled for the purpose of hearing him
explain his views for giving up his parish and emigrating to
America and the reasons which induced him to leave this
country etc. Hore commenced by saying . . . it might seem
strange to them that a man of his age and position in the
country should think of doing so. He then stated his
reasons were chiefly these:

That he commenced his mission in America where he

remained many years and therefore was more competent to judge the relative interests and prospects of both countries. That he done so as he had was with the permission of his late Bishop and to encourage younger clergymen as well as the laity of this country to follow his example, believing as he did that the clergy were required more there than here and that the mass of the people would benefit their condition by going . . . He saw no hope of their prospects improving by remaining in this country but the certainty of inevitable ruin should they remain.

He then proceeded to dwell in forceable language on the contrast that existed between America and this country, stating that the independence, prosperity and comfort which the American people enjoy, while in this country there exists misery, degradation and starvation.

He said that he believed the people had in great measure initiated these evils on themselves through their Party animosity, bigotry and ill-will which they entertained towards each other . . . that such has been the curse of Ireland, the evil consequences of which left Ireland and Irishmen as they were – the bye-word and scorn of all civilised nations – that Catholic as well as Protestant were alike to blame for keeping alive those feelings of animosity towards each other . . . that England always fostered it and by which she was able to make use of either party at her will for her own purposes.

He then said that as this was probably the last time he would address them on this subject, he would speak to them freely and went on to say that Ireland had to thank England and English legislation for all the miseries and sufferings which this country had endured and under which it still suffered. That he was no Prophet, but that he could see that at no distant day England would suffer for her misgovernment and ill-treatment of Ireland. That it was a notorious fact that England was at present despised and distrusted by nearly every nation in the world and had not scarcely a friendly power in Europe to assist her in the event of a war which every day threatened her.

That her Irish subjects were every day flying from the country in thousands and he believed and trusted that the tide of emigration was only commencing to flow . . . That the time would come when England would want Irishmen to aid her in her battles but would not have them to get; that the downfall of England was certain at no distant day and that Ireland too would sink with her.

He then dwelt for a long time in describing the climate, soil, etc. of America; the comfort and prosperity of its inhabitants etc. – and mentioned as a mark of the growing prosperity of the former emigrants from this country, the vast sums they were daily remitting to their friends at home to enable them to join them . . . and quoted several cases of individuals with whom he said he was personally acquainted, who in a few years became men of independence and fortune, and who, if they had remained in this country would never have been anything better than paupers. That their lands were free soil, no rent, tithe or tax to pay. That there was no such thing as bigotry known there, that there every man might worship his God in the form he liked, without incurring the ill-will of his brother man, as was unfortunately too often the case here where man made God and His Scripture the causes of ill-will and hatred instead of love.

He went on to say that he intended leaving this country about the commencement of September next and that he would that day commence to take down a list of the names of such as were willing to accompany him, as by going with him it would be a great saving to them as he intended to charter a vessel if he found he had as many ready to go as

174

would enable him to do so and that he expected each applicant would be ready to deposit the sum of 10s as a guarantee to him and as a portion of their passage money.

He said his place of destination was one of the best in the Union for climate, soil, etc. – that he intended to purchase land there himself and hoped to be able to form a colony there of his own people. Mr Hore then concluded by exhorting all such as could accompany him to do so if they valued their own and their families' future welfare and as he believed there was not the slightest hopes of doing good by remaining in this country but on the contrary inevitable destitution.

About 2,000 persons were present, many of whom came a distance of seven and ten miles. I understand that about 100 persons gave down their names with the intention of accompanying Mr Hore and it is supposed that from 600 to 700 persons will leave the country with him.

The constable's predictions, like the priest's expectations, were both in fact too low. In the end, over 1,200 emigrants left Ireland with Hore. Their story is recorded in *Farewell to Famine* by Jim Rees who traced every step of the emigrants' journey. Hore first planned to charter just one sailing ship for the voyage to New Orleans, 5,000 miles across the Atlantic Ocean, and take a paddle-steamer up the Mississippi River to find fresh pastures. As the priest of a parish set in farming country, Hore well understood the type of farming land that would best suit his parishioners. As farmers, many of them tenants of small holdings on Earl Fitzwilliam's estate, they could probably afford the £5 fare (US $7.50 today but more like $25 then), the equivalent of about six months' salary; and about 100 deposits to reserve a passage were handed over at the end of the service. Father Hore's eloquent sermon had clearly moved his audience, and over the summer months, many beyond the parish boundaries sought to join the priest and his flock. Four months later, 400 families, a total of 1,200 emigrants, left their land and their homes in Wicklow and Wexford counties, with as many agricultural tools as they could carry, and with pooled savings amounting to £16,000 for the purchase of new farms in America.

Originally, Hore chose Arkansas as their destination, with a far flung sector of land much further north, in the state of Iowa, as a fall-back. He was influenced by Dr Andrew Byrne, born in Meath, but serving as the first Bishop of Little Rock. Byrne spent much time recruiting priests and nuns to develop the church in his new diocese and when the two men met in Liverpool, he handed a document to Father Hore which read:

To all whom these presents may come, health and blessing. Know ye that we by these presents give the Very Reverend Thomas Hore, late of the Diocese of Ferns in Ireland, full and ample jurisdiction to preach, teach and administer throughout our diocese all the sacraments usually administered by a clergyman of his order. And we moreover appoint the said Very Reverend Thomas Hore our Vicar-General and to the especial charge of the flock by whom he is accompanied from Ireland until revoked by me.
Given at Liverpool
under our hand and seal
this 22nd day of October 1850
Andrew Byrne, Bishop of Little Rock

When Hore and his party set off on the first stage of their journey, the darker days of Autumn had already arrived and his flock faced the prospect of several bitterly cold weeks on the Atlantic. Undeterred, they set off by horse-and-cart for the two-day journey to Dublin, where animals and vehicles would be sold for a pittance or abandoned on the dock-side.

In Dublin, the priest had to charter not one but three ships to cross the Irish Sea to Liverpool.

Both Bishop Byrne and Father Terence Donoghue, Vicar-General of Dubuque, Iowa, had encouraged and supported Hore in his courageous enterprise. The dioceses close to the American frontier cried out for more clerics and more parishioners. The attractions for Father Hore were both temporal and spiritual – fertile, inexpensive farmland and the proximity of a church or monastery.

In Liverpool he found two American ships preparing to return to New Orleans and an English brig, the *Ticonderoga*. She was big and fast and, with a crew of 28, she could carry up to 30 sails. Captain John Farran enrolled Father Hore as a ship's officer and accepted 450 passengers. The remainder of the group joined the smaller *Chacsa* and the *Loodianah*, owned in Liverpool. Their £5 fare bought 10 cubic feet of luggage space and a bunk bed. The ship's rations amounted to 6 pints of water daily, and a weekly allotment of 1lb of flour, 5lbs of oatmeal, 2lbs of rice, 8ozs of both sugar and molasses, plus 2ozs of tea, for every passenger.

Whether by divine intervention, good fortune or even better seamanship, Father Hore's vessel arrived on December 3rd, after only 40 days at sea. The *Loodianah*, under Captain Dallimore, arrived 17 days later, while the *Chacsa*, under Captain Wise, was blown off course into the Caribbean. Wise stocked up provisions at St Thomas in the Virgin Islands, and tied-up in New Orleans on January 11th. Father Hore had long since departed, with some 300 parishioners, heading for the Mississippi. The rest of the original group had splintered, some remaining in the city while others headed for Refugio in Texas, though local records fail to show whether they ever reached their destination. The fate of the late arrivals remains unknown. After many weeks on the roaring, rearing seas of the ocean, the calmer waters of the

Mississippi River held no terrors for the priest's party. The life they witnessed daily on the riverbank must have excited the younger folk who had been confined below decks for most of their time on the *Ticonderoga*. Their paddle-steamer took them up the Arkansas River and they reached Little Rock in the third week of December. Bishop Byrne was away in Ireland at the time. His assistant, who had been told to expect the group from Wexford, had recently died while out on a mission. The locals were justifiably surprised by the arrival of the emigrants, but welcomed them and put them up over Christmas. Sadly, fever broke out among the emigrants. They were cared for in a converted church, but at least 20 died according to a local newspaper report. Of the rest, too few were able to find work and settle successfully in the state capital. The large stretches of land they had hoped to occupy had already been sold and, with the outbreak of fever, the majority decided to move on, and they took to the river again.

A group of eight families pressed on westwards to Fort Smith on the very edge of the frontier. The surrounding land was Indian territory – the traditional hunting lands of the Comanche and Shoshone tribes which stretched from Fort Smith to Oklahoma. Then a tiny town of little more than 1,000 people, Fort Smith was built on the site of a former American Cavalry outpost named after General Thomas Smith. Some families settled in and around Fort Smith, where their descendants live today, such as the Breens and Hendricks and, in the near vicinity, the Keatings and Kellys.

Father Hore left to continue his search for decent farmland while the bulk of his party headed east by boat, intending to meet Hore at St Louis. Hore journeyed to Iowa, arriving in Dubuque, nearly 900 miles from New Orleans, on January 23rd 1851. Travelling still further north into Allamakee County, close to the Wisconsin state line, he finally settled at New Melleray in a Cistercian monastery built only two years earlier. Here, where the woods and meadows resembled the green valleys of his homeland, he fulfilled his dream, buying rich farmland for the emigrants with the residue of pooled savings. In a matter of weeks he purchased a total of 2,157 acres at US $1.25 an acre, territories formerly held by the Winnebago Indians for which the United States government had paid only 10 cents an acre.

Hore took the good news to St Louis, but found that many of the Irish group had already settled down, having found homes and jobs in St Louis. Yet 18 families – nearly 100 men, women and children – remained loyal to Hore, and followed him to Iowa. Boarding the river steamer *Franklin*, they arrived at Lafayette Landing on March 25th 1851. With the timber cleared from their new land, they built homes and they lost no time in building a church as well. On April 23rd, the feast day of St George, their new church was ready for dedication to the saint in 1851. Around St George's Church they created a small community, named Wexford in deference to the birthplace of their devoted leader. Among the first landowners in Wexford were some of the *Ticonderoga*'s passengers, whose names are recorded in the ship's manifest: Catherine Bulger, John and Mary Ryan, Timothy Collins, John Gavin, Timothy Howe, Edward and John Kelly, Patrick McNamara, William Heatley, Austin Joyce, John Brophy, Edward O'Neill, John Lamb, Catherine McKeogh, James Murphy and Thomas Mullins. Some married within the emigrant community, while others moved off, but still there are many residents in both Wexford and Fort Smith whose origins go back to the original voyagers on the *Ticonderoga*.

Of the remaining descendants in Fort Smith today, Janie Hendricks married Jack Freeze who recently became the town's mayor. James and Fanny Breen had crossed the

Atlantic with 12 children having left one behind, in an Irish convent. Two of the Breens' great-grandsons, William Breen, born in 1913, and Joseph Breen, born in 1910, live happily in retirement in Fort Smith while today, some younger descendants still work in the town, one as a garage-owner and two as bankers. But the heroine of the family is a very sharp lady of 93, Margaret Mailor. Born in 1903, she was a Breen before she married in the 1930s and knows the family history down to the last crucifix. She recounts:

I can still remember my great grandmother talking about the crossing. She was a youngster in her teens when her family came over from Ireland; they were on the *Ticonderoga* and I used to listen to her stories when I was just about going to school. I suppose she was 70-something then. She didn't talk much about Ireland or the Famine. She may have been too young to remember Ireland but her brothers, her sisters and her folks, apparently they never stopped talking about the voyage and the journey up the Mississippi. They all had scads of kids and there's a lot of us still in these parts, well we wouldn't be here today if they hadn't pulled up all their roots and followed that priest along with everyone else.

One of Margaret Mailor's first cousins, Peter Breen, a retired printer, lives in Wexford. His great-great-grandfather left Fort Smith five or six years after the voyage, and settled in Wexford where six generations of the family have continued to live. The first two generations were farmers. Peter's grandfather was a dealer in farm implements and machinery, his father a grain merchant and car dealer. Peter's children, the sixth generation of the Wexford Breens, were raised in Wexford but then moved on as Peter explains: 'One son was in the army and then in transportation and the other is out on the west coast, in the computer business.'

The 6,000 miles from Wexford to Wexford proved to be a momentous journey. The families who with their own hands built homes, and a church where they could worship freely, marry, baptise their off-spring and one day be laid to rest, created a community which thrives today. They are fondly remembered by the community, and so is Father Hore who returned to Ireland in 1857 and died, still in the priesthood, in Cloughbawn, County Wexford, in 1864.

19

The Smallest in the Famine Fleet

*H*annah, at 59 feet long and 19 feet wide, was by far and away the smallest vessel in the famine fleet. Imagine four medium-sized family cars, parked bumper-to-bumper to gain some idea of *Hannah*'s compact size. How small she must have seemed when moored at Limerick quayside on the River Shannon, waiting to embark for New York. Barely large enough for 60 passengers, she was manned by a small eight-strong crew of which two were teenage apprentices, yet she crossed the Atlantic eight times.

Other ships bore her name. Another Irish-owned *Hannah* was wrecked by an iceberg a year earlier. During the 1840s ten more ships of the same name carried cargo across the Atlantic, to Australia, to India and the Far East, occasionally across the Pacific or busying between countless European ports. But the most remarkable *Hannah* was also the smallest. When she first appeared in Lloyd's Register of Shipping, numbered (1) 4832, the *Hannah* was described as a Limerick Coaster. Built in 1824, she was originally a small brig of 132 tons with just two masts. A sound, profitable little workhorse, she initially ferried cargo around

Limerick, 50 miles down the River Shannon to reach the ocean, then America.

the Irish ports and occasionally to London or Liverpool, Bristol, Newport or Glasgow, and even to the closest of the French ports. These round trips of 200 or 300 miles rarely lasted more than a week.

By the time of the Famine, *Hannah* had more than earned her price when she was bought and rebuilt by John Norris Russell, a Limerick corn merchant. In 1849, *Hannah* was again surveyed and re-registered by Lloyd's. Her survey revealed that she had been transformed from a brig into a barque with the addition in 1838 of a third mast and new topsides, and with large repairs made in 1845 and further small repairs in 1848. Despite having passed her survey, she seemed too fragile for a rough Atlantic crossing. It took an extra degree of bravery to board such a small ship before a long ocean voyage. The accommodation below was built with rough planks of timber, nailed and wedged into place; three tiers of bunks on either side of the hold, with a narrow aisle down the middle, covered no more than the space of an average room today. Yet however tortuous the voyage, what promise of life was there at home?

The *Hannah* typically berthed at Limerick on the Shannon, where the waters, 50 miles inland from the ocean, are wide and deep. The ancient city of Limerick was built over a thousand years ago on an island in the river Shannon; later, the city expanded across the river and beyond its five bridges. Famed for its eventful and bloody history, Limerick was laid under siege at least three times: in 1651, for a year, by Cromwell's army, again in 1690, following the Battle of the Boyne 150 miles away, and once more in the following year. The siege and the war in Ireland ended famously in October 1691, with the signing of the Treaty of Limerick. When William III broke the promises made in the treaty, Limerick became known as The City of the Violated Treaty. The first article of that treaty guaranteed religious rights to the Catholics of Ireland. One of the Irish signatories, Patrick Sarsfield, is commemorated by a statue standing proudly in the city, and by one of the Shannon bridges, named after him. A general and a hero, he was regarded as

A 'fortunate ship', said the advertisement. Quite true – everyone was saved and walked ashore when the Constitution *ran aground on Long Island and broke up.*

the most gallant of Ireland's soldiers, and among the greatest of its patriots. It was probably fortunate for him that, dying in battle in 1693, he did not live to witness the introduction of the Penal Laws (see pp 20–21) in 1695 – the most savage of which would remain in force until 1780, and was only fully repealed in 1829.

During the Famine, the quaysides of Limerick were, surprisingly, daily lined with rich produce for export from farms lying in the most fertile stretch of land in the country, known as the Golden Vale. Pork, butter, oats, eggs, sides of ham and beef, ploughs and scythes and farming implements, bales of linen and wool were stacked on the quayside before being loaded and sent to English markets. A Limerick merchant and ship owner, Francis Spaight, recorded the exports flowing through the port from June 1846 to May 1847. These included 386,909 barrels of oats and 46,288 barrels of wheat. The irony of the situation was aptly described by the Dublin-born playwright George Bernard Shaw in his play *Man and Superman*:

Malone:　My father died of starvation in Ireland in the Black 47. Maybe you've heard of it?
Violet:　The Famine?
Malone:　No, the starvation. When a country is full of food and exporting it, there can be no famine.

In the Golden Vale, however, even the peasants enjoyed its fruits: in the summer months when the breadnut trees by the river bore their fruit, the hungry peasants lit fires to roast the breadnuts. Another source of nourishment was the turnip, and the turnip cake was invented in the Golden Vale by Eyre Lloyd. His successful recipe, made from a mix of turnips, meal and flour – then virtually barbecued – was published in the *Freeman's Journal* and spread through Ireland.

Just to the north of Limerick lies County Mayo which was hard hit by the Famine, with over 400,000 destitute in 1847, and only 13,000 employed, according to the annual census. When the British Parliament appointed a select committee to inquire into the horrors of 1847, Francis Spaight, a Limerick merchant and British magistrate, gave evidence. As a farming landlord, with a castle in Tipperary, he had himself transported many of his own tenants in 1847. Of his actions he commented: 'I found so great an advantage of getting rid of the pauper population upon my own property that I made every possible exertion to remove them; they were a dead weight and prevented any improvement upon the land they

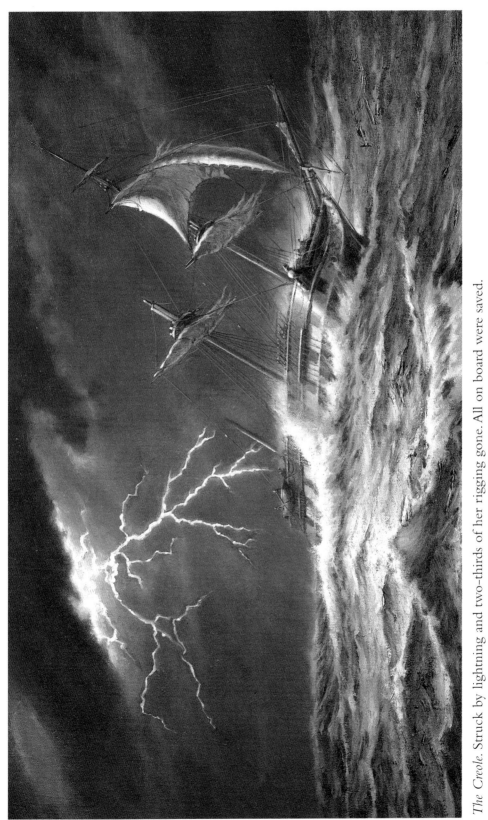

The Creole. Struck by lightning and two-thirds of her rigging gone. All on board were saved.

The Hannah. Treacherous icebergs wrecked their ship, yet 129 passengers and crew survived.

Washington Irving. The founder of the Kennedy dynasty on board in 1849.

The Constitution. The last day of the voyage and at midnight she went aground on Long Island.

Ticonderoga. Passengers from Wexford, Ireland, will take the Mississippi paddle-steamer for Wexford, Iowa.

Odessa. Ship's cook for a shilling.

Erin go Bragh – 'Ireland Forever' – and America is at the other end of the landing line.

occupied.' He added, 'I consider the failure of the potato crop to be of the greatest possible value in one respect in enabling us to carry out the emigration system.' Three years later his views had not changed, the potato crop continued to fail while food exports continued to flow and many continued to flee Ireland.

One emigrant trip, the *Hannah* left Limerick on April 26th, a beautiful spring day in 1850. From the deck of the *Hannah*, the Galty Mountains far off in Tipperary, showed clear, and the river, running through the shallows below King John's Castle, gurgled its own farewell. The *Hannah* was commanded by John Mills, a 31-year-old Englishman from the Isle of Wight, whose small crew comprised the mate, George Fisher, a local cook, Martin McCarthy, three seamen and two apprentices. Down below in steerage, the converted hold housed 65 emigrants. Of these, a dozen young spinsters berthed with 15 bachelors, violating recent regulations under the Passengers' Act. Fellow passengers probably acted as chaperones. There were few families on board, though young mothers travelled with their children, hopefully on their way to a joyful reunion with their loved ones. Sarah Walsh journeyed with two sons and two daughters; Johanna Scanlon with a little boy and three-month-old Mary; Ellen Stark with four-year-old Norry; and Mary Moloney travelled with Tom, just a year old. The three young Hogan girls were travelling without parents. Mary was the oldest at 13, her sister, Margaret, was nine, and Bridget was five. John Dwyer, a 12-year-old, travelled all alone.

As the *Hannah* glided out to sea, she was watched wistfully by the passengers of the stationary *Triumph* which would delay another four tides before slipping her moorings and gliding gently down the Shannon. She was a larger vessel than the *Hannah*, 75 feet long, but as she carried half as many passengers again, conditions aboard would be very similar.

Another vessel, the *Maria Brennan*, was considerably bigger and due out at the end of the week. Both were heading for New York. At the same quay, the *Congress*, bound for Quebec, prepared to sail, with 200 emigrants aboard.

What were the scenes at the quayside as the emigrant ships left Limerick? Did those left behind write? Did those departing beg others to follow? So many of the emigrants abandoning their country were young men and women who would meet, marry and raise their families far from their homeland. They would bring prosperity and vigour to another nation, while depriving Ireland of its vital middle generation. How many decades would recovery take?

The Famine ship optimistically named the *Triumph* had the distinction of being one of very few emigrant ships to have been built in Ireland – in Youghal, County Cork – 11 years earlier. Owned by Francis Cherry Sikes, a local merchant, she was built of oak, elm and black birch. Though a tiny ship, she had already made several successful emigrant crossings and in April 1850, set sail again, bound for New York. The eight-strong crew included one young apprentice, John Winders, who had never been to sea but was signed on as ship's carpenter, with free passage, as he was good with his hands. The passenger list numbered 97, of which 23 were bachelors and 27 spinsters. Several young children and single mothers travelled alone: Maria Lynch was accompanied by her seven children but not her husband; young Michael Edgar, at only eight, was sole guardian to his brother, Patrick, a babe in arms. One bleak entry was noted in the log on arrival: Mary-Ann Cunningham, three, died at sea.

For the smaller ship, the *Hannah*, the spring voyage was uneventful despite her heavy load. After 43 days at sea, she arrived safe and sound on June 7th at South Street Seaport. The *Maria Brennan* came in on the next tide, followed by the *Triumph* four days later.

TRIUMPH 11 JUNE 1850

From Limerick

NAMES OF PASSENGERS	AGE	SEX	OCCUPATIONS	DATE PORT SHIP
GILMORE, Thos.	21	M	Laborer	11Ju06Ao
DILLON, Johanna	22	F	Unknown	11Ju06Ao
HOWE, Thos.	23	M	Unknown	11Ju06Ao
LUCKMAN, Dennis	25	M	Unknown	11Ju06Ao
BOVENIZER, Margt.	28	F	Unknown	11Ju06Ao
LOODY, William	22	M	Unknown	11Ju06Ao
CALLAHAN, C.	31	M	Unknown	11Ju06Ao
STANTON, Mary	20	F	Unknown	11Ju06Ao
HARNNASSEN, Dennis	40	M	Unknown	11Ju06Ao
Bridget	30	F	Unknown	11Ju06Ao
James	10	M	Unknown	11Ju06Ao
Norry	.00	F	Infant	11Ju06Ao
BRAHAN, Cath.	20	F	Unknown	11Ju06Ao
BOYLE, Hannah	20	F	Unknown	11Ju06Ao
L., Johanna	16	F	Unknown	11Ju06Ao
STINDON, John	19	M	Unknown	11Ju06Ao
HOGAN, John	47	M	Unknown	11Ju06Ao
RYAN, Will	36	M	Unknown	11Ju06Ao
DROZEL, Michl.	23	M	Unknown	11Ju06Ao
Eustice	18	M	Unknown	11Ju06Ao
Johanna	14	F	Unknown	11Ju06Ao
CAREY, Michl.	55	M	Unknown	11Ju06Ao
Margt.	50	F	Unknown	11Ju06Ao
Thos.	20	M	Unknown	11Ju06Ao
George	13	M	Unknown	11Ju06Ao
Peter	12	M	Unknown	11Ju06Ao
Margt.	9	F	Child	11Ju06Ao
James	.00	M	Infant	11Ju06Ao
MOLONEY, Margt.	20	F	Unknown	11Ju06Ao
OHALLAN, Mary	30	F	Unknown	11Ju06Ao
OBRIEN, Thos.	20	M	Unknown	11Ju06Ao
ENWRIGHT, Michl.	25	M	Unknown	11Ju06Ao
BRECK, Ellen	20	F	Unknown	11Ju06Ao
MCGRATH, John	17	M	Unknown	11Ju06Ao
SWEENEY, Margt.	20	F	Unknown	11Ju06Ao
MORONEY, Patt	20	M	Unknown	11Ju06Ao
COMMENS, Dennis	23	M	Unknown	11Ju06Ao
LYNCH, Maria	30	F	Unknown	11Ju06Ao
Brdgt.	19	F	Unknown	11Ju06Ao
Martin	17	M	Unknown	11Ju06Ao
Honor	13	F	Unknown	11Ju06Ao
Daniel	11	M	Unknown	11Ju06Ao
Patt	6	M	Child	11Ju06Ao
Michl.	4	M	Child	11Ju06Ao
Margt.	.00	F	Infant	11Ju06Ao
MADIGAN, John	26	M	Unknown	11Ju06Ao
CLANCY, Nancy	10	F	Unknown	11Ju06Ao
MADDEN, Ellen	30	F	Unknown	11Ju06Ao
MCMAHON, Michl.	20	M	Unknown	11Ju06Ao
Margaret	.00	F	Infant	11Ju06Ao
MCINERTY, Mary	26	F	Unknown	11Ju06Ao
Michl.	.00	M	Infant	11Ju06Ao
LYNCH, Cath.	18	F	Unknown	11Ju06Ao
COSTELLO, Thos.	25	M	Unknown	11Ju06Ao
MAHONEY, Kate	20	F	Unknown	11Ju06Ao
DUGGAN, Michl.	26	M	Unknown	11Ju06Ao
Cath.	22	F	Unknown	11Ju06Ao
LYKEN, Michl.	22	M	Unknown	11Ju06Ao
GOULD, Hannah	30	F	Unknown	11Ju06Ao
OSHAUGHNESSY, Ellen	20	F	Unknown	11Ju06Ao
MOLONEY, Bridget	17	F	Unknown	11Ju06Ao
OCONNOR, Ellen	20	F	Unknown	11Ju06Ao
EDGAR, Michl.	8	M	Child	11Ju06Ao
Patt	.00	M	Infant	11Ju06Ao
DWYER, Mary	26	F	Unknown	11Ju06Ao
RUE, William	20	M	Unknown	11Ju06Ao
Timothy	19	M	Unknown	11Ju06Ao
Ellen	25	F	Unknown	11Ju06Ao
Mary	17	F	Unknown	11Ju06Ao
FARREL, Cath.	22	F	Unknown	11Ju06Ao
CONNELL, Mary	16	F	Unknown	11Ju06Ao
LANGHAN, Daniel	30	M	Unknown	11Ju06Ao
CARTHY, Dan	20	M	Unknown	11Ju06Ao
OBRIEN, Mary	26	F	Unknown	11Ju06Ao
Bridgt.	30	F	Unknown	11Ju06Ao
HEFFERNAN, Patt	21	M	Unknown	11Ju06Ao
James	17	M	Unknown	11Ju06Ao
NEALON, James	16	M	Unknown	11Ju06Ao
COONEY, Lawrence	35	M	Unknown	11Ju06Ao
MCCALLY, Daniel	25	M	Unknown	11Ju06Ao
DONOHUE, Mary	22	F	Unknown	11Ju06Ao
BOLAND, Ellen	20	F	Unknown	11Ju06Ao
ANDERSON, John	35	M	Unknown	11Ju06Ao
CUNNINGHAM, Honor	30	M	Unknown	11Ju06Ao
Mary-Anne	3	F	Child	Died-At-Sea
REAVES, Ellen	35	F	Unknown	11Ju06Ao
MURPHY, Mary	35	F	Unknown	11Ju06Ao
MADIGAN, Bridget	10	F	Unknown	11Ju06Ao
FARRELL, Mary	18	F	Unknown	11Ju06Ao
MAXWELL, John	40	M	Unknown	11Ju06Ao
James	30	M	Unknown	11Ju06Ao
Cath.	20	F	Unknown	11Ju06Ao
WINDER, Cath.	25	F	Unknown	11Ju06Ao
ODONNELL, Ellen	28	F	Unknown	11Ju06Ao
Johanna	30	F	Unknown	11Ju06Ao
CALLAHAN, Ellen	30	F	Unknown	11Ju06Ao
MAHONEY, John	20	M	Unknown	11Ju06Ao

CONQUEROR 11 JUNE 1850

From Liverpool

NAMES OF PASSENGERS	AGE	SEX	OCCUPATIONS	DATE PORT SHIP
WELCH, Mary	20	F	Unknown	11Ju02Ar
CONNOLLY, Martin	25	M	Unknown	11Ju02Ar
BROWN, Charles	25	M	Unknown	11Ju02Ar
FINLAN, Edward	35	M	Unknown	11Ju02Ar
Ann	30	F	Unknown	11Ju02Ar
Patrick	.00	M	Infant	11Ju02Ar
CLINCH, Bridget	.00	F	Infant	11Ju02Ar
FINNIGAN, Elizabeth	45	F	Unknown	11Ju02Ar
GARRIGAN, Pat	17	M	Unknown	11Ju02Ar
JENNISON, Thomas	25	M	Unknown	11Ju02Ar
CARPENTER, John	21	M	Unknown	11Ju02Ar
Ann	20	F	Unknown	11Ju02Ar
DUGAN, John	23	M	Unknown	11Ju02Ar
Ellen	25	F	Unknown	11Ju02Ar
MOLTOY, Thos.	25	M	Unknown	11Ju02Ar
FURLONG, Nicholas	25	M	Unknown	11Ju02Ar
NEILL, Thos.	28	M	Unknown	11Ju02Ar
DOYLE, John	20	M	Unknown	11Ju02Ar
SCOTT, James	25	M	Unknown	11Ju02Ar
CORBETT, Thos.	16	M	Unknown	11Ju02Ar
HESTIN, John	16	M	Unknown	11Ju02Ar
Ned	12	M	Unknown	11Ju02Ar
PADDIN, Ned	17	M	Unknown	11Ju02Ar
DOGHERTY, Tim	21	M	Unknown	11Ju02Ar
MURPHY, Mary	50	F	Unknown	11Ju02Ar
DELANY, Margaret	25	F	Unknown	11Ju02Ar
Bridget	.06	F	Infant	11Ju02Ar
HENNESSY, James	20	M	Unknown	11Ju02Ar
Mary	22	F	Unknown	11Ju02Ar
MYERS, Moses	22	M	Unknown	11Ju02Ar
WREN, James	15	M	Unknown	11Ju02Ar

16

The passenger list for the Triumph, *sadly missing Mary-Ann Cunningham, who was buried at sea. She was only three years old.*

20

The Absence of Evidence

O n the first day aboard the *Washington* 900 passengers lined up on deck to receive their water ration of six pints each, as prescribed by law. Thirty filled up their cans at the barrels when suddenly the ship's mate who was supervising the operation ordered: 'That's all, no more.' Bewildered, 870 Irish emigrants turned away empty-handed and dry-mouthed until a few hours later when they were again called out for their water allowance. This time, 30 received water before the rest were again turned away and roughly herded back to their steerage accommodation by brutal and abusive mates who kicked and cursed the passengers without provocation. As it turned out, water was not the only commodity in drastic short supply on board the *Washington*.

She left Liverpool on October 27th in 1850, bound for New York on what would become an infamous voyage. For, by a stroke of luck, an enterprising passenger, Vere Foster, kept a diary of events which he later published on his return to Ireland, provoking a public outcry and debates in Parliament.

The *Washington* was one of 18 big, fast packet ships operated by the Black Star Line, whose vessels sailing from

Liverpool carried emigrants of many nationalities: German, Polish, Russian, Scandinavian but in the main, Irish and especially the slightly better-off Irish who could afford a cabin. At 200 feet long and with a wide beam, the *Washington* was quite spacious, compared to the much smaller, English and Irish-owned converted cargo ships. Even in steerage, passengers could enjoy considerably more comfort as these American packets were built exclusively for the passenger trade, and their crews were generally superior.

Vere Foster was a rich, well-connected and well-intentioned philanthropist who took a special interest in the plight of the Irish emigrants. He had already helped several reach America by paying their fares. Concerned about bad reports of emigrant travel, he resolved to discover for himself the quality of life aboard a Famine ship. On board the *Washington*, he kept a meticulous diary of events which he sent, with a letter, to his relation, Lord Hobart, a minister at the Board of Trade in London. His letter, dated December 1st, was posted on arrival in America:

As the weather is very beautiful today and the wind and sea perfectly still, I will take advantage of so fair an opportunity of writing you some account of my voyage thus far, during the intervals between the performance of my household duties as cook to our mess. We are now, and have been for several days, within one day's sail of our destination if we had a fair wind, but unfortunately there is now no wind.

This is a magnificent vessel of 1,600 tons register burthen with two lofty and well-ventilated passenger decks, each between seven and eight feet high and very high bulwarks, over six feet, to protect the deck from the spray of the sea. She is a new vessel and very strong and dry, and probably as well furnished with all necessary conveniences as the best of the emigrant ships between Liverpool and New York. Her crew consists of 31 men, three boys and five officers; namely the captain and four mates and she has on board upwards of 900 passengers whose sleeping berths are a shelf along each side of the whole length of the two decks, with low boards dividing the shelf into berths, all of one size and each containing from four to six persons.

One end of the upper deck is divided off as a separate apartment containing 12 enclosed cabins, each having two, four or six berths, and each berth containing two persons. The passengers in this part of the vessel pay a somewhat higher price £5 instead of £3 15s or £4 [US $25 instead of $18.75 or $20]. I occupy one of the berths in a cabin containing four berths.

He described his companions, and went on:

The quantity of provisions according to Act of Parliament and according to the stipulation of our contract tickets, in which their price is included, besides three quarts of water daily and the supply of sufficient firing, is 2½lbs of bread; 1lb of wheaten flour; 5lbs of oatmeal; 2lbs of rice; 2ozs of tea; 8ozs each of sugar and molasses; vinegar and John Taylor, Crooke and Co., agents to this company, the Black Star Line of Packets, engage to supply in addition to the above, 1lb of pork free-of-bone, to each passenger weekly.

The extra provisions which I have brought on board for the use of my bedfellow and myself, in addition to the ship's provisions, are the same as I have been in the habit of supplying to such passengers as I have sent at my expense to America . . . flour, sugar, salt, soap, soda, tea plus a 4lbs loaf of bread, 2½lbs of butter and 6lbs of bacon. These extra provisions cost 10s 6d [US $2.55]

I also brought some cooking utensils and other tinware, bedding, towels and dishcloths. I consider the above quantity of provisions to be plenty so far as necessity is concerned, with the exception of a pint of vinegar in summer. A cheese, more flour, a few herrings and some potatoes, would however be a palatable and desirable addition particularly during the first fortnight, until the stomach becomes enured to the motion of the ship.

All the passengers who arrive at Liverpool a day or more before the sailing of an emigrant ship, have to be inspected by a surgeon appointed by Government, who will not allow anyone to go on board who has any infectious disease of a dangerous character. I passed before him for inspection which occupied only one or two seconds. He said, without drawing breath, 'What's your name? Are you well? Hold out your tongue; all right,' and then addressed himself to the next person. We were again all mustered and passed before him on board the ship while sailing down the river.

There was no regularity or decency observed with regard to taking the passengers on board the ship; men and women were pulled in any side or end foremost, like so many bundles. I was getting myself in as quickly and as dexterously as I could when I was laid hold of by the legs and pulled in, head foremost down upon the deck, and the next man was pulled down on top of me. I was some minutes before I recovered my hat which was crushed flat as a pancake. The porters in their treatment of passengers, naturally, look only to getting as much money as they possibly can from them in the shortest space of time, and heap upon them all kinds of filthy and blasphemous abuse, there being no police regulations and the officers of the ship taking the lead in the ill-treatment of the passengers.

The *Washington* went out of dock on the 25th [October]

and anchored in the river. I went on board the next day and witnessed the first occasion of giving out the daily allowance of water to the passengers. In doing so there was no regularity, the whole 900 and odd passengers were called forward at once to receive their water pumped out into their cans from barrels on deck. The serving out of the water was twice capriciously stopped by the mates of the ship who, during the whole time without any provocation, cursed and abused and cuffed and kicked the passengers and their tin cans.

And having served out water to about 30 persons, in two separate times, said they would give no more water out till the next morning, and kept their word. I gently remonstrated with one of the mates who was cuffing and kicking the poor steerage passengers, observing to him that such treatment was highly improper and unmanly and that he would save himself a great deal of trouble and annoyance, and win instead of alienating the hearts of the passengers, if he would avoid foul language and brutal treatment, and use civil treatment and institute regularity into the serving out of the water. But he, in reply, said that he would knock me down if I said another word. I was happy to find however, that my rebuke had the effect of checking for the moment, his bullying conduct.

Provisions were not served out this day, notwithstanding the engagement contained in our contract tickets, and notwithstanding that all the passengers were now on board, the most of them since yesterday and had no means of communication with the shore. Many of them being very poor, had entirely relied upon the faithful observance of the promises contained in their tickets, the price of which includes payment for the weekly allowance of provisions.

I was on board a fine vessel of the same size as the

Washington five weeks ago, the *Constellation*, one of Tapscott's line of packets, on which I sent some passengers. There were 875 passengers on board and the provisions were served out punctually on the day appointed for sailing, although she was yet in dock and did not sail for several days afterwards.

Foster continued with entries from his diary, begun on the day of embarkation:

October 27th: While a steamer towed the *Washington* down the river all the passengers were mustered on deck and answered to their names. One little boy was found hid, having made his way on board thinking to escape notice, and he was sent ashore.

October 28th: We were so fortunate as to have a most favourable wind which carried us out of the Irish Channel, being that part of the voyage in which we expected the greatest delay.

October 29th: I went the round of the lower deck with Mr Charles Reynolds, surgeon of the ship, observing him take down the numbers in each berth. The doctor noted down in many instances, persons between the ages of 14 and 16 as 'Under-14' for the purpose of making a saving in the issuing of provisions, as half-rations are only served out to passengers under 14. The doctor remarked that 16-years-of-age on board the *Washington* constituted an adult.

October 30th: No provisions have yet been served out and the complaints of the poorer passengers in the steerage are naturally increasing, as they have no means of living excepting on the charity of those who had brought extra provisions. At their request I drew up a petition addressed to the captain of the ship Master A. Page.

October 31st: Respected Sir We, the undersigned passengers on board the ship *Washington*, paid for and secured our passages in her in the confident expectation that the allowance of provisions promised in our contract tickets would be faithfully delivered to us. Four entire days having expired since the day on which the ship was appointed to sail – some of us having been on board from that day, and most of us from before that day – and three entire days since she actually sailed from the port of Liverpool, without our having received one particle of the stipulated provisions excepting water, and many of us having made no provision to meet such an emergency, we request that you will inform us when we may expect to commence receiving the allowance which is our due.

Signed Vere Foster; James Molony; John Collins; James MacNamara; John Hickey; Samuel Thorn; James Ward; Thomas Hotchin; Denis Mangan; Charles O'Donoghue and H. Hopkins.

P.S. From want of conveniences of writing but particularly from the fear of being interfered with by the officers of the ship, no more signatures have been proceeded with otherwise nearly 900 might have been added. While writing the former part of this letter at the request of my fellow passengers, the first mate Mr Williams knocked me down flat upon the deck with a blow in the face. Another day has elapsed without provisions being served out.

Vere Foster's diary records the rest of the story:

October 31st: When the mate knocked me down which he did without the smallest intimation or explanation, he also made use of the most blasphemous and abusive language. I said not a word, knowing the necessary severity of the laws of discipline on board ships, but retired, as he bade me, to my own cabin. A passenger heard him make use to the cabin cook, of the observation that if he caught me in tween decks again, he would not hit me but he would throttle me.

I presented the letter to Captain Page. He asked me the purport of it and bade me read it. Having read one-third of it he said that was enough, that he knew what I was, a damned pirate, a damned rascal and that he would put me in irons and on bread and water throughout the rest of the voyage. The first mate then came up and abused me foully and blasphemously and pushed me down bidding me to get out of that, as I was a damned b———. He was found by one of the passengers soon afterwards, heating a thick bar of iron at the kitchen fire. The cook said, 'What is he doing that for?' and the mate said 'There is a damned b——— on board, to who I intend giving a singeing before he leaves the ship.'

Provisions were issued for the first time this day. I took the precaution of bringing a weighing machine on board, weighing as low as 2ozs, in order to compare the allowances issued with the quantities due, which afterwards proved extremely useful for my own purposes and to other persons.

Throughout his letter Foster could not bring himself to spell out the worst of the officers' abusive words. He admitted that he received more flour than he was due and most of his sugar, but only half his allowance of biscuits, rice, oatmeal and tea, no pork and only a third of his molasses. The steerage passengers fared even worse, though food continued to be issued throughout the voyage. But whenever passengers made a mistake, they would be abused and beaten by the mates, punched and lashed with the end of a rope. Foster's diary conveys the passengers' anxiety and uncertainty:

November 9th: The captain never appears to trouble himself in the slightest degree about the passengers, nor ever to visit the part of the ship occupied by them. I hear occasionally some of the passengers complain to the first mate or to the captain, of the favouritism shown by the passengers' cooks to those who give them money or whiskey, and who consequently get five or six meals cooked daily.

No one knows the whereabouts of the vessel except the captain and first mate and they keep that a profound secret from the ship's company and passengers. No groceries were issued, as they should have been this day.

November 13th: I have spoken frequently with different sailors, asking them if this was the first time of their sailing in this ship. All answer yes and that it will be the last and some of them express an opinion that the first and second mates will get a good thrashing at New York.

The diary went on to record that on November 14th provisions were issued and on November 16th groceries. Another vessel was sighted on November 18th only the second since leaving Liverpool. On November 19th, a mock collection for the ship's doctor expressed the passengers' growing mistrust and black humour: 'Would a shilling each be enough to buy rope to hang him? The doctor has received a great deal of money from the passengers.' After noting, on November 21st, the issue of provisions and the start of a violent gale, the diary went on to describe the storm:

November 22nd: The gale became perfectly terrific; for a few minutes we all expected momentarily to go to the bottom for the sea, which was foaming and rolling extremely high, burst upon the deck with a great crash and made us all believe some part of the vessel was stove in. The wave rushed down into the lower deck and I certainly expected every moment to go down. Some of the passengers set to praying, the wind blew a perfect hurricane, there was several feet of water on the deck and we had up only two sails.

November 25th: Another child, making about 12 in all, died of dysentery for want of proper nourishing food and was thrown into the sea sewn up, along with a great stone, in a cloth. No funeral service has as yet been performed, the doctor informs me, over anyone who has died on board; the Catholics objecting, as he says, to the performance of any such service by a layman.

As there was no regular service, the man appointed to attend to the passengers seized the opportunity, when the sailors pulling at a rope raised the usual song of,

'Haul in the bowling, the Black Star bowling

Haul in the bowling, the bowling haul . . .'

to throw the child overboard at the sound of the last word of the song, making use of it as a funeral dirge.

November 30th: The doctor came down to the second cabin with the second mate, roaring out, 'Now then, clean out and wash out your rooms every one of you, God damn and blast your souls to hell.'

Tea and sugar as usual.

December 2nd: A beautiful day and a favourable breeze, took a pilot on board. Many of the passengers have at different times during the voyage expressed to me their intention of making a public complaint respecting their ill-treatment on board this ship so to meet their wishes I wrote the few following lines which was signed this evening by those persons whose names are attached.

Ship Washington, *off New York, 12 December 1850*
We testify as a warning to and for the sake of future

emigrants, that the passengers generally, on board of this noble ship the Washington, *commander A Page, have been treated in a brutal manner by its officers, and that we have not received one-half the quantity of provisions allowed by Act of Parliament and stipulated for by us in our contract tickets.*

The complaint was signed by 34 women and 95 men, and the diary continued:

December 3rd: A few of the passengers were taken ashore to the hospital at Staten island and we arrived alongside the quay at New York this afternoon.

December 6th: I met this afternoon with some friends of mine who came out two months ago in the *Atlas*, Captain Osborne with 415 passengers. They describe the treatment on board that vessel by the officers, as considerably worse than what I have related respecting the *Washington*. The provisions on board were not served out at all till about the end of the first week and no pork excepting to such persons as were willing to buy it. The *Atlas* is also one of the Black Star line of packets.

I also met today some friends who came out on the *St Louis* which arrived the day before yesterday and they described their treatment as kind and considerate, provisions and water as ample and there were no deaths from dysentery among the 350 passengers.

I have since met with passengers I sent out in the *Washington* on her previous voyage. No provisions were served out in the first fortnight and no meat during the whole of her voyage. I met passengers sent out in the *William Rathbone*, another Black Star packet, whose treatment by the officers and as regards provisions, was similar.

On receiving this report in London, Lord Hobart immediately raised the matter in both the House of Commons and the House of Lords, provoking a flurry of mail between civil servants, MPs, the Chief Emigration Officer in Liverpool, the British Consul in New York and American lawyers. Despite similar reports of injustice, only three previous complaints had been formally lodged during 1850, and none against an American master.

When the *Washington* returned to Liverpool, Captain Page was challenged but he denied all allegations. In the absence of evidence, it was impossible to take the matter any further under British law, for a British court had limited jurisdiction over acts done at sea on a foreign ship. Everyone expressed their regret that Foster and the other passengers had not taken proceedings to New York. Though Foster had campaigned valiantly, and taken positive steps to reform practices on board emigrant ships, the political and legal climate was unhelpful. Famine emigrants continued to suffer at the hands of corrupt captains, owners or agents. Prosecutions were rare and when made, were often quashed in the absence of evidence. Yet, on returning to Ireland, Foster did manage to publish a helpful guidebook for emigrants. Entitled *Emigrants' Guide*, it offered many useful tips for surviving on board and on shore.

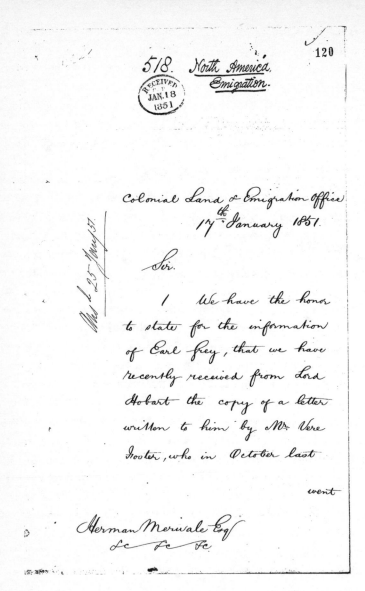

518. North America,
Emigration.

RECEIVED
JAN. 18
1851

120

Colonial Land & Emigration Office
17th January 1851.

Sir,

1   We have the honor
to state for the information
of Earl Grey, that we have
recently received from Lord
Hobart the copy of a letter
written to him by Mr Vere
Foster, who in October last

went

Herman Merivale Esq
&c   &c   &c

Mr Vere Foster sent his diary to Lord Hobart at the Foreign Office in London, chronicling the ill treatment of Irish emigrants. Nothing came of his efforts.

2

went out to New York as a
Steerage Passenger in the United
States Ship "Washington": From
this letter it would appear
that Mr Jooter and his fellow
Passengers were constantly
assaulted, and ill used, by the
Officers of the Ship, and that
they were also defrauded of the
provisions which the United
States Law as well as the
Passenger Act, entitled them
to receive.

   2   In Lord Hobarts'

                  and

and Mr. Foster's letters, it is
asserted that what occurred on
board the Washington, has
occurred also on board other
Ships. We have no means of
testing this statement, but it
is not intrinsically improbable.
At the same time, we feel,
that we are powerless in this
Country to prevent this ill
treatment of Emigrants, since
independently of the difficulty
of procuring evidence against

the

4

the Master and officers on
the return of the Vessel, it
appears very doubtful, whether
the tribunals of this Country
could take notice of acts done
on the high seas by Foreigners
under a Foreign Flag.

5   Upon the whole, we
consider that the only chance
of affording Emigrants real
protection on the voyage,
would be by inducing those
who are ill treated, or

defrauded

defrauded of their allowances,
to appeal to the Courts of the
United States immediately on
their arrival. The United
States Law requires a Dietary,
at least as ample as that
prescribed by the Passenger
Act, in all cases where
Passengers do not provide
themselves — so that an offence
against the spirit of the
English Law, would almost
always be equally an offence

against

to the proposed notice, a
recommendation to Emigrants
to apply for assistance to Her
Majesty's Consuls at those
Ports.

We have the honor to be
Sir

Your obedient
Humble Servants,

T. W. C. Murdoch

Alexander Wood

21

Finding a Scapegoat

T rial by newspaper was very much in vogue in the 1850s, and could sometimes help curb corruption more effectively and immediately than the rather sluggish British legal system. Even when legal action was successfully pushed through the overcrowded courts, fines were often relatively meagre. A case in point is the *Sophia* which left Liverpool carrying well over her limit of 30 emigrants and so violating the Passengers' Act. When she was forced by storm to dock in Belfast, she was found to have nearly 50 passengers in steerage. Yet the master was fined just £20 (US $100) in Belfast and the broker £10 (US $50) in Liverpool.

Compared to such minor legal penalties, bad newspaper publicity was immediate and damaging in its effects, and might effectively deter captains and owners. In 1850 when the laws of libel were practically non-existent, journalists were free to adopt a flamboyant, accusatory style, inciting strong reactions and steering public opinion. An infamous case concerns the British ship *Blanche*. She set out from Liverpool in February 1851, on her maiden voyage, bound for New Orleans with 470 emigrants on board. Despite the early season, the weather was warm, sultry and occasionally stormy. Tragically, fever broke out en route, and 25 passengers died and were buried at sea. Soon after, the master Thomas Duckitt, the first and second mate and 13 of the crew went down with the fever. On arrival in New Orleans, a further 140 of the Irish passengers fell ill and were carried ashore.

Since the fever year of 1847 (see pp 38–44), such outbreaks were, fortunately, rare and so prompted an immediate inspection by the port health officer. He examined the remaining food and found the bread and biscuits mouldy. When he measured the ship, he discovered that she had been loaded with 84 extra passengers – above the limit allowed by either the American or the British Passengers' Acts. The inspector suspected that the cramped conditions and lack of fresh air in steerage might have forced the spread of fever. He complained, the British Consul complained, the Customs and Immigration officers complained. In London the Colonial Office turned the spotlight on Liverpool where the Chief Emigration Officer was ordered to investigate. He too complained – about a work-load so heavy that there was not enough time to measure a new ship. With only one assistant to help him, there were days when he would be sometimes faced with up to a dozen ships to check in a day, while 2,000 emigrants waited to leave on the same tide. Instead he had accepted the measurements given by the ship's owner and builder, and the government's official surveyor.

News of the *Blanche*'s tragedy, originally reported in New Orleans, quickly spread to Liverpool where its ten newspapers picked up the story, covering the subsequent arguments and investigations. As the hue and cry mounted in the American newspapers, Captain Duckitt felt bound to express his side of the story and wrote to the *True Delta* on April 5th.

I hereby Certify that I have actually on board the Ship *Blanche*
for the use of the Passengers, amounting in all to **425** Statute Adults, the full quantities
of Provisions and Water, stipulated by the Passengers' Act, as particularly specified below, as well
as a sufficiency of Fuel for the Voyage; that I am satisfied with the accommodations for the
Passengers, as regards the size, stability, and arrangements of the Berths; and that the Ship is in
all respects seaworthy; and that there is not on board, as cargo, any Gunpowder, Vitriol, Guano,
Green Hides, or any other Article likely to endanger the safety of the Ship, or the Health or Lives
of the Passengers; all of which I attest, with a due sense of the personal responsibility it involves.

Irrespective of any Provisions, the Passengers may find themselves.

Provisions not inferior in quality to the Sample inspected.

86 August 30 Barrels Biscuit.................... 10625 Lbs.
     90   „   Oatmeal.................... 21250 „
     21   „   Flour .... 4250 „
            Bags Rice.......................... 8500 „
                        Total 44625 „

            Chests Tea...................... 531 „
                 Sugar...................... 2125 „
               Molasses.................... 2125 „
            Barrels Pork.................... 4250 „
                 Water in sound and sweet Casks,
     110 Casks of   210   Gallons 23100 on clearing
            Casks of   Gallons   the Ship
     Total 110 Casks containing   23100   Gallons.
Provisions in addition for my crew of 28 Men, and   2   Cabin Passengers, for
Seventy Days.
     Water for my Crew and Cabin Passengers 2800 Gallons.

                                   Master.

Dated at Liverpool, this   22 day of January 18 57

The Blanche *was overloaded for her voyage to New
Orleans.*

His letter also appeared in the *Liverpool Mercury*, the most
influential paper in the city.

Quite apart from answering his detractors, Duckitt's letter
described the dramatic story of events aboard the *Blanche*:

Several very severe and in my opinion unjust articles having appeared in the papers, relative to the British ship *Blanche*, – and the sickness on board that vessel – from Liverpool under my command, I think it a duty I owe to myself and the owners to give a plain statement of the facts.

The ship *Blanche* now on her first voyage, was surveyed for passengers by a sworn government officer and the number of superficial [square] feet between decks and in the poop, ascertained to be 6,650 as is provided by the document signed by the government officer and the Collector of Customs at Liverpool. I accordingly took on board only the number of passengers allowed both by the American and the English laws, namely one adult to every 14 superficial feet, and if there be any blame it rests upon the measurer.

The ship had all the provisions, water etc., required by law, which were regularly served out as the Act directs. The passengers had their regular allowance of water per day and flour, oatmeal, bread, tea, sugar and molasses served out regularly twice a week, in full quantities and no complaint has been made by any of the passengers either of the quality or quantity of the provisions.

For our first four weeks after I left Liverpool everything went on well. No sickness appeared amongst us and the passengers seemed happy and contented. They attended to the rules and regulations for cleanliness and airing their berths. When we got into the trade winds, the wind came round to south-west with heavy rain and close weather and many of the passengers, contrary to my remonstrances, persisted in sleeping upon deck. Their clothes became soaked and the fever, as a natural consequence, broke out amongst them. On the first day we had five cases and by care and medicine, administered by myself, they all recovered. From five to six appeared every day, subsequently, and no exertions were spared by myself, officers or crew in ministering to the wants and alleviating the sufferings of the poor, unfortunate sick.

The berths were kept clean, the between decks ventilated and everything was done to arrest the disease until my first and second officers, and 13 of the crew were prostrated from their exertions and struck down with the fever. Left to my own resource and having no physic, I had to enforce habits of cleanliness among the passengers, I begged and entreated them for their own sakes to continue the regulations which had been enforced during the early part of the voyage, but in vain.

Many of them became apathetic and indifferent, finally by toiling amongst the passengers myself and assisting them in every way that I could think of, I was also struck down by the fever, and then there was no one left to look after the passengers but themselves, there being only four seamen left fit for duty, and not sufficient to work or steer the ship. Under these circumstances, the pestilence in the midst of us, I considered that it was a miracle that I was enabled under a Merciful Providence, to bring the ship to the pilot ground.

In reference to the alleged overcrowding of the vessel, I deny it altogether. The owners and myself have acted in strict accordance with both the United States and the English law, and if the sworn governmental surveyor measured the vessel wrong, he is to blame not the owners. They gain nothing by taking more passengers than authorised by law, the between decks being chartered for a round sum to the passengers' agents, and not for a sum for each passenger, and it is therefore quite evident that it could not be for their interest to overcrowd the vessel.

The measurement of the vessel by the officer's survey, as

appears by the official document in the Consul's office is 6,650 superficial feet, which, by law, allowed me to carry 475 adult passengers, and I had only 361 adults and 100 children, or 470 passengers counting each child as an adult passenger. I ought to mention I found five stowed away after we got to sea. Of all this number I lost 25 by death – not an excessive mortality under the lamentable circumstances.

It ought to be marked that not one of the English passengers died, though under the same circumstances, and having the same diet as the rest, who were from Ireland. Nor did I lose one of my crew. I forebear to assign a reason for this exemption from disease to which the others fell a prey, leaving to better judges to determine the effect, debility and previous habits might have produced.

I have thus given a simple statement of facts which can be verified by written evidence, and is perhaps the best answer to the abuse and vilification which have been heaped upon me by some portions of the Press. Recovering only from a bed of sickness myself, brought on by my unceasing exertions to relieve the sick – increased by mental anxiety at the heavy responsibilities devolving upon me, both as regards life and property – conscious of having done my duty to my passengers, though claiming no sympathy for myself, my feelings have been deeply wounded at finding myself, arriving in a strange country and in a foreign port, arraigned before the world as an inhuman monster and a murderer. But I rely upon the justice of the citizens of New Orleans, and they will not condemn a man upon one-sided statements without a fair hearing.

Since the article in the *True Delta* of the first instant was published, which is characterized as much by good taste in its unscrupulous attacks upon my country and its government, as it is remarkable for its ignorance of the law and disregard of facts – nearly 50 of my passengers remaining in the city have voluntarily come forward and signed the annexed testimonial.

Trusting that you will, as an act of justice, insert this communication, I remain, Yours, very respectfully

Thomas Duckitt, Master of the British ship *Blanche*.

The testimonial, signed by 50 former passengers, read:

We the undersigned passengers of the *Blanche*, state that the provisions, water, bread etc., were of good quality and served out regularly as prescribed by law . . . that Captain Duckitt and his crew did all in their power to make us comfortable . . . and we do not consider him at all to blame in the matter . . . and had the captain not disposed himself, we might never have reached New Orleans.

Along with the captain's letter the *Liverpool Mercury* published an editorial, part of which stated:

We would be the very last to defend any abuse of the wholesome laws of the country in relation to emigrant passengers who are so often subject to impositions. We believe the captain to be a generous, humane man . . . it is proper we should say, upon the authority of the British Consul, that the provisions of the ship have been examined and found to be sound and in good order, and that the official documents in reference to the measurement of the ship, are duly authenticated.

Though the good captain was publicly exonerated, the Colonial Office scrutinised the actions of the crew members, in particular those of Lieutenant Hodder, and of the

Chief Emigration Officer. Sworn affidavits were taken from the agents who had chartered the ship, and from the bakers who had supplied fresh breadstuffs and who confirmed the quality of their product.

Yet, despite the rigour of the investigation, no clear reasons emerged for either the fever or overcrowding on the *Blanche*. Nothing remains today among the official papers to explain the mistake made by the government's surveyor. After the inquiry, Hodder's pay was cut by half, but it was the Chief Emigration Officer who suffered most. As the official scapegoat, he was formally found negligent by the Colonial Minister, Earl Gray, and was dismissed, after 16 years of service. Six of these had been spent at Liverpool where he had seen the best part of 3,500 emigrant ships leave for America, Canada, Australia and South Africa.

22

Ship's Cook for a Shilling

As the millions of emigrants struggled on and off their ships, it was a time which often revealed mankind at its worst. Pragmatic and uncaring politicians, inhuman landlords, brutal crews, ruthless brokers, dockside racketeers, corrupt ship owners, land agents and high-minded statesmen in London all in their own way profited from the hungry days in Ireland. Yet looking right across the fabric of the Famine period, as many stories emerge of heroism and triumph as of tragedy and cruelty. A closer look reveals deeds of bravery and kindness towards the Irish emigrants, helping them on their way to a new life across the seas.

The western skies were beginning to glow when a young Irishman, Patrick Crotty, reached the dockside at Cork, early on the morning of Tuesday, August 19th in 1851. The days stretched long at this time of year and in fine weather the spectacle of the sun dropping gently into the ocean each night was an inspiration for somewhere beyond the sun lay the Promised Land. The special light on the western horizon, symbolised the hope of a new life in America always promising, always inviting. The decks of the sailing ship

Odessa were busy: with just three or four hours to go before departure, the crew prepared for another voyage to America. The last of her passengers had boarded, totalling 142 men and women, children and babes-in-arms. When high tide came in at mid-morning, Patrick faced the awful prospect of standing on the quay and waving goodbye to his younger brother on board the *Odessa*, as their meagre savings would only extend to fares for one of them.

In all Ireland no one had suffered more throughout the Famine than the inhabitants of Patrick's home county of Cork. The town of Skibbereen witnessed the very first blights and starvation, and the first of the British Government's infamous soup kitchens. The Famine graves, dug beside a ruined Cistercian cell, attracted pilgrimages for more than a hundred years. Cork's great natural harbour at Cove, named Queenstown since 1848, was also popularly known as the Harbour of Tears for it was the site of many anguished goodbyes as floods of emigrants left for America during the Famine years. The River Lee flows out of the cove through the former wetlands and swampy marshes to Cork (from the Gaelic 'Corcaigh' meaning marsh) and divides to enclose an island right in the heart of the city. The island itself and the opposing banks of the North South Channels, provide 22 quays, at one of which the *Odessa* was tied-up. Beyond the city, the river meanders through woods and water meadows and just to the north stands Blarney Castle, built four centuries earlier and home of the ever-famous Blarney Stone.

As Patrick Crotty stood on the quay on that August morning, his heart was clearly set on making the journey, though he had never been to sea before. His desire was to wave his goodbyes from up on the deck, rather than down on the dock. Young Patrick must have been blessed by the Blarney Stone itself for amazingly, he talked himself aboard

No. 2_ _ _ **Certificate of British Registry.**

THIS is to Certify, that in pursuance of an Act passed in the Eighth and Ninth Years of
the Reign of Queen VICTORIA, intituled, " An Act for the Registering of British Vessels,"

William Carson of the city of Dublin Merchant

having made and subscribed the Declaration required by the said Act, and having declared that ~~He~~
~~together with~~

Canc'd and Reg'd Denovo
27th August 1850 No. 29

_is_ ___ sole Owner (in the proportions specified on the Back hereof) of the Ship or Vessel called the
___ _Odessa_ ___ of _Dublin_ ___ which is of the Burthen of
Three hundred & twenty three Tons, and whereof _Henry Selby_ ___
is Master, and that the said Ship or Vessel was _built at Denov in the Province of_
New Brunswick in the year one thousand eight hundred and
thirty nine, as appears by the Certificate of last Registry No. 7.
granted at this Port 25th February 1848, now delivered up,
and cancelled, property changed ___
and _Henry Mentire Tide Surveyor at this Port_ having certified to us that
the said Ship or Vessel has ___ _One_ ___ Decks and ___ _three_ ___ Masts, that her length from
the inner part of the Main Stem to the fore part of the Stern Post aloft is _Ninety nine_ ___
___ feet _One_ ___ tenths, her breadth in Midships is _twenty three_ ___
___ feet _Seven_ tenths, her depth in hold at Midships is _Seventeen_ ___
___ feet _three_ tenths, that she is _Barque_ ___ rigged, with a _Standing_ ___ Bowsprit;
is _Square_ ___ sterned _Carvel_ ___ built; has ___ _No_ ___ Galleries, and _a common Bust_
Head; and the said subscribing Owners having consented and agreed to the above Description, and having
caused sufficient Security to be given, as is required by the said Act, the said Ship or Vessel called the
___ _Odessa_ ___ has been duly registered at the Port of _Dublin_ ___

Certified under our Hands, at the Custom-House, in the said Port of _Dublin_ ___ this
_18th_ Day of _June_ ___ in the Year One Thousand Eight Hundred and _forty nine_

Collector.

Comptroller.

United Kingdom. No. 267—Certificate of British Registry. (Copy.) 8, New Act.
2 Rms.—Feb., 1849.

Odessa, *veteran of the Atlantic crossing.*

the *Odessa*. We cannot know what words passed between the fledgling sailor and the *Odessa*'s master, but shortly before the anchor chains rattled into the hold, Crotty was signed on as one of the crew. This curious fact was noted in the ship's papers, now faded blue manuscripts covered in the captain's copper plate handwriting and stamped by the Consul in New York. The papers show that Patrick Crotty was the last man to be hired but unlike the rest, he was hired on the very day that the *Odessa* sailed. The ship's papers also reveal that though Patrick had never been to sea before and he was not an apprentice seaman, he was signed on as passengers' cook for the princely sum of 1s (25 cents in 1851). What exactly occurred when the old sea captain, Henry Selly, exchanged a few words with the spirited young man on the dock, hoping to talk his way to America? We can only speculate: perhaps Selly took pity on young Patrick? Perhaps he had sons of his own, perhaps a brother from whom he was parted at an early age. Whatever the exact cause, Seaman Patrick Crotty found himself aboard the *Odessa* as a result of the captain's unsung act of kindness. Selly even advanced Crotty his pay – a shilling – and he signed up, swearing to, 'conduct himself in an orderly, faithful, honest and sober manner' and to be at all times diligent in his duties.

Selly had hired the rest of his crew in Dublin a week earlier, including his usual mate, Eddie Dempsey, the bosun, William Denstow, ship's carpenter, James Kelly, the cook, and deck-hands all of whom were experienced seamen; in addition a dozen Irishmen, four Englishmen, an American and a Canadian were hired. Dempsey was paid £2 10s (US $12.50) a month with a bonus on their return, while ordinary seamen received £1 5s (US $6.25). All hands also enjoyed the perk of free provisions which guaranteed a good solid meal, every day during the voyage. Dublin, the ship's home port, was the usual point of departure, and the *Odessa* had made

*The River Lee and the quays in the centre of Cork —
where the Fords boarded their ship, and where Patrick
Crotty found a kindly captain.*

the crossing three times already, and a fourth time from
Limerick.

The *Odessa* was a decent size for the crossing – triple-
masted and 99 feet long at the water-line, she weighed 323
tons. Built in 1839 in New Brunswick, Canada, she was
owned by William Carson, Dublin's foremost shipping

merchant. When surveyed in 1850, she had been given a 'First-Class, Division Two' rating. For the summer trip, she arrived in Cork on August 17th. She loaded a small cargo and embarked her passengers. The ship's list shows that Mary O'Neill sailed alone with her four daughters, one being the small, new-born Catherine. In all, there were 20 children under the age of ten aboard, plus two dozen teenagers. Nine young families travelled without husbands or fathers, under the sole care of young mothers. By 1851 this pattern of family travel was becoming increasingly common as few families could afford to get there. Sometimes, instead, a husband might have died, leaving a young mother to continue alone, with no one but her children by her side at the start of their new life. The four teenage Murphy girls had neither parent with them. The oldest men on board, Pat Barry and William Rockey, both aged 50, travelled alone. Had they left families at home in Ireland who would follow them? The rest of the passenger list records young married couples, a few brothers and sisters, a small number of spinsters and, among the young bachelors, listed by itself, the name of 20-year-old Simon Crotty, Patrick's younger brother.

The ship spent most of the first day cruising down the river, borne along by the tidal flow and the moderate south-westerly breeze, through the cove before she burst into the ocean. Seaman Crotty was doubtless earning his wages as Captain Selly hardened his sails and steered the ship towards America. On deck, the passengers cherished their last glimpse of Ireland, her tiny inlets and harbours lying beneath green hills which melted into the distance – a beautiful and heartbreaking scene. No seaman's skills were required for Patrick's task up on deck, where he organised the passengers' provisions and possibly kept them from bickering about turns at the fire box. If the weather was bad, Patrick could have the day off, as no cooking was allowed in the hold.

On arrival in New York, 41 days later, Patrick was discharged, according to the crew roll. Now free to join his brother and the friends he had made among the passengers, he walked ashore on Monday, September 29th. Captain Selly had once again brought his ship and her human cargo safely into port.

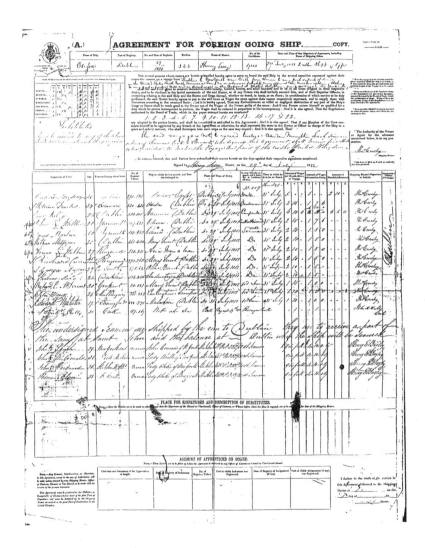

According to the Crew's Agreements for the Odessa,
stored in London, a young man was hired as 'passengers'
cook' for the one-way journey.

23

The Brave Men of Nantucket

Ireland heaved a sigh of relief when the time came for lifting the potatoes in the late summer of 1851. Though it was yet too early for complete confidence, it was clear that the worst of the blight was over and it was time to face the long road to recovery. The flight of hungry men and women from Ireland would continue, along with the harsh winter sailings, for some years to come. Ship owners and shipping agents kept the prices of fares fluctuating, accurately gauging the ratio between supply and demand – they had years of practice.

One of the oldest vessels on the Atlantic during the mid-19th century was named the *British Queen*, not perhaps the best name for a ship carrying Irish emigrants fleeing the Famine. Victoria, the stern-faced monarch, and her Parliament in London, stood accused of doing too little to save Ireland from her plight. The 225-ton barque had been at sea for 66 years. She had seen out the last two decades of the slave trade and then earned her owner further profits during the six Famine years. As an emigrant ship, she had sailed from the Irish ports of Dublin, Sligo, Belfast and Liverpool, bound for America and Canada. Her worthy service ended dramatically in December 1851, when she went aground in the ice around Nantucket Island, but her passengers and crew were rescued by the islanders in a spectacular mission which remains part of the proud maritime history of the old whaling port of Nantucket Island.

The *British Queen* left Dublin with 228 passengers on October 22nd 1851. It must have been a difficult voyage, as she was still on passage eight weeks later. Yet even with unfriendly headwinds, another two or three days might have seen her safely berthed in New York, in time for her storm-battered passengers to celebrate Christmas in the new country. But luck deserted them just as they came within sight of land. The full might of winter descended; snow, one of the hazards of Atlantic trips, blinded their ship and shrouded the shore in a blizzard. Around Nantucket Island, dangerously narrow channels lie between shifting sand bars and shallow waters, creating a hazardous passage, feared even by the most able mariners. When Captain Christopher Conway reached this treacherous stretch of water, navigation became nigh impossible. He maintained little canvas at the masts but a northerly gale blew his barque too close inland. The snowstorm obstructed his look-outs who shouted constantly for adjustments on the wheel as jagged chunks of ice, bumping alongside, grazed the aged timber hull. It was still snowing hard when darkness settled over the ocean in the afternoon. The shortest day of the year was less than a week away.

Crew and passengers alike knew their voyage was almost at an end, but how would it end? The anxiety of the experienced few up top transferred itself to the unknowing mass down below whose uncertainty turned to fear as the night stretched before them and suddenly they went aground. The ebbing tide had caught the ship in a particularly

225

dangerous channel off Muskeget, close to Martha's Vine-
yard, 12 miles from Nantucket Harbour. The crew hastily
stowed the rest of their sails and set their distress signal. They
could not be sure just how many miles now separated them
from land. Their best chance of rescue lay in being seen by a
passing vessel but, as they knew, most shipping steered a very
wide berth around this dangerous spot. The storm showed
no signs of abating. Now time was of the essence – would
anyone spot the stricken ship in time before she started to
break up? She was stuck fast on the sandy seabed and
beginning to keel over dangerously as the tide subsided.
The overnight temperatures dropped far below freezing.
The blustering wind shrieked and rattled through the rigging, while the sound of the waves crashing over the deck
alternated with the bump, bump, bump of ice floes bouncing
off the exposed hull. As dawn arrived, the travellers could
only hope and pray. There was no means of sending a signal,
no emergency flares. Yet, though no one aboard realised,
they had been spotted already, almost as soon as daylight had
lifted. As the snow eased briefly, a look-out in the south
tower of the Unitarian Church on Orange Street, had seen the
stricken ship through his long-glass and recognised the red
duster – a quartered Union Jack and red-surround – the flag
of the British merchant fleet. The look-out had been on fire-
watch but, at a height of 120 feet above the harbour, visibility
on a good day stretched for 20 miles and though he could see
barely half that distance, it was just enough on that wretched,
December day to notice that the flag was flying upside down.
'Ship in distress,' he had cried and his description of the big
three-master was relayed to the men in the harbour.

The ship's flag was identified and the initial stages of a
rescue attempt were under way, but hampered by the storm.
The stranded passengers would spend another day and
another fearful night out on the ocean. On shore, at Nan-

tucket everyone was aware of the ship's precarious situation, and primed to act, as soon as the storm blew itself out. Winter had set in early in Nantucket that year and for days the howling winds had forced ice floes into the Sound. But, as the islanders strained to see through the snowy shroud, at last brief windows began to appear in the white wall of snow, and through the telescope in the church tower could be seen masses of passengers gathering on the main deck. But there was still no movement in the harbour, the gales, the tides and the freezing weather rendered any immediate rescue impossible.

Five years earlier, when the island was already in decline as a whaling base, fire had destroyed the harbour. The Nantucket waterfront was now lined with empty wharves and abandoned warehouses. Old sea captains lived on their memories while a small band of younger men lived off their wits and ship-handling skills, and grasped whatever opportunities came their way. For a seaman with sufficient nerve and competence as a pilot, salvaging a ship was a lucrative business, with potential rewards of up to a third of the value of the ship itself and half the value of her cargo.

Out in the shallow channel, Captain Conway ordered the foremast and mizzen mast to be chopped away to prevent the *British Queen* tearing herself apart. The main mast now carried a distress flag but he realised that, with the approaching darkness, there was no chance of getting his passengers off until the next day, assuming that they managed to survive that long. They settled down to pray again, huddling together on the open deck for warmth and comfort. There was little the crew could do; provisions had long since disappeared and the water-barrels had run dangerously low. If they were spared, they would begin their new life in tattered clothes, stripped of their few, treasured possessions. Forced to ride out two more tides, Conway was resigned to losing his ship and he reasoned that, given the weather, they would be fortunate to survive at all. Indeed, as 11 feet of water settled in the hold overnight, two passengers died from the cold.

The rescue of the British Queen *began on December 19th 1851.*

On the Island, soon after the alert was raised, a small group of men gathered in the waterfront offices of Joseph Macy, a ship owner and a leading merchant on the island, to devise a rescue plan for the next day. The *Telegraph*, a paddle-steamer which maintained a regular ferry service to the mainland, would tow the schooners, *Hamilton* and *Game Cock*, over the sand bar and up to the mouth of the harbour, where they could raise sail. But the steamer could not move until high tide, due around midday, as she needed at least

228

8 feet draft, and would stand-off some way from the wreck, as the ice could damage her paddle wheels. The schooners, sailing close to the wreck, would carry out the rescue. There was no shortage of volunteers to crew the rescue vessels. The people on Nantucket would join in the prayers and see what tomorrow would bring. Another dawn bared the scene and they were relieved to see little had changed. Aboard the *Telegraph*, as she built up steam next morning, Captain George Russell and a professional wreck master, Captain Thomas Gardner, were on duty. The schooners were commanded by the Patterson brothers, William on the smaller *Game Cock* and David on the *Hamilton*. He declined the tow at the last minute and made his own way out to the wreck. In the early afternoon of December 19th, with the northerly gale still persisting, the rescue began. Out over the bar the aptly named *Game Cock* cast off her tow, set her storm sails and plunged through the wind and waves while the *Telegraph* followed at a more sedate pace.

Sight of the ships heading out must have gladdened the hearts of all the half-frozen men, women and children on board the *British Queen*. This was the first indication in more than 36 hours that they might be saved and their prayers had been answered. Anchoring as close to the *British Queen* as they dared, Nantucket's expert mariners conferred. The breakers were baring their teeth as their combined crews took to the boats and rowed across to the stranded ship. Captain David Patterson and the wreck master Captain Gardner then climbed aboard the *British Queen* where Captain Conway informed them: 'We have no cargo and the ship is a total loss, it is not insured. All I want is to get my passengers to safety. The water has been up over the lower decks all night and they are in a horrid condition.' The rescuers signalled the *Game Cock* to lay alongside the wreck and all the seamen worked together to transfer passengers to the schooner. It was a hazardous operation; the smaller ship frequently rose above the rail of the wrecked barque then plunged into a trough as the waves roared around them. When some 60 passengers were aboard the *Game Cock* she started striking the bottom. As the tide was turning, there was no time to transfer the survivors to the paddle steamer. Instead, the *Game Cock* headed back to the harbour. The *Hamilton* eased in alongside the wreck to continue the rescue. The Nantucket records state:

> The *British Queen* was now headed north and listed heavily to starboard, with the waves smashing against her stern. The *Hamilton* approached her bow, dropped an anchor, and payed out her anchor cable until she lay across her bow, then slowly worked down her starboard side.
>
> Clinging to the wreck with mooring lines, the *Hamilton* was heaved high above the ship with each rising wave, then smashing down on the shoal. Meanwhile, the passengers were jumping or being thrown from the wreck to the schooner where they were hustled below and wrapped in blankets.
>
> As the day darkened and the tide turned, every one of the passengers was rescued without the loss of a single person. Shortly after five o'clock the *Telegraph* and *Hamilton* reached Straight Wharf where the *Game Cock* was already tied up and a large crowd waited in the cold and dark to take charge of the immigrants.

The survivors were taken to a variety of fire houses, church halls or private homes where they spent six days recovering from their dreadful ordeal. On Christmas Day itself most of them went aboard the old paddle steamer, the *Telegraph*, and set off for New York to complete their journey. But there were many who wanted nothing more to do with the sea and were happy to stay among people who had made them so welcome, and who had risked their own lives to bring them ashore. Among the survivors who settled on the island was a young Irish couple: 29-year-old farmhand Robert Mooney with his new bride Julia, who was 21. They raised a family of seven children and became tenant farmers until Robert earned the money to buy his own 200-acre spread. With his older son to help on the farm, he grew corn, potatoes and a variety of vegetables, and bred a large dairy herd. Robert's son and then his grandson succeeded to the farm. His grandson later became a police officer and in the early part of this century, was appointed Nantucket's Police Chief. His

BRITISH QUEEN.

The nameboard, all that survived of a gallant ship.

son, also named Robert, after his great-grandfather, the original Famine emigrant, became a lawyer. Robert C Mooney still practices law in Nantucket and is himself the father of three sons, in their mid-20s a construction worker, a truck driver and a local handyman on the island.

One of the Mooney family's treasured links to the past, to their Irish heritage and to that memorable event in 1851, is the *British Queen*'s nameboard. Robert C Mooney is the current guardian of this polished piece of wood, recovered when the wreckage washed up on shore. It hangs splendidly above the fireplace in his home. 'One of the islanders found it on the beach some days after the ship broke up,' the lawyer explained, 'and made a present of it to my great-grandfather. It has remained a proud possession of the family ever since and been handed down through four generations. There was one further piece found on the beach among all the drift-wood. It's a crucifix and I have that here as well. The wreck itself was sold as she lay, on the shoals out in the Sound for US $290. Amazing isn't it, worth so little but she did the job, I'm here today to prove it.'

24

Ireland Forever

The modern Catholic cathedral in Liverpool is known irreverently but affectionately as Paddy's Wigwam, in deference to its shape and to the antecedents of the masses who worship within the diocese today. The six years of the Famine sailings saw a million Irish emigrants arrive in Liverpool's port. The majority had just completed the short trip across the usually turbulent Irish Sea – the first stage of their journey to America or Canada. Nearly a quarter of them would have nothing more to do with that cruel sea and those inhuman ships. Some travelled to England and Scotland but many an Irishman and his family remained in Liverpool. For some the city symbolised the end of all their travels and a section of the city came to be known as Little Ireland.

For nearly two centuries, from *c*. 1700–1900, Liverpool's port enabled Britain to dominate rival maritime nations. Liverpool sent out ships to explore the world but also ships full of human cargo, first slaves, and then emigrants. Known as the slavers' port in the 18th century, Liverpool rapidly became an emigrants' port in the 19th century, though

Liverpool's ship owners continued to trade in slaves until slavery was abolished by Britain in 1807. During that final year, 185 ships transported as many as 50,000 slaves. Soon the commercial rule of 'slaves-out and sugar-back' gave way to 'emigrants-out and timber-back'. On ships bound for New York or Boston during the Famine, it cost 6 cs to insure US $4 worth of baggage but only 4 cs to insure your life. But the Irish were only part of the emigration story. During the 19th century, a total of nine million emigrants spilled out of Europe, sailing from Liverpool to America. Liverpool enjoyed unique commercial and geographical assets. Sited strategically close to the Irish Sea, the city lay only 3 miles up the River Mersey. Liverpool was also one of the first posts to forge a rail-link with Hull, 100 miles away. Hull, in turn, enjoyed busy trade with the ports of Hamburg and Bremen, Gothenburg and Danzig, from where a remarkable ethnic mix of people journeyed, sometimes fleeing their homelands for various reasons. The crossing from Europe to Hull over the North Sea, was as short as that over the Irish Sea, and the rail fare was only a few shillings. Of course, at this particular time the mainland Europeans formed only a minor part of the emigrant population in Britain.

It was logical for the Irish to aim for Liverpool as their launching pad into the New World, not merely because it was the nearest port of convenience, but also because it was a familiar site and source of summer work. Thousands of Irish farmhands regularly crossed to Liverpool, seeking work at the back end of summer on England's farms. Too few opportunities existed at home at harvest time and the wages in England were better. Additionally, many more ships were available in Liverpool, with its big, fast vessels and speedy American packet ships. The fast packets grabbed a good half of the emigrant trade towards the end of the Famine years, averaging 40 days westward and 23 days eastward. Liverpool was also one of the world's busiest shipping ports, with over 36 miles of quays and a massive ship tonnage registered as three times the overall tonnage owned in America at that period. Into this teeming city sailed the Irish families from their rural communities. Already overawed by the Irish cities of Dublin, Belfast or Cork, the rural emigrants had to survive the streetwise con-men and racketeers of Liverpool, and later of New York or Boston. At various levels the Liverpool fraternity was engaged in the business of exporting people and, as human cargo was regarded as a commodity, every trader sought to extract his ounce of flesh from that commodity. Yet help was at hand, if only the emigrants knew where to look and who to ask. Various publications offered guidance, and government circulars advised on how to find lodgings, how to seek a passage and buy a ticket, where to exchange money, what to avoid at the docks, on the ships and on arrival.

The priority for the emigrant in Liverpool was to obtain a ticket for a ship sailing within a few days. Space on most of the Atlantic ships was often sold in one block by the owners to the passenger brokers and competition was so intense that fares varied from day to day, sometimes changing by the hour. A berth in steerage ranged between £3 10s to £5 (US $17.50 to $25). The port authority licensed 21 brokers who each provided a bond plus two sureties totalling £200 (US $1,000). The brokers paid a small commission to dock-runners for each emigrant delivered to their office. Given half a chance, a runner would lead his unsuspecting victims from the brokers to a lodging house, and then on to a chandler for provisions and suitable clothing, earning further commission, if he could persuade his prey to part with his last few pennies. Before the day of departure, each emigrant had to appear before a medical officer who was paid by the ship owner or charterer £1 (US $5) for every hundred passengers he inspected. After a very rudimentary examination, he would stamp each ticket as proof of inspection. Passengers were entitled to board the ship 24 hours before departure. Once settled, if lucky to have among them a fiddler or a piper and while spirits were high, the passengers might enjoy a song and dance. Once out on the ocean, the sloping decks and strong south-westerly winds would soon restrict their activities. Occasionally, there were scenes at the quayside if passengers arrived late, after the gangway had been raised, the mooring lines cast off and the ship had sailed away. The late arrivals would be rushed to the dock-gate and as their ship passed close by, their luggage and boxes would be flung aboard, followed by the passengers themselves, hopefully landing on the deck. If they or their luggage missed the ship and splashed into the water, there was usually a man in a rowing boat positioned for a rescue, and a reward.

Steam tugs usually towed a sailing ship into position down-river. As tugs were not always available during these early days of steam, outgoing ships were sometimes steered by a practised pilot with a single-sail cutter in attendance. The pilot's local knowledge of navigational hazards, tides, currents and winds and his regular practice in handling a ship were invaluable. During the short voyage down-river, the ship's crew searched for stowaways. All legitimate passengers were mustered on deck during the search, while dubious bundles were poked with long, sharp sticks and suspect barrels were turned upside-down. Many a barrel or trunk concealed a body or two. Once discovered, the guilty stowaways were transferred to the tug and returned to shore where they would be tried before a magistrate. A lucky few survived the search and made their appearance two or three days later when the crew would be grateful as the successful stowaways worked their passage by doing the most unpleasant jobs on board.

More famous drawings from the Illustrated London
News . . . *The initial medical inspection before boarding
ship . . .*

*. . . Dancing between the decks, but only at the start of a
voyage . . .*

237

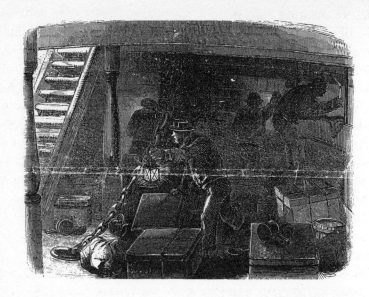

...Searching for stowaways before leaving Liverpool...

...And the roll-call.

Before hoisting his sails for the ocean, the captain took a roll-call of all the passengers aboard, and would prepare his list which would be handed to Immigration officers on arrival in America. Next the ship's doctor inspected the passengers again. While the medical examination on shore was undertaken by government decree to prevent any outbreak of contagious disease on board, the second inspection was carried out for the benefit of the ship's owners. They had to pay a poll-tax to the American port authorities US $1.50 for each passenger. If any passengers were found to be ill or deformed, unable to support themselves and without relatives, then the ship's owners were fined and forced to enter a bond of up to US $1,000 a head, to compensate for the likely drain on the public purse.

Once on board ship, emigrants were subject to the same discipline as the crew, and all were subject to the captain's rule. Aptly dubbed 'Master Under God' by the Board of Trade, the captain exercised almost absolute authority at sea. Even a passenger could be charged with mutiny, for showing any form of rebellion or defiance, and the penalty for mutiny was death by hanging. Once out of Liverpool, the Irish sailed back the way they had come, towards Ireland with the prevailing winds dictating their routes north around Mallin Head, south by the Waterford Estuary, Cove and Cape Clear. Optimistic or unenlightened passengers often mistook the sight of land, their homeland, for their final destination, the Promised Land. Perhaps those who were denied a last glimpse of their homeland, by virtue of bad weather or a more southerly route, got off to a better start. There were no easy voyages for the Irish. The sea was a stranger to them, the ships were alien and, if America seemed like a dream, the Atlantic passage was all too often a nightmare. Both extremes were faced on two voyages from Liverpool to New York. The first, nightmarish trip on the *Aberfoyle* began in the first year of the Famine sailings; the second, happier voyage, in the last year of the Famine. Few, if any, ship's logs exist for this period, as many which had been carefully stored for 90 years were destroyed by fire. However, events of the first voyage are recorded in a sworn affidavit by the ship's master, Thomas Jones.

Jones' feet had barely touched the cobblestones in South Street, before he made his way to the British Vice Consul, with his first mate, Robert Metcalf, and a senior mariner, Robert Innes. At the dock, the Immigration officers were still clearing the ship's 192 passengers while the crew aboard set the remnants of canvas to dry. Jones and his men intended to record under oath the extraordinary events of the 69-day crossing. Jones carried the ship's log, proof of their words for he feared that few would believe their story. The Vice Consul, Anthony Barclay, escorted the men to an official public notary, John H Lyell, who recorded their sworn statements on March 10th 1847. On the *Bible of the Holy Evangelists of Almighty God*, they swore that, on leaving Liverpool on December 30th 1846, their ship had been: stout, staunch and strong; had her cargo well and sufficiently stowed and secure; was well masted, manned, tackled, victualled, apparelled and appointed;' and was in every respect fit for sea and the voyage she was about to undertake. The full story of the voyage was recounted in the ship's log:

Day 1: Variable winds and weather, making and short-ening sail as required. Nothing of importance occurred until . . .

Day 4: Winds freshen considerably, weather becoming squally. We deemed it prudent to shorten sail.

With the weather no worse than could be expected in January, they sailed on, heading westwards in the Atlantic, until they encountered rough weather.

Day 15: Strong gales. Close-reefed topsails, took in top gallant sails and spanker, heavy squalls bent new main trysail . . .

Day 16: The wind continued to blow very hard; the cargo shifted and stove in several cask heads. Pumps regularly attended; lost sails.

Day 18: Ship labouring heavily; shipping a great deal of water, a quantity of which all goes down the hatchways.

The ordeal continued for two long weeks, with strong gales and rain, with reefing and furling sails and heavy seas crashing over deck and hatchways. The ship laboured on, while the crew checked the pumps constantly. Is it possible to imagine the suffering of the wretched passengers freezing and wet in the hold below, beneath shattered hatchways, wondering when and how it would all end? The log's entries graphically describe their ordeal:

Day 27: Passengers' water ration cut to four pints a day.

Day 29: A cross, confused sea, ship labouring very much and making more water than usual.

Day 34: Ship's company allowed four pints of water per man. Nothing of any importance occurred for several days; weather generally very calm.

Day 51: A continuation of calms with hot, sultry weather. Passengers' water reduced to two pints per man.

Day 55: Ship's company reduced to two pints of water per day.

Day 56: Strong breezes and a heavy, cross sea, ship labouring and straining very much.

Day 58: Put ship's company on allowance of 1lb bread per day.

Day 59:   Passengers allowed 8ozs bread per day. Strong gales and squalls, took in more sails.

Day 61:   At midnight strong gales. At noon wind blowing very hard, we hove the ship to under close-reefed main topsail and main trysail.

Day 62:   A continuation of blowing weather and squalls. The ship labouring heavily and shipping a quantity of water.

Day 64:   We spoke to the brig *Independence* of Philadelphia, from Palermo [Italy] 105 days out, supplied them with some provisions and lamp oil.

Day 66:   Strong gales. At 4 am the ship rolling heavily shifted the cargo and stove-in the heads of several casks containing the cargo. The pumps always regularly attended.

Day 69:   At 2 pm made the land. At 8 pm [the ship] sounded and grounded in eleven fathoms of water.

A Revenue cutter met the *Aberfoyle* outside the port and transferred 180lbs of bread for the ravenous passengers. The steam boat *Hercules* towed them into port where they moored alongside another barque, the *Apollo*. In the curious legal style of the era, the affidavit closes:

. . . and thereupon the said Master doth publicly and solemnly protest against winds, weather and seas, and against all and every accident, matter and thing . . . the said vessel or her cargo have suffered or sustained damage or injury . . . and that no part of such losses do fall on him, the master, his officers or crew.

The most amazing statistic after such a wicked voyage was not recorded on the affidavit but revealed on the ship's manifest lodged with the Immigration officials. Of the 194 passengers who boarded her in Liverpool, two infants died at sea. The rest had suffered untold agonies every day, every hour perhaps, but they reached shore in the end and the nightmare was over.

Others would follow and others would dream, and a dream can do wonders for those with faith and determination. After so much heartache at home, imagine the joy of finding passage out of Liverpool on a ship bound for America, a ship named *Erin Go Bragh*, meaning Ireland Forever. Such good fortune was shared by 273 Irish passengers on March 22nd 1851. Pat Kelly, Pat Cahill and James Duffy each headed a family of eight, accounting for 24 of the passengers. Among the remainder were five McGraths, seven Barratts, and another nine large families, a sprinkling of spinsters and some 50 young, unattached men ready for work. *Erin Go Bragh* was a grand title for a fully-rigged, three-masted ship. Owned in Cork by Joshua and Abraham Hargreaves, she was built of oak and tamarac, beech and elm. Captain Jeremiah Casey and his crew of 15, plus four teenage apprentices, set a spanking pace across the Atlantic and she reached New York after 32 days at sea on April 23rd, 1856. What a bustling, colourful scene greeted them on arrival at the very same South Street Seaport where the stricken *Aberfoyle* had moored. After hiring a pilot at Sandy Hook, Captain Casey used the current to force the ship over to the Manhattan side of the East River. For the handful of bewildered passengers allowed up on deck, the spectacle changed every minute. As the ship passed by a cluster of barges, some labouring dockhands looked up and were the first to greet the passengers. The fortunate few on deck called down below with details of the stunning scenes along the river. Quays turned into market places overnight as fishing smacks disgorged their catch, and schooners unloaded fresh fruit on to roughly-made stalls.

A preacher on a box, exalting a small crowd to resist evil, was ignored by a knot of ship's captains intent on exchanging their news. The notes of a song floated across from the Brooklyn bank, as a ship's crew rhythmically hauled on lines to secure their vessel. No fear showed on the faces of the shipping agents, nor anxiety among the stevedores or sea-men, children at play, or anyone else moving along the quays, save for a few women clasping their bonnets against the wind. No one fought over food; there were no beggars, but signs of plenty all round: sacks of grain were off-loaded on to barges which disappeared into the city on a network of canals. A gang of boys at play, intent on taking cotton from a cart drawn by a tired horse, waited their chance. The steep sloping roofs of tall, square warehouses three storeys high looked down on all the activity and, amid the forest of masts at South Street, many flags of the Stars and Stripes fluttered their welcome to the new Americans.

The *Marion* from Cork and the *Lady Miller* from Dublin had docked on the previous tide. Ahead in the East River was the *Princeton,* also from Cork, followed by the *George Washington* which had left Liverpool five days earlier. The voyage on the *Erin Go Bragh* was nearly over. Suddenly America, the Land of the Free, lay at the end of the mooring line which was spinning through the air from the hands of the second mate, Eddie McDonnell, as the *Erin Go Bragh* prepared to berth. The dream had just come true for 1,100 Irish men, women and children who arrived in New York on two tides on that momentous day in April, 1851. A thousand ships would make a similar voyage during 1851 there was but one *Erin Go Bragh*.

While some faced their new life alone and unprepared, the lucky ones met families waiting for them on arrival. For

Age	Sex	Occupations	Date Port Ship	Names of Passengers	Age	Sex	Occupations	Date Port Ship
24	M	Farmer	25Ap16Bx	BURK, Thomas	9	M	Child	25Ap16Bx
18	F	Unknown	25Ap16Bx	SELLY, U-Mrs.	60	F	Farmer	25Ap16Bx
12	M	Unknown	25Ap16Bx	MOORE, Catherine	24	F	Unknown	25Ap16Bx
17	M	Unknown	25Ap16Bx	Michael	.09	M	Infant	25Ap16Bx
25	M	Farmer	25Ap16Bx	Ann	3	F	Child	25Ap16Bx
17	F	Farmer	25Ap16Bx	SELLY, Ann	26	F	Unknown	25Ap16Bx
20	M	Farmer	25Ap16Bx	Marln	18	F	Unknown	25Ap16Bx
20	F	Servant	25Ap16Bx	Margt.	24	F	Servant	25Ap16Bx
13	M	Servant	25Ap16Bx	MARKEY, Thomas	25	M	Unknown	25Ap16Bx
28	F	Dressmaker	25Ap16Bx	GARTLEN, Owen	17	M	Unknown	25Ap16Bx
.11	M	Infant	25Ap16Bx	Pat	12	M	Unknown	25Ap16Bx
20	M	Unknown	25Ap16Bx	CLIFFORD, Ann	20	F	Servant	25Ap16Bx
50	M	Unknown	25Ap16Bx	Catherine	16	F	Unknown	25Ap16Bx
28	F	Unknown	25Ap16Bx	BOYLE, Catherine	18	F	Unknown	25Ap16Bx
20	M	Unknown	25Ap16Bx	WARD, Mary	15	F	Unknown	25Ap16Bx
49	M	Farmer	25Ap16Bx	TIMOTHY, Francis	53	M	Farmer	25Ap16Bx
42	F	Farmer	25Ap16Bx	Mary	21	F	Unknown	25Ap16Bx
11	M	Farmer	25Ap16Bx	Pat	18	M	Unknown	25Ap16Bx
9	M	Child	25Ap16Bx	Sarah	16	F	Servant	25Ap16Bx
5	F	Child	25Ap16Bx	Frank	15	M	Unknown	25Ap16Bx
18	F	Farmer	25Ap16Bx	FEE, Ann	45	F	Unknown	25Ap16Bx
16	M	Unknown	25Ap16Bx	Bridget	14	F	Unknown	25Ap16Bx
19	M	Unknown	25Ap16Bx	Henry	14	M	Unknown	25Ap16Bx
50	M	Farmer	25Ap16Bx	Ann	12	F	Unknown	25Ap16Bx
17	M	Farmer	25Ap16Bx	WALSH, John	20	M	Paper Maker	25Ap16Bx
26	F	Servant	25Ap16Bx	ALLICE, Eliza	16	F	Unknown	25Ap16Bx
24	F	Servant	25Ap16Bx	BALLARD, Joseph	29	M	Farmer	25Ap16Bx
22	F	Unknown	25Ap16Bx	U-Mrs.	30	F	Unknown	25Ap16Bx
20	F	Unknown	25Ap16Bx	U-Miss	5	F	Child	25Ap16Bx
18	F	Servant	25Ap16Bx	Joseph	1	M	Child	25Ap16Bx
16	F	Unknown	25Ap16Bx	BUTLER, U-Mrs.	35	F	Servant	25Ap16Bx
29	F	Unknown	25Ap16Bx	CRAFFORD, Melaney	29	M	Farmer	25Ap16Bx
6	M	Child	25Ap16Bx	ODONNEL, James	33	M	Unknown	25Ap16Bx
2	M	Child	25Ap16Bx	MALLDERICK, John	36	M	Unknown	25Ap16Bx
44	F	Unknown	25Ap16Bx	BLAKE, James	28	M	Unknown	25Ap16Bx
18	F	Unknown	25Ap16Bx	WALSH, Joseph	24	M	Plumber	25Ap16Bx
13	F	Unknown	25Ap16Bx					
9	M	Child	25Ap16Bx					
20	F	Unknown	25Ap16Bx					
20	F	Unknown	25Ap16Bx					
19	F	Unknown	25Ap16Bx					
19	F	Unknown	25Ap16Bx					
55	M	Unknown	25Ap16Bx	ERIN-GO-BRAGH 25 APRIL 1851				
20	F	Unknown	25Ap16Bx					
25	M	Laborer	25Ap16Bx	From Liverpool				
24	F	Unknown	25Ap16Bx					
10	M	Unknown	25Ap16Bx					
7	F	Child	25Ap16Bx	DOHERTY, Michael	20	M	Laborer	25Ap02By
5	M	Child	25Ap16Bx	GARVEY, Malachi	20	M	Laborer	25Ap02By
25	M	Unknown	25Ap16Bx	Ellen	18	F	Laborer	25Ap02By
24	F	Unknown	25Ap16Bx	COMMONS, Michael	24	M	Laborer	25Ap02By
9	F	Child	25Ap16Bx	NOHILL, Barthe	32	M	Laborer	25Ap02By
.06	F	Infant	25Ap16Bx	Biddy	30	F	Laborer	25Ap02By
22	M	Farmer	25Ap16Bx	Margt.	13	F	Laborer	25Ap02By
25	F	Unknown	25Ap16Bx	HAKER, Thomas	45	M	Laborer	25Ap02By
.09	M	Infant	25Ap16Bx	Ann	45	F	Laborer	25Ap02By
30	F	Unknown	25Ap16Bx	Eliza	22	F	Laborer	25Ap02By
10	M	Unknown	25Ap16Bx	John	12	M	Laborer	25Ap02By
8	M	Child	25Ap16Bx	BUTLER, Bridget	45	F	Laborer	25Ap02By
.11	M	Infant	25Ap16Bx	James	21	M	Laborer	25Ap02By
6	M	Child	25Ap16Bx	John	19	M	Laborer	25Ap02By
14	M	Unknown	25Ap16Bx	BOYD, Hm.	39	M	Laborer	25Ap02By
12	M	Unknown	25Ap16Bx	Martha	40	F	Laborer	25Ap02By
60	M	Farmer	25Ap16Bx	BUTLER, James	18	M	Laborer	25Ap02By
50	F	Unknown	25Ap16Bx	Ann	15	F	Laborer	25Ap02By
20	M	Unknown	25Ap16Bx	Margt.	13	F	Laborer	25Ap02By
17	M	Unknown	25Ap16Bx	John	11	M	Laborer	25Ap02By
13	M	Unknown	25Ap16Bx	Elizabeth	9	F	Child	25Ap02By
10	F	Unknown	25Ap16Bx	Mary	6	F	Child	25Ap02By
9	M	Child	25Ap16Bx	CANNAN, Michael	40	M	Laborer	25Ap02By
12	M	Unknown	25Ap16Bx	Kate	40	F	Laborer	25Ap02By
8	M	Child	25Ap16Bx	Mary	26	F	Laborer	25Ap02By
5	F	Child	25Ap16Bx	Pat	10	M	Laborer	25Ap02By
.06	M	Infant	25Ap16Bx	Ann	13	F	Laborer	25Ap02By
60	M	Farmer	25Ap16Bx	BURKE, Patt	27	M	Laborer	25Ap02By

91

Erin Go Bragh – *Ireland Forever* – *they all arrived safely.*

245

NAMES OF PASSENGERS	AGE	SEX	OCCUPATIONS	DATE PORT SHIP	NAMES OF PASSENGERS	AGE	SEX	OCCUPATIONS	DATE PORT SHIP
CAMANA, Mary	.06	F	Infant	25Ap02By	RYAN, Jas.	35	M	Laborer	25Ap02By
FITZPATRICK, Mary	20	F	Laborer	25Ap02By	TIMLON, Eliza	20	F	Laborer	25Ap02By
MORAN, Biddy	20	F	Laborer	25Ap02By	MCGRATH, Ann	16	M	Laborer	25Ap02By
MORRISS, Patt	21	M	Laborer	25Ap02By	MURRAY, Kate	16	F	Laborer	25Ap02By
HALDRON, Mary	18	F	Laborer	25Ap02By	MATTHEWS, B.	12	M	Laborer	25Ap02By
COSTELLO, Ceila	20	F	Laborer	25Ap02By	Lar	8	M	Child	25Ap02By
QUINN, Kate	13	F	Laborer	25Ap02By	WARD, M.	25	M	Laborer	25Ap02By
MURRAY, Thos.	25	M	Laborer	25Ap02By	KANE, John	21	M	Laborer	25Ap02By
PYERS, Dermod	20	M	Laborer	25Ap02By	Mary	20	F	Laborer	25Ap02By
HOUGHTON, Martin	45	M	Laborer	25Ap02By	HOPKINS, Honor	20	F	Laborer	25Ap02By
Kate	40	F	Laborer	25Ap02By	SMITH, Pat	30	M	Laborer	25Ap02By
COYNE, Pat	18	M	Laborer	25Ap02By	Ann	7	F	Child	25Ap02By
Bridget	13	F	Laborer	25Ap02By	MONE, Chas.	58	M	Laborer	25Ap02By
MILKEN, Sarah	18	F	Laborer	25Ap02By	MONAGHAN, Pat	25	M	Laborer	25Ap02By
KEAN, Patt	20	M	Laborer	25Ap02By	BREHENY, John	27	M	Laborer	25Ap02By
MULLINS, John	25	M	Laborer	25Ap02By	Mary	25	F	Laborer	25Ap02By
KEEGAN, Patt	22	M	Laborer	25Ap02By	Maria	9	F	Child	25Ap02By
Kate	38	F	Laborer	25Ap02By	CUDDY, Honor	50	F	Laborer	25Ap02By
MAHON, Bridget	45	F	Laborer	25Ap02By	Honor	16	F	Laborer	25Ap02By
Thos.	9	M	Child	25Ap02By	John	13	M	Laborer	25Ap02By
Kate	6	F	Child	25Ap02By	FARNEY, Ellen	18	F	Laborer	25Ap02By
MCMULLEN, Alex.	22	M	Child	25Ap02By	HOGAN, Ann	18	F	Laborer	25Ap02By
OBRIEN, Jas.	22	M	Child	25Ap02By	CORCORAN, John	25	M	Laborer	25Ap02By
Ellen	24	F	Laborer	25Ap02By	Mary	25	F	Laborer	25Ap02By
CATAGAN, Thos.	22	M	Laborer	25Ap02By	Mary	.06	F	Infant	25Ap02By
FINN, Pat	10	M	Laborer	25Ap02By	KILLAN, Ellen	30	F	Laborer	25Ap02By
CAMPBELL, John	24	M	Laborer	25Ap02By	Kate	.06	F	Infant	25Ap02By
MCFADDEN, Francis	26	M	Laborer	25Ap02By	MCGUIRE, Thos.	21	M	Laborer	25Ap02By
GILLESPIE, John	19	M	Laborer	25Ap02By	MALONEY, Thos.	26	M	Laborer	25Ap02By
CONWELL, Patt	13	M	Laborer	25Ap02By	FITZPATRICK, Mary	20	F	Laborer	25Ap02By
Mary	40	F	Laborer	25Ap02By	MORAN, Bridgt.	20	F	Laborer	25Ap02By
Margt.	20	F	Laborer	25Ap02By	GIBBONS, Tobias	18	M	Laborer	25Ap02By
DEVERNEY, Mary	12	F	Laborer	25Ap02By	FLINN, Thos.	24	M	Laborer	25Ap02By
CONWELL, John	30	M	Laborer	25Ap02By	Margt.	24	F	Laborer	25Ap02By
MCBRERTY, Brian	30	M	Laborer	25Ap02By	Brigt.	18	F	Laborer	25Ap02By
Mary	25	F	Laborer	25Ap02By	MCCANN, Pat.	40	M	Laborer	25Ap02By
BOYLE, Jas.	35	M	Laborer	25Ap02By	MARTIN, Mgt.	35	F	Laborer	25Ap02By
GALLAGHER, Jas.	29	M	Laborer	25Ap02By	MCGINNIS, Mgt.	22	F	Laborer	25Ap02By
Mary	22	F	Laborer	25Ap02By	KELLY, Pat	36	M	Laborer	25Ap02By
John	.06	M	Infant	25Ap02By	Brigt.	38	F	Laborer	25Ap02By
LIVINGSTON, Jas.	40	M	Laborer	25Ap02By	Mary	17	F	Laborer	25Ap02By
Mary	35	F	Laborer	25Ap02By	Jas.	15	M	Laborer	25Ap02By
Rose	7	F	Child	25Ap02By	Pat	12	M	Laborer	25Ap02By
Biddy	.06	F	Infant	25Ap02By	Ellen	12	F	Laborer	25Ap02By
MCQUADE, Ellen	40	F	Laborer	25Ap02By	Jas.	2	M	Child	25Ap02By
Patt	13	M	Laborer	25Ap02By	Honora	.06	F	Infant	25Ap02By
TAGNE, Dan.	18	M	Laborer	25Ap02By	FOLEY, Barbara	17	F	Laborer	25Ap02By
GALLAGHER, Peter	25	M	Laborer	25Ap02By	CONLON, Eilz.	17	F	Laborer	25Ap02By
Biddy	21	F	Laborer	25Ap02By	GIBNEY, Joh.	10	F	Laborer	25Ap02By
TEAGUE, Joney	22	M	Laborer	25Ap02By	CAHILL, John	17	M	Laborer	25Ap02By
SWEENEY, John	24	M	Laborer	25Ap02By	Ellen	56	F	Laborer	25Ap02By
Ellen	22	F	Laborer	25Ap02By	Pat.	50	F	Laborer	25Ap02By
Mary	.06	F	Infant	25Ap02By	Mary	30	F	Laborer	25Ap02By
REILLY, Jas.	18	M	Laborer	25Ap02By	Thos.	23	M	Laborer	25Ap02By
John	18	M	Laborer	25Ap02By	Mary	30	F	Laborer	25Ap02By
BURNES, Ann	18	F	Laborer	25Ap02By	Mergt.	20	F	Laborer	25Ap02By
KILFEATHER, Rose	18	F	Laborer	25Ap02By	John	.06	M	Infant	25Ap02By
DUFFY, Pat	20	M	Laborer	25Ap02By	CLARK, Sarah	18	F	Laborer	25Ap02By
Rose	20	F	Laborer	25Ap02By	COSROVE, Brigt.	18	F	Laborer	25Ap02By
Jas.	.06	M	Infant	25Ap02By	Jas.	10	M	Laborer	25Ap02By
Mary	40	F	Laborer	25Ap02By	Ann	7	F	Child	25Ap02By
Jas.	60	M	Laborer	25Ap02By	CORAN, Ell.	10	F	Laborer	25Ap02By
Peter	12	M	Laborer	25Ap02By	COSROVE, Kate	30	F	Laborer	25Ap02By
John	19	M	Laborer	25Ap02By	Mary	6	F	Child	25Ap02By
James	18	M	Laborer	25Ap02By	BUTLER, Ricd.	54	M	Laborer	25Ap02By
Denis.	20	M	Laborer	25Ap02By	Jane	51	F	Laborer	25Ap02By
WALSH, Anty	18	M	Laborer	25Ap02By	John	14	M	Laborer	25Ap02By
WILSON, Wm.	30	M	Laborer	25Ap02By	Jane	12	F	Laborer	25Ap02By
Ellen	30	F	Laborer	25Ap02By	Ricd.	9	M	Child	25Ap02By
Anastasia	3	F	Child	25Ap02By	SHAUGHNESSY, Thos.	20	M	Laborer	25Ap02By
GREEHY, Jas.	26	M	Laborer	25Ap02By	HEFFEREN, Mick.	35	M	Laborer	25Ap02By
MURRAY, Margt.	27	F	Laborer	25Ap02By	FLYNN, Pat	20	M	Laborer	25Ap02By
BRIEN, Bridget	25	F	Laborer	25Ap02By	HENLEY, Con	21	M	Laborer	25Ap02By
Alice	24	F	Laborer	25Ap02By	ALLEN, Thos.	34	M	Laborer	25Ap02By
BARRATT, Ellen	25	F	Laborer	25Ap02By	Ellen	60	F	Laborer	25Ap02By

92

246

aspiring farmers, there might be news of enticing land offers, publicised in the emigrant circulars. The official *Colonization Circular*, for instance, published each spring in Britain, gave details of farmland for sale in Canada. The circular of 1851 listed several areas where cleared-land was available at 5s (US $1.25) an acre and stated, 'One-fourth of the purchase money will be payable in five years from the date of purchase. The remaining in three equal instalments at intervals of two years between each, all with interest.' The limit was set at 100 acres but the reasonable terms of such offers indicate the eagerness of the Canadian and American governments to hang on to the Irish emigrants to work the land. In Nova Scotia, land was sold at even less – half that in Canada and, if the full amount were paid on purchase, a 100-acre farm could be bought for £8 15s (US $43.75).

Although it had no official backing, a booklet entitled *Nine Years in America* was in great demand in Ireland. It was compiled from a series of letters sent from Thomas Mooney, who had travelled all through America and Canada, to his cousin Patrick Mooney, a farmer in Ireland. The opening words were bound to appeal to the hard-pressed Irish peasant: 'The American farmer never pays any rent, when he takes a farm he buys it forever . . . two, three or possibly seven years may pass over before he is called upon by the government to pay the purchase money.' Mooney noted that food in America cost only two-thirds the price in Ireland and public taxes about a quarter; while clothing, fuel and house-rent were about equal. But, the facility for acquiring 'housing and lands, and education for the children [was] a hundred to one greater'. The emigrant passengers had much to look forward to.

The first census in Ireland, taken in 1841 showed a population of 8,175,124, though this figure is now regarded as too low, given the unaccounted numbers living in rural communities. Ten years later, the census returns gave a figure of 6,552,385. Sociologists have since decided that, allowing for a normal increase in population, the population of 1851 should have been in excess of nine millions. Death by Famine or departure by emigration, can logically claim a loss to Ireland in real terms, of two and a half million people – more than one in four.

Dr Mary Robinson, the President of Ireland, made an official visit to London in 1995 and diplomatically reminded the politicians of Britain that a century and a half has passed without a single expression of sorrow or remorse for the Famine. 'It was the darkest moment in Irish history,' she said, The Famine commemoration will also be important . . . that it does not simply open old wounds. Instead, if it were to foster a sense of historical reconciliation, a willingness to shoulder appropriate responsibility on both sides of the Irish Sea, and a capacity to express genuine regret for what was done or left undone, then the commemoration of the Great Famine would be a significant moral act of deep relevance to our bilateral relations.' Before leaving London the President added, 'Even now, it is not too late to say sorry. That would mean so much.'

Index

Page numbers in *italics* refer to illustrations

INDEX

250

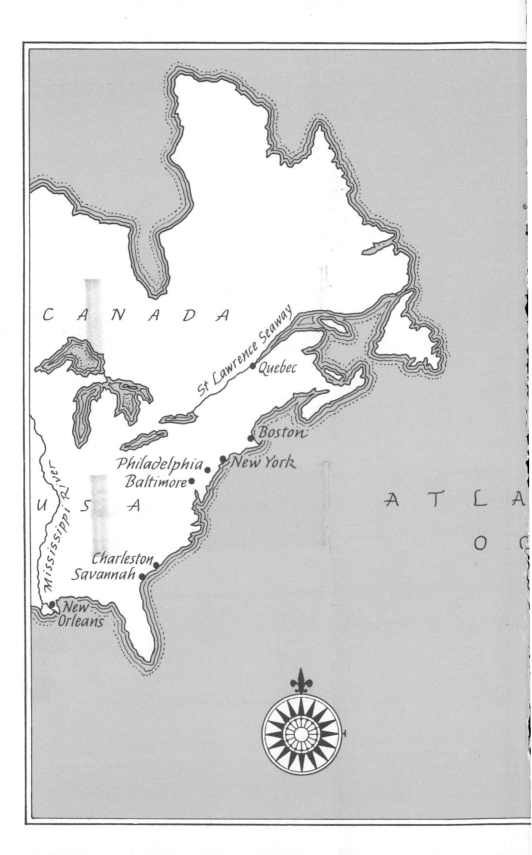